CONNOR

The Life Story of
GEORGE CONNOR

CONNOR

The Life Story of
GEORGE CONNOR

By Jack Connor

CONNOR
The Life Story of George Connor

10 9 8 7 6 5 4 3 2 1

Written, published and printed
in the United States of America.

www.GeorgeConnorBook.com
Chicago Publishing
2559 W. 111th Street
773-233-4270

Library of Congress Cataloging-in-Publication Data

Connor, Jack 1928-
    Connor : the life story of George Connor / by Jack Connor

    ISBN 0-9743658-0-7 : $24.95
1. Connor, George 1925–2003. 2. Football players-United States-
Biography. 3. University of Notre Dame-Chicago Bears-Football-
History-20th century.

TXu 946-395

Contents

DEDICATION VII

FOREWORD IX

INTRODUCTION XIII

PROLOGUE XV

CHAPTER ONE: A Rough Start 1

CHAPTER TWO: The Early Years 5

CHAPTER THREE: Holy Cross 21

CHAPTER FOUR: The Navy 41

CHAPTER FIVE: Notre Dame, 1946 Season 47

CHAPTER SIX: Notre Dame, 1947 Season 65

CHAPTER SEVEN: The Chicago Bears 83

CHAPTER EIGHT: 1955 Season 133

CHAPTER NINE: Turning Points 149

CHAPTER TEN: Life After Football 161

CHAPTER ELEVEN: Paying The Price 179

CHAPTER TWELVE: Giving Back 185

CHAPTER THIRTEEN: Leahy's Lads Stories 199

CHAPTER FOURTEEN: Looking Back 207

CHAPTER FIFTEEN: Summing Up 231

CHAPTER SIXTEEN: Coaches, Teammates
and Friends 241

CHAPTER SEVENTEEN: What His Friends Say 255

EPILOGUE 269

ACKNOWLEDGEMENTS 271

PUBLISHER'S NOTE 273

Dedication

Dr. Charles and Esther Connor had four children – Mary Ellen, Chuck, George and Jack (the author). With George's concurrence, this book is dedicated to our parents who gave all of us a loving home, a model of living our Catholic faith, and instilled in us the values and Christian principles that would sustain each of us through life.

We lost our brother Chuck in 1975. Although it has been over 27 years since he passed away, he is always with me and never far from my thoughts. He was an exceptional person – so full of cheer and love for his family and friends. This book is dedicated to Chuck, along with Dr. Charles and Esther Connor.

Foreword

He changed the game. Chicago Bears and Notre Dame legend George Connor will be long remembered as one of the greatest players in the history of the 100-yard wars. He was also a very good man and in this remarkable portrait by his brother Jack, his story is chronicled for the first time and for future generations.

It is difficult to compare athletes of different eras. But there is no debate about Connor's legacy of accomplishment. A devastating blocker and ferocious tackler, he is a member of both the Pro Football and College Football Halls of Fame. For two decades he was also the driving force in the Chicagoland Sports Hall of Fame.

Connor, whose nickname was "Moose," was the toughest of the 60-minute men. According to NFL records, he averaged 54 minutes a game, which was far more than any player. That record will never be broken.

As the first of the big, fast linebackers of the modern era, he changed the structure of the game and became the prototype for successors from Bill George through Brian Urlacher.

"He was the first of the big linebackers," according to his plaque at the Pro Football Hall of Fame, "and his success in that position made it almost mandatory that linebackers who followed him be as he was: big, fast and mobile."

George also had a reputation as the smartest guy on the field. "If you try to follow the ball, any slick quarterback can fool you," he said, "but if you concentrate on watching a few offensive players, they'll lead you right to the play."

Connor, who also played offensive and defensive tackle, became the first player to be selected as all-pro on the offensive and defensive teams in the same year. He was all-pro eight times in five years and was the only player to earn offensive and defensive honors for three consecutive seasons. There will never be another.

When the NFL celebrated its 75th anniversary, Connor was selected on the All Decade team for the Forties. On another occasion, he was an offensive and defensive first-team selection on an NFL All-Decade team for the Fifties.

His college career was even more extraordinary. Before World War II, he earned All America honors at Holy Cross. After serving in the Navy, he transferred to Notre Dame where he played for the great Frank Leahy. As a tackle playing both ways, Connor was the strongest and quickest lineman on the most dominant team in the history of college football. In 1946, the Irish defense, led by Connor, was so overpowering that opponents managed to score only four touchdowns all season and failed to score an extra point. "We wore down a lot of teams," said Connor, who in 1946 became the first winner of the Outland Trophy as the nation's most outstanding lineman. With the Golden Dome in the background, he was featured in *Life* magazine.

On the 100th anniversary of the first college football game, *Sports Illustrated* selected Connor as a member of the All Century team. "George Connor was the best tackle college football has ever pro-duced," recalled former Irish quarterback John Lujack. "He was equally good on offense and defense."

Jack Connor discloses in this volume that George was among the athletes and actors who were given a screen test to replace former Olympian Johnny Weissmuller as Tarzan. He didn't get the part. "If George was playing Tarzan and was in a fight with a lion," the pro-ducer later commented, "the lion would be the underdog."

It is to Connor's great credit that he stood up against racism. In 1952, when the Bears were playing at Detroit, he was appalled when several members of the Lions began taunting Chicago's Eddie Macon with racial slurs. "I don't appreciate the names you're calling him"

Connor shot back, "so I'm here to tell you to knock it off." According to Jack, the hecklers stopped.

Jack Brickhouse once told me that he thought George would have done very well if he had gone into politics. I share that view. He was a natural leader, good speaker, and had more friends than anyone in Chicago.

Anyone with a passion for the game will love this book. Jack's previous book, the best-selling "Leahy's Lads," ranks with Roger Kahn's "The Boys of Summer" as as one of the best volumes ever written about a team. What makes these books special is that Jack Connor, like Kahn, not only lived through the era that they are writing about but were participants in the drama. Kahn was a New York sportswriter covering the Brooklyn Dodgers. Like his brother, Jack was among Leahy's Lads. It is because they write from this perspective that Kahn and Jack Connor are good at making sports history come alive. What also makes Jack's book fresh and original is that he has conducted dozens of interviews with college and professional players of this era and also makes extensive use of sports archives, newspaper microfilm, and other primary sources.

I met George in the early 1980s and got to know him better through my pals Jack Leahy and Ed McCaskey. There was no one more enjoyable to spend an afternoon with than these guys. Connor, a great storyteller, had vivid memories of Elroy "Crazylegs" Hirsch, Gino Marchetti, "Joe the Jet" Perry, Norm Van Brocklin, and Bobby Layne. In the golden age of football, they were the heroes of my youth. So was George Connor.

Steve Neal
Author and Chicago Sun-Times Columnist

Introduction

From the time we were kids, my brothers, Chuck and George were my heroes. Although Chuck died over twenty-five years ago, he and George are still my heroes. But it was more than brotherly love that generated the idea of a book about George. Yes, he was a premature baby who grew up to be one of the best football players whoever lived, which is in itself an amazing story. However, the real story of George is the way he has lived his life, his passionate love of people, his overwhelming drive and determination to succeed and his loyalty to his family, friends and the schools he attended. The story of such a man had to be told. And, to be perfectly honest, being Irish, I love to tell a story.

George and I have had a close bond as brothers – it has been that way all our lives. With this in mind, I am aware of the burden I have in writing this book to be as objective as possible. This I attempted to do, with one caveat. When there is an opinion or comment about George not attributed to someone else or not concerning factual matter, my admiration, respect and love of George might show through. I hope it does.

One other aspect about the book should be noted. As the author, I originally intended to keep myself almost entirely out of the story so as to be as objective as possible. However, it became increasingly more difficult to do so since I was present for so many of the events in George's life. Further, I realized that in some respects, it is also a Connor family story. Because of these factors, I decided to include myself in the story in a limited way as needed. In so doing, I hope I have not overstepped the bounds of objectivity or propriety.

During the writing of this book, George and I had many sessions where we talked about his youth, his football career and his life after football. These sessions were enjoyable for both of us and if anything, they strengthened our bond. In researching the events in George's life, I used family scrapbooks, newspaper clippings, and many books about Notre Dame and professional football to obtain the facts I needed to be accurate. Most of the insights about George were obtained through the many interviews I conducted with him, his family (Sue, George Jr. and Al), his teammates and his friends from various walks of life. In addition, there are my own personal recollections as well as those of our sister, Mary Ellen.

George's story will take us from his early youth to De La Salle Institute, Holy Cross College where he gained football stardom as a 17-year-old freshman on through his days at Notre Dame and with the Chicago Bears, his work as a CBS color analyst and with the Chicagoland Sports Hall of Fame and beyond. In reading about George's life, the reader will get an inside glimpse of some of the notable men of his time – such men as: Mayor Richard J. Daley, George Halas, Red Grange, Frank Leahy, Sid Luckman, Monsignor McDermott, Ziggie Czarobski, Father John Smyth and many more.

If there are inaccuracies in the book, the fault is all mine.

Prologue

On March 29, 2003, I completed the work on the manuscript for this book. Later that day I visited George at the Warren Barr Pavilion where he had lived for over a year. I told him the manuscript was completed, and he was thrilled. We then had a wonderful visit, the best in many months. Two days later on March 31st, and before the manuscript was submitted for publication, George passed away. Although he had been ailing for some time, his death came as a shock to the whole family, particularly since he had been so good just two days before.

The date of George's death, March 31st, kept nagging at me until I realized it is the same date that Notre Dame's legendary coach, Knute Rockne passed away. Although it has been 72 years since the plane he was on crashed in the fields of Kansas, Rockne is still regarded by many as the greatest college coach of all time. And although it has been 56 years since George captained the 1947 National Championship team, he is still regarded by many as the best college lineman of all time. Two of Notre Dame's legends are forever bound together not only by their fame and accomplishments as coach and player, but by the date they left this world.

Since George's passing, one of the great consolations for his family has been the memory of George's 78th birthday party. On January 21st, his birthday, George was feeling good and was in excellent spirits. His wife Sue and their sons George and Al, and George Jr.'s wife Angela, decided on the spur of the moment to throw a birthday party. With only twenty-four hours notice, they contacted family members and some of George's closest friends to gather at one of George's favorite haunts, Butch McGuire's on nearby Division Street.

When George was wheeled into McGuire's, he was stunned to see about 100 people gathered there to help him celebrate his birthday. The only friends who couldn't attend were out of town at the time. George, who has a long history of rising to big occasions, rewarded the assembled crowd by breaking into that well-known big smile of his to the cheers of the people gathered. During the course of the evening he greeted all there – calling them by name and obviously overjoyed to be among family and friends. The cake at the party, brought by the Goldens, read "#81 is 78." He told his son, Al, that he was so happy, he couldn't stop crying. It was a vintage George performance.

George was laid to rest on April 5, 2003. Everything about the Mass of celebration for George's life was class, as befitting the way he lived his life. At the end of the liturgy, personal tributes to George were given by his sons, George and Al, and by me. George was always so proud of his boys and after their heartfelt tributes to their Dad, I'm sure he was smiling from above. As Tony Golden put it, "If there is such a thing as a great funeral, this was a great funeral."

Reflecting on the wake and Mass, it was obvious how many lives were touched by George as evidenced by the huge crowd in attendance. One thing that struck many of us was the range of people who were there, from the famous to the not-so-famous. There was Richard M. Daley-the Mayor of Chicago, the McCaskey family-owners of the Chicago Bears, Chuck Comiskey-former owner of the Chicago White Sox, Johnnie Red Kerr-the "voice" of the Chicago Bulls, representatives of the College and Pro Halls of Fame. Also present was the doorman from George's building-Ronnie, George's barber, and a man who identified himself as having met George 15 years ago for ten minutes. Although he hadn't seen him since, he wanted to pay his respects to the man who was so nice to him.

One was inspired by the famous people who came to pay him last respects. Almost more touching however, and symbolic of the way he lived his life, were all the others who were proud to call a famous football star a friend.

Prologue

In the chapel at All Saints Cemetery in Des Plaines, Illinois, George's close friends, Father John Smyth and Monsignor Ignatius McDermott, presided over the final blessing. Father Smyth began by telling those attending not to be alarmed if they heard some rumblings or strange noises because it was the cemetery where George's former sidekick Ziggie Czarobski was buried. There were many smiles as we realized the irony and appropriateness of George and Ziggie being together again.

What was it that made George not only such an outstanding football player, but the kind of man who friends from all walks of life honored for his commitment to others?

What follows is George's story. It is much more than a story of a once-frail baby that went on to gain athletic fame. It is the story of how a southside Chicagoan ascended the heights but never lost touch with his humble roots.

CONNOR

The Life Story of
GEORGE CONNOR

CHAPTER ONE

A Rough Start

Baby Connor was not expected to live more than a few days. Being on the staff at Mercy Hospital in Chicago gave Dr. Charles Connor and his family access to the best doctors at the hospital but even the best care seemed not enough to save the new arrival.

The day had begun at about 1:30 a.m., January 21, 1925 when Esther Connor woke her husband Charles and said, "I'm having some problems. I think the baby is in trouble." Esther was only six months pregnant, the mother of two small children and herself a nurse, so her call for help was not something Charles took lightly. After a brief medical exam, Charles was sure he had an emergency on his hands. He immediately called his neighbor and close friend Jimmy O'Brien to ask if he and his wife could look after three-year-old Mary Ellen and one-year-old Chuck while he rushed Esther to the hospital.

Charles bundled Esther in the car and nervously drove down snow-swept South Park Boulevard for the seven mile trip to Chicago's Mercy Hospital. Several hours later, Mother gave birth to a three-month premature baby boy who weighed two pounds eight ounces. The Connor baby was rushed to a warming cradle that served as a sort of incubator for premature babies.

Mother and Dad had agreed some time before that if she were to have a boy, they would name him George, after Charles' brother, Monsignor George S. L. Connor. Dad talked with Dr. Walter Black, the noted head of Pediatrics at Mercy, about who should break the bad news to Mother. Dr. Black told Dad that as the primary doctor on the case it was his job to inform Esther. She knew young George might not live, but she was praying that something could be done to save him. When she saw the look on Dr. Black's face as he entered her hospital room, she knew she would not hear good news.

"Esther," began Dr Black in his most gentle voice, "I am afraid I have some bad news for you. The baby, despite all we can do, is just not strong enough to survive. Charles agrees with me, as do all the other doctors who have examined your little one." He held Esther's hand as he continued. "You have two fine, healthy children, and there is no reason you can't have other children, but this one just isn't developed sufficiently to make it. I'm sorry." Mother had been expecting the news, but to actually hear the words was harder than she imagined. She fought back the tears as she thought of losing her son. She said nothing, and after being left alone with her thoughts, she finally drifted off to sleep.

When Mother was strong enough to leave the hospital a few days later, she and Dad took George home to die in the surroundings of a loving home as was the custom in those days. Dad, although brokenhearted, completely accepted the verdict about George. Mother, however, had other ideas. Before they were married, she had worked for the Infant Welfare Society under Dr. Herman Schluter. She had witnessed first hand some remarkable recoveries of infants who were suffering from malnutrition and not expected to live. It was under Dr. Schluter's care that these recoveries took place and Mother thought maybe he could do the same for George. She felt that it was certainly worth a try.

That first evening at home she broached the subject with her husband. As she was afraid might happen, he was dead set against the idea of bringing in another doctor, particularly one he had never met. In answer to Mother's plea, he said, "George has been examined by some of the best doctors in the city of Chicago and they say there is no hope. Why prolong the agony of accepting what has to be?"

The following morning, despite Dad's reservations, Mother called Dr. Schluter as soon as Dad left for the day. At first, given Dad's opposition to the idea, Dr. Schluter did not want to come. But, on Mother's insistence, and with the agreement that Charles would be told but not present when he came, he agreed to the visit.

That afternoon, Dr. Schluter, baggy suit and all, with tobacco stains on his wrinkled tie, entered the room where Esther and the baby were. After a thorough examination of the baby, he said, "Esther, this little baby of yours is one of the littlest babies I have ever seen. He is so small and wrinkled, I think he could fit into one of my cigar boxes." Mother was used to his colorful language and said nothing. Dr. Schluter, who could be as compassionate as he was gruff at times, said kindly, "Esther, if you do exactly what I tell you to do, I think we can save this baby."

He proceeded to give detailed instructions on how to accomplish this. The baby should be kept in a room heated to 80 degrees. He should be fed boiled cabbage and carrot juice every hour on the hour, twenty-four hours a day until further notice. If Charles agreed, he promised to visit daily until he thought George was on the way to recovery.

Dad wasn't the least bit happy when he came home late that afternoon and was told of Dr. Schluter's visit. However, when Mother told him of Dr. Schluter's prognosis, and harboring some hope that the baby could recover, Dad not only accepted Dr. Schluter's consultation, but did everything he could to make the recovery a reality.

Dad had a friend, a carpenter by trade, construct a reclining chair. Since Mother would have to spend virtually all her time in this 12 by 15 foot room, such a chair was necessary for her to catch some sleep between feedings. The nursery room was heated as instructed. And so, Mother began a life devoted almost entirely to taking care of baby George. This meant hourly feedings. The feedings were slow and painstaking as George had to be fed the boiled cabbage and carrot juice through an eyedropper because he was so tiny. When Mother finished a feeding she barely had time for a quick catnap before she had to start the process all over again. Dad hired a young Irish girl to live at the house and take care of Mary Ellen and Chuck.

After several months of hardship for the entire family, the cabbage and carrot juice and Mother's loving care paid off. George not only lived, but Dr. Schluter pronounced the baby well enough to take regular baby food and be treated as any other infant his age.

It is hard to conceive of anyone who was more devoted in caring for a son than Mother was during George's first few months of life. When one considers the hardships she endured, the hourly feedings and lack of sleep, the strain on her emotional and physical well being, her lack of complaining, it boggles the mind to consider the love she demonstrated to save her son. Through the years Mother never talked about those days. Knowing her, I can only assume she did not want to bring attention to herself but rather was content to hold those precious times in her heart – in that special place that only mothers understand.

Years later, Dad recalled "Every doctor at Mercy who examined baby George, including myself, gave George less than a 1 in 10 chance to live a week – he was no bigger than my fist." Then Dad's eyes would fill with tears as he told of Mother's remarkable dedication to saving the life of their son.

As they thought about the future, Dad and Mother must have wondered what was in store for their prematurely born son. Would he always be weak and never have the stamina of a normal child? Could this frail little body ever adapt to the rigors of life? Would he grow up to be a normal child? They didn't have the answers, but they knew one thing – George seemed to be a determined little guy.

CHAPTER TWO

The Early Years

There were two landmarks in the Park Manor area on Chicago's south side where George grew up. One was St. Columbanus Church and grammar school. The other was Meyering Park, located across the street from the school on Calumet Avenue between 71st and 72nd Streets. In the 1930s the Connor family lived in a bungalow at 7321 Indiana Avenue, just five blocks from St. Columbanus where the four Connor children received their early education from the Adrian Dominican nuns. St. Columbanus was one of the many well-known Catholic parishes that flourished during the 1930s and 1940s era of the depression and the war years.

Those were the days when a family's world pretty much revolved around the parish neighborhood, and in particular, the church and school. Dad had his doctor's office just one block from the school, above Neary's Drugstore at 71st and South Park (now Martin Luther King Drive). It was a time when milk was delivered by a horse-drawn buggy, ice by the "ice man" who drove an old truck down the alley with chunks of ice (25 pounds, 50 pounds, etc.) to fill the "icebox," and coal for the furnace was shoveled down the coal chute on the side of the house. There was a special police convertible touring car painted orange that patrolled the neighborhood. Less than half the families had a car, soda pop cost five cents, a loaf of bread 10 cents, a movie 11 cents, the street-car six cents and a new car could be had for $750.

Dad was one of the best known people in the parish because he was the doctor for the nuns and priests as well as half the people in the parish. A typical family living in the parish at that time had two or three children and some other relative living with them. All went to

5

Dad for their medical care. In the days before specialization, he delivered the babies, took their appendices out, stitched up the many cuts, treated the colds, flu, pneumonia and all the other ailments that families suffer from.

Dad was known as a very good diagnostician and very caring doctor. There are many stories attesting to this such as the one my good friend Frank Morrissey, a prominent lawyer and legal scholar, tells about his father. The Morrissey family lived in an apartment in St. Columbanus parish in the early 1940s. Frank's father was very ill. His mother instructed Frank, who was about ten years old at the time, to go to Dad's office (the Morrisseys had no telephone), about three blocks away and ask Dad to make a house call. When Dad heard the request, he promised to go to the Morrissey residence as soon as he was finished with his office hours.

Upon entering the bedroom of Frank's father, Dad saw a man who was bloated and had difficulty breathing. Dad asked him if he worked with brass. Mr. Morrissey at first said he didn't, but then remembered that he had laid a linoleum floor where he had used brass strips and had cut himself on a sharp edge of the brass. Because of his vast experience in treating patients, Dad immediately diagnosed Mr. Morrissey as having brass poisoning. He wrote out a prescription and had young Frank run to the nearby drugstore to have the prescription filled. In quick order Frank was back with pills which he described as "the size of horse pills." In a matter of hours, Mr. Morrissey was feeling much better and in days he was completely cured. Frank Morrissey, in concluding his story said, "I have always admired all of the Connor family but Doctor Connor will always be special to me because he saved my father."

Dad loved sports and, through his office window, enjoyed watching the boys in the neighborhood play at Meyering Park. He was known to stop at the park to watch a game on his way to and from his office. Because of his medical practice and from watching games at the park, he knew most of the boys who played sports in the area. Occasionally, he would notice one of the boys missing from the games. He would make a mental note of this fact and when he encountered the boy's mother or father in the neighborhood, at church or in his office, he would inquire why the particular youngster wasn't playing as before. Invariably the answer was because the parents could not afford the doctor bills in the event the boy was injured.

To ease the parent's fear of medical bills connected with sports, Dr. Connor issued an edict. The edict which became known throughout the neighborhood was simple and effective. "Any neighborhood boy who was injured playing sports at Meyering Park could be treated by Dr. Connor for free." Through the years, many a young lad continued playing sports because of Dad's expertise and generosity.

Among the families who always paid their medical bills was the Capone family. Al Capone, the notorious Chicago gangster, owned an apartment on Prairie Avenue two blocks from the Connor house where his mother, his brother Ralph and his family lived. Al lived elsewhere but was close to his mother whom he visited often. Dad was Al's mother's personal doctor. One night in the early 1930s, Dad received a call from the Capone residence saying that Mrs. Capone was ill and could he come right over. It seems Mrs. Capone wasn't sick at all. The reason Dr. Connor had been called is that one of Capone's men had been shot.

Always the healer, Dad treated the wound and then told Al's brother Ralph that as soon as he got home he was going to call the police. Ralph told Dad, "That isn't a good idea." Dad didn't say anything and left. When Dad arrived home he called the police and reported what happened.

The following day he received a personal phone call from Al Capone. Capone apologized for the fact that he was called to attend to a gunshot wound. He went on to say he appreciated Dad taking care of his mother and promised if he would continue to do so that he would never again be called for that kind of medicine. Dad continued to attend to Mrs. Capone for several more years.

Dad was raised in Holyoke, Massachusetts, one of eight boys. As a young lad he and his brothers were involved in one sport or another as soon as they could walk. The Connecticut River was at the bottom of the hill where the Connor boys were raised. During the summer months they spent many a day swimming in the river down through the canals that ran behind the many paper mills in Holyoke. When they weren't swimming, they were playing baseball. As a result, Dad became an excellent swimmer and baseball player.

As a young man, Dad worked in the local paper mill until he turned 18. Then he enlisted in the Marines. At 5-feet-11 and 185 pounds, he was every inch an athlete. One day, a Navy Commander who was the head medical doctor of that area and also from Holyoke visited the Marine base where Dad was stationed. According to Dad, he had the opportunity to visit with the Commander and told him how he hated Marine duty and longed to be a naval corpsman. The Commander arranged for Dad to be discharged from the Marine Corps and enlisted in the Navy for a new four-year hitch.

Dad served in the Navy as a medical corpsman from 1906 to 1910. In 1907 Dad was assigned to the battleship *Ohio*. This was during the era that President Teddy Roosevelt developed his famous policy of "Speak softly and carry a big stick." To show the world the "big stick" part of his policy, Roosevelt sent "The Great White Fleet" (so called because of white-painted hulls) on an around-the-world mission of "Gunboat Diplomacy." From December 16, 1907 to February 22, 1909 the fleet of 16 battleships, including the *Ohio*, called on ports the world over to show the foreign dignitaries that the United States did have a "big stick."

As part of the "speak softly" segment of Roosevelt's policy, the fleet put on exhibition baseball games in most ports where they docked for any length of time. Dad, who was an exceptional baseball player, was the captain of the fleet baseball team. If the country the fleet visited had a baseball team, the fleet all-stars would play that country's team. If the country did not have a team, the various battle-ship teams would play an exhibition game. Because of this, Dad played in numerous baseball games in ports around the world during the

White Fleet's world tour. With that kind of athletic background it is not surprising that Dad passed on his love of competitive athletics to his sons.

Dad had an endless number of stories about his days aboard the battleship *Ohio*. One that always brought laughter from the Connor kids was the story about his battleship leaving port when a British ship passed by. As the British sailors on deck spotted the big letters OHIO, one of them hollered, "There goes the OH and the bloom'n 10."

Dad would usually tell his stories at the end of dinner. We heard the stories so often that Mary Ellen would get up from the table on the pretense of helping Mother. Then Chuck would slip away followed shortly by George. That left me at the table as the sole audience for Dad's stories. One night Dad launched into one of his stories before the others could make their usual exit. He was telling what a great All-Star baseball team they had when they played the Japanese team in Japan; a story I had heard on numerous occasions. Dad said, "The infield was amazing. We had 'Soup' Campbell at first, George Baker at second, and a cracker-jack third baseman named, er...." Before I realized it, I filled in the missing name by saying, "Muck Waters." Dad said, "Muck Waters – that's right" and kept right on with his story.

The others, particularly George, almost fell out of their chairs laughing. After that, anytime George and I were together and one of us couldn't remember a name, any name, the other would say, "Muck Waters." The "Muck Waters" story is well-known to all the Connor clan. Even the grandchildren supply the name Muck Waters when one is needed.

After Dad's tour of duty with the Navy, he was honorably discharged and he returned home to Holyoke. For several years he worked in a local pharmacy and played semi-pro baseball for one of the many teams sponsored by the paper mills in the area. He then applied to Loyola Medical School for admission as a medical student. In those days it wasn't necessary to have a college degree to be eligible. Dad passed an entrance exam and left Holyoke for Chicago where he enrolled as a freshman.

After his first semester in medical school, Dad ran out of money and sought full time employment. He found it as a nurse to a wealthy man who lived in Chicago. He returned to medical school after about six months of attending his patient. It soon became evident that he would have to find additional employment to pay his way through the remainder of medical school. With this in mind, and at the suggestion of someone at the medical school, Dad took the State of Illinois nurse's exam. He passed the exam and thus became the first male nurse ever registered in the State of Illinois.

Dad graduated from Loyola Medical School and served his internship at Mercy Hospital. It was during this internship that he met nurse Esther Keeley who was destined to be his wife. After his internship, Dad joined the U.S. Medical Corps and was given the rank of Captain. This was during World War I and he was assigned to care for wounded soldiers aboard the medical-troop trains that took soldiers from the ports of New York and Philadelphia to the various military hospitals around the country. After his discharge from the Army, Dad returned to Mercy Hospital to serve a surgical residency under the world-renowned surgeon Dr. John Murphy. Upon its completion he entered private practice and service as an associate professor at Loyola Medical School.

Dad married Esther Keeley on September 1, 1920. She had left her home in St. Joe, Michigan in 1915 to come to Chicago and study nursing at Mercy Hospital. As the story goes, she met Dad who was an intern at Mercy when they bumped into each other in the hallway near the coffee shop. Dad was attracted to this beautiful brunette, so he asked her for a date. After a relatively short courtship, they were married in Plainfield, Illinois. About a year after they were married they had their first child, Mary Ellen. Two years later Chuck was born, followed eleven months later by George. I entered the world three and a half years after George.

George, like his older brother Chuck, became hooked on sports at a very young age. When one of the Connor boys reached the fifth grade, they were told the rules of the Connor house for participating in any organized sport at St. Columbanus. First, you had to be on the honor role and second, you had to play in the school band. So in fifth grade Chuck took up the trumpet and George opted for the tenor saxophone. Chuck was an excellent trumpet player and by the time he was in eighth grade placed second in the city-wide grammar school solo contest. George, on the other hand, despite trying his best was not very good. But, as with all the eighth grade members of the band, he entered the solo contest. George practiced his solo endlessly at home. We were all very grateful when the day of the solo contest finally arrived so we would not have to listen to George's rendition of "Beautiful Colorado" ever again.

Late on the Saturday afternoon of the solo contest, George bolted through the front door of the house dragging his saxophone case in one hand and waving a medal in the other. He proudly proclaimed, "I won second place." The family was stunned. Mother beamed at the news. As his reward, George was served his favorite meal and dessert that evening, and for about a week thereafter.

Sometime later he confessed there had been only two entrants for the tenor sax solo competition. George had his piece memorized which gave him an automatic ten points against his opponent, yet the other guy handily beat him. But George got the second place medal and milked that fact for all it was worth.

Within the next few days, George was playing football at Meyering Park and when he dove to make a tackle, he had a front tooth kicked out. With a front tooth missing, he could no longer bite correctly on the reed of his saxophone. Figuring his saxophone days were over, George, without telling Mother or Dad, pawned his saxophone. The following evening, our Dad said, "Let's have some music." That was his signal to have Mary Ellen, Chuck and George play as a trio with Mary Ellen at the piano, Chuck the trumpet and George the saxophone. There was a pause until Mary Ellen, who always covered for us boys, said, "We can't play together. George pawned his saxophone." Dad never said a word about it. I suspect that he was probably as happy as the rest of the family to know that we would never again have to listen to George attempt to play that instrument again.

By this time George's interest in sports was obvious to any observer. There was a backboard with a hoop attached to the grape arbor in the Connor's backyard and he practiced his shots at all hours – before school after 6:30 a.m. mass, after school and sometimes in the evening. Even at that early age, George demonstrated a passionate determination to reach his goals.

George had the benefit of some marvelous role models growing up in St. Columbanus Parish. The parish and Meyering Park both sponsored many athletic programs. When George wasn't playing some sport, he was watching the older players perform in the various basketball and baseball tournaments put on in those two settings; there were some great ones. As a result of his attendance, George became the ball boy for the parish's CYO (Catholic Youth Organization) City-Wide championship team in the late 1930s.

It was a time when sports flourished because it was still the Depression and young men spent most of their free time playing some sport. Every Saturday at Meyering Park the older boys would meet for the weekly round-robin 16-inch softball games. Once the sides were chosen by the Captains, each man chipped in a nickel and the games were played with an intensity of a World Series game. Many of the same players participated in both basketball and baseball. Men such as Walter "Pug" Boyle, Pete McDonald and Joe Dockery were among the best. They were the heroes of the neighborhood not only because they were great athletes, but also because they lived exemplary lives. As one of the St. Columbanus priests once said, "We didn't need priests at St. Columbanus when there were such men as Pug, Pete and Joe to set an example for the younger kids." Such was the local scene where George grew up.

When George was in seventh grade, one of the neighborhood policemen, Gordie Powers, arranged a football game with St. Kevin's on the east side. St. Kevin's had a small kid playing in their backfield who could punt the ball 50 yards. His name was Babe Baronowski. (Babe would go on to be one of the greatest high school athletes in Chicago's history. While playing for Leo High School his performances earned him recognition in the Chicagoland Sports Hall of Fame.) St. Kevin's beat George's team 14 to 0. Years later Babe told George the reason they beat them was because they had them scouted. As Babe told it, "We knew who was going to carry the ball – it was the guy wearing the helmet." George's team had one helmet and passed it around.

One of George's early sports heroes was Jay Berwanger who played halfback for the University of Chicago in the mid 1930s. George would ride the street car to Stagg Field on the east side of Chicago where the Chicago team played to watch his hero, number 99, Jay Berwanger. George was never disappointed as Berwanger was a one-man-team and the most electrifying runner in college football. His superlative play earned Berwanger the Heisman Trophy in 1935, the first player ever to receive football's most coveted individual award. (Actually, Berwanger received the Downtown Athletic Club's Trophy as the Outstanding College Football Player East of the Mississippi River. It was named the Heisman Trophy the following year.)

Years later, George and Berwanger saw each other often and became good friends. George asked Jay how he learned the uncanny ability to cut so sharply, he replied, "I learned as a young high school player how to cut sharply dodging trees and hedges while running full speed in the hills of Dubuque. I had an incentive as I was being chased by some older guys when I dated a girl who lived in a neighborhood where I wasn't welcome."

In those days Mt. Carmel High School had a grammar school basketball league that played games on Saturdays. George played on the St. Columbanus team that got to the finals. On the day of the championship game George and his teammate, Louie Knox, returned to the neighborhood after the game where they met Pug and Pete. The two asked George how they did. George replied, "Oh, we lost. The other team got hot." The final score was 6 to 4.

George played in a game that year that had even a lower total score. In a game against St. Kilian's, their arch rival, the two teams played the entire game without either team scoring a point by the end of regulation play. George's team won in overtime by the score of 3 to 2. Louie Knox was high point man with two points as George scored one.

There was something about the way George played sports, even at that early age, whether it be football or basketball, that caught the eye of discerning sports watchers. It wasn't his coordination or natural athletic ability that got their attention. It was his all-out style of play that singled him out from others. Whatever the game, for however long it took, George played with an intensity rarely seen in such a young athlete. It was this dedication and all-out effort that would be his trademark for as long as he played sports. As his pals, Lou Knox and Iggy Richards said, "You could tell even then that George was special."

George followed Chuck to high school at De La Salle Institute at 35th and Wabash on the south side of Chicago. As a freshman at DLS, George was 5-feet-5 and weighed 135 pounds, which made him average size. As George recalled, "I wasn't big enough to be a lineman so I tried out for the backfield and was cut from the squad the first day. The next day I put on my equipment and went to practice. The coach spotted me and said, 'I thought I cut you yesterday.' I said, 'You did and if you cut me again, I'll keep coming to practice,'" which he did. George's persistence paid off. He eventually made the first team and had a good year. What George lacked in speed, size and mobility, he made up for in heart and determination.

By his sophomore year George had grown four inches and gained 30 pounds. He played tackle on the varsity and could more than hold his own against the best on the team. One day when Dad was visiting with the football coach, Emmett Murphy, the coach told Dad that the reason he didn't play George very much in the games was because he was afraid George would "burn out." Murphy explained that George played with such intensity and appeared to be still growing that playing him at this stage might not be in George's best interest. He went on to say that he was sure George would be a great ballplayer once his body was fully developed.

The summer between his sophomore and junior years, George's

growth exploded. He grew to six-feet-three and 200 pounds. He devoured every morsel of food put in front of him, but often that wasn't enough. I vividly recall one evening at about 8:30 after he had eaten a huge dinner two and a half hours earlier. George told mother he was hungry; Mother made George a few bacon, lettuce and tomato sandwiches. Seeing that wasn't enough, she kept making them. George consumed eight sandwiches, then about half a Devils' food cake, washed down with a quart of milk. Each morning as George came to the breakfast table he looked as though he grew an inch or two from the previous day. Mother used to say that the hardest part of George's phenomenal growth period was seeing that he had pants that fit him. He seemed to grow out of new pants in a matter of weeks.

Along about this time in George's life, he was unwittingly put to the test by some older guys in the neighborhood. It seems that because of construction work on 71st Street the streetcar tracks were torn up. There were sections laying on the side of the street. One summer evening, Chuck and George, then about 15 years old, walked to the drugstore on 71st Street to see some of their pals. Some of the older guys hanging around the drugstore thought they would have some fun with George who was already getting noticed as someone to keep your eye on – a tough football player. They told George that they had been having a contest to see who could lift a section of the track the highest and did he want to try. "Sure," said George and asked who did the best. They told him that Skippy Carroll, one of the acknowl-edged strong guys in the neighborhood and then a star tackle at Leo High School, had lifted the track over his head. George bent down, grabbed the section of track firmly and lifted it to eye level, strained to go higher and then dropped it saying, "I can't do it." The guys gathered there couldn't believe what they had seen. They had been leading George on. Skippy was the best of all the guys who made an attempt and he could barely lift it above his knees. From that day on, George was tabbed as a "comer."

In his junior year at De La Salle, George was not only the first string left tackle but was one of the best players in the Catholic

League. Playing next to him on the line at guard was Chuck who was also an outstanding player. In addition to his football ability George was also a very good basketball player. In his junior year, George became a force as a scorer and rebounder on the De La Salle basketball team. Going into the team's final game of the season, George was the second leading scorer in the Catholic League. At the dinner table the evening of a game, Chuck, who was a senior and captain of the team, told George to get his usual 14 points or so in the game and he would guard Johnny Payette (the league's scoring leader) and hold him to under eight points. "That," said Chuck, "should give you the scoring title."

In the game that evening, George did get his usual number of points, but despite Chuck's defensive work as he was practically draped all over Payette, the Fenwick star couldn't miss and ended up with over 20 points. George had to settle for second place.

In George's senior year, De La Salle hired a new football coach, Joe Gleason, who had played his college ball at Notre Dame. During one of the first practice sessions, Gleason ordered the tackling drill called "Murderers' Row." Wearing his gold Notre Dame football pants he was going to run against the linemen himself. George stationed himself first in line and did so in every row which meant he tackled Gleason each time he ran against a row of players. By the fifth row, George hit Gleason so hard that he limped away and never again tried to run against the team, especially not against George.

That year George was the dominant lineman in the Catholic League. He was such a hitter and terror in practice that Gleason often held him out of drills and scrimmages for fear he would hurt his teammates. George recalled one practice when the live drill was a tackle against the wingback and the end: "I loved that drill. One day I hit the end Willie Horvath so hard he got up, spit out a couple of teeth and was ready to go again. He was one tough player who later went on and played at Purdue." That year, 1941, George was named to the All-Catholic, All-City and All-State teams. What is so amazing about George's accomplishments is the fact that he was only 16 years old.

Being raised in an Irish-Catholic home George was used to hearing the Notre Dame Victory March and cheering for the Irish football team in the fall. Perhaps different from other homes with similar backgrounds, it was our mother who had the Notre Dame connection. When Mother began her nursing studies at Mercy Hospital her roommate was Rose Cavanaugh who later became a nun in the Holy Cross order. Mother spent many weekends at the Cavanaugh house where she met many Holy Cross priests including Fathers Tom and Eugene Burke – legends at Notre Dame. After graduation from nursing school in 1918, Mother, along with Rose Cavanaugh, went to the University of Notre Dame to work in the student infirmary because of a severe flu epidemic. It was during that period that she dated John Cavanaugh, Rose's cousin. John was a rising star at the Studebaker Company in South Bend. He later entered the Holy Cross order to study for the priesthood and after ordination advanced to become President of Notre Dame in 1946 which was the year George, Chuck and I first attended Notre Dame.

Upon her return to Chicago, Mother did some private-duty nursing. One of her patients was the son of the owner of Mandel Brothers, a very large, prosperous department store. It seems that young Mandel, who was about Mother's age, had a thing for Mother. The Mandels, who were very wealthy, planned a trip around the world and asked Mother to join them and continue her private-duty nursing of young Mandel. In telling the story to our sister Mary Ellen, Mother said she turned down the offer and then pondered aloud, "I wonder what would have happened?"

Mother was well-known in the neighborhood for her hospitality and caring nature. She not only made numerous extra sandwiches for George during his fantastic growth period, she seemed to be making sandwiches every day for the many visitors at the Connor house. Our house was the place where our friends gathered. Mary Ellen, Chuck, George and I all brought our friends home as we were encouraged to do by Mother and Dad. We had the basketball hoop in the backyard and a ping-pong table in the basement as attractions but the main attraction was a happy home and Mother as a much-loved person by all who came to our house.

All of us Connor kids got along very well with each other. Chuck, George and I all adored Mary Ellen. She taught each one of us how to dance before prom time and made sure we looked presentable when going on a date. If Chuck or George wanted to use the car, Mary Ellen would go to the piano and play, "Little Sir Echo." If Dad responded from the kitchen as the echo, Mary Ellen would tell the particular one that Dad was in a good mood and to ask for the car. When asked in his early twenties when he was going to marry, Chuck replied, "Not until I find a girl like Mary Ellen." That sums it up.

Since they were only eleven months apart in age and had many of the same friends, Chuck and George were together most of the time. Naturally, there was a little friction occasionally, but Chuck was so easy-going that these occasions were rare. As for me, being the youngest, Chuck and George always looked out for me. I can't remember ever having a cross word with either of them.

George at this stage of his life displayed many of the same qualities he showed throughout his life. With a task at hand, George was serious, intense and always exhibited that determination. Most other times, George showed his lighter side with a fun-loving attitude, coupled with a marvelous sense of humor.

In George's words,

> I know I had a great upbringing in a warm and loving household with a mother and father who were always interested in what we kids were doing and who we were with. They knew where we were at all times and supported us not only in school, school plays and sports but in everything we did. When Chuck and I were altar boys we were always assigned to the early masses because the priests and nuns at St. Columbanus knew the Connor boys would be there. Mother was a good Catholic. She loved God but didn't wear her

religion on her sleeve. I remember going to early mass with her. We would always stop at the bakery on the way home from mass to buy some rolls for the family. It was a great thrill for me to be with her.

Dad was always there when we needed him. He did not have a lot of time to spend with us because in addition to his hospital rounds he had office hours from 3 to 5:30 p.m. and from 7 to 8:30 p.m. and was always taking care of patients even in the middle of the night. I'll never forget when I was in high school, he would leave the office early to come and watch our football practice at McKinley Park. After practice he would give some of the boys a ride home. He never interfered with us or told us how to play. He was a good athlete himself but never suggested plays or second-guessed the coaches. In my senior year, I had a knee injury and missed some school days. Many of the days I spent with the heating pad and hot packs but Dad let me play on Sunday. He didn't think that was too bad that I missed a little school because I was doing what I wanted to do.

With the wonderful parents George had, it was no wonder that he grew up with Christian values that sustained him through life. When it came time for George to select a college, he remembered:

Various schools and scouts became interested in me but Dad and I had kind of an unwritten rule that we wouldn't talk to anyone. The most important thing for me was to concentrate on my studies but down deep I knew there was a Holy Cross connection with the family. (Dad's brother, Monsignor George Connor was a star football and basketball player at Holy Cross in the early 1900s and was then the

President of the Holy Cross Alumni Association.) Dad wanted me to go there but I didn't know how strong his feelings were.

The only coach I talked to after the season was Coach Frank Leahy of Notre Dame. He came to the house with Scrapiron Young, the team trainer and he was very nice and gentlemanly, not overpowering. He said they wanted me at Notre Dame – that it was up to me and he wouldn't keep pestering me. My coach, Joe Gleason was the same way. When scouts would come to him asking about me, he told them that my father and I did not want people talking to us.

Finally it got down to decision time. One night I asked Dad, "How much does it mean to you that I go to Holy Cross?" Dad in his own way said, "Son, it would be very meaningful but I won't ask you to do it." I said, "That's it – I'm going to Holy Cross."

I never regretted the decision. I thought it was a good one. Freshmen were eligible to play football at Holy Cross, at Notre Dame they were not.

I'll never forget. I wasn't ashamed that my father got on the train with me to go away to college. It was the first train ride I ever had in my life. I was never on the IC (Illinois Central) or any kind of a train. I got on the train at 63rd and Englewood with Dad and we went to Springfield, Massachusetts to see Father George who then drove us to Holy Cross in Worcester, Massachusetts, where I started my freshman year.

In the days that followed, George would begin his rise to stardom as one of the all-time greats at Holy Cross.

CHAPTER THREE

Holy Cross

In mid-August of 1942, George joined a Holy Cross team coached by Anthony "Ank" Scanlon. Scanlon had come from Philadelphia where he had coached St. Joseph's Prep team to several championships. He brought with him his premier line coach, Ludlow "Lud" Wray, as well as many of the area's top players including Reds McAfee, Joe Campbell, Tom Kenny and Tom Smith.

What George didn't realize when he reported for practice was that he wasn't on a football scholarship. (His uncle, Monsignor George Connor was paying his way.) Nor did the coaches know of George's accomplishments on the football field. So George arrived on the scene without any fanfare. He was, in today's words, "a walk-on." George recalled,

> I was on the fifth team. They never heard of me. Because I was Monsignor Connor's nephew, they begrudgingly allowed me to come to practice. I'll never forget that first practice. I was with all the hamburgers (reserves). After the first practice, Dad left to go back to Springfield to visit Father George (Monsignor Connor) and I said to him, "You tell Father George that I'm going to make this team."

Dad returned to Springfield and spent a few days at Holy Name Rectory with his brother. During the course of their chats, Dad relayed George's predication that he would make the team. Father George, who knew the Holy Cross football team well, told his brother not to get his hopes too high. He went on to inform Dad that at starting left tackle, which was George's position, was a veteran player named Jim Landrigan who was All-American material. Further, he explained, the Holy Cross team had many standout players. He felt that as a 17-year-old freshman George would be lucky to get in a game or two. Very few people ever disagreed with Father George. However, Dad knew his son and replied, "You don't know George as I do. He is an outstanding player with more determination than you can imagine. I wouldn't be surprised if George was a starter before the season was over." Father George probably thought his brother was blinded by parental pride and not willing to offend merely said, "We'll see what happens."

George's Holy Cross teammate and life-long pal, Reds McAfee recalls:

> When I first saw George and his size, I thought he must be one of the coaches. It wasn't long before the coaches recognized George's talent and they put him over with the starters. George was not only big and strong but he was also very fast and heady. There were few players who were as intelligent as George. He was amazing in what he could do on the football field. We knew George was something special the very first day of practice. As a wingback, I had to double team the tackle along with the offensive end. In blocking drills with two of us against George, he almost knocked our heads off as he would split us apart. There was no way we could block him. After days of this, the end, Bill Swiacki (a 1946 All-American at Columbia) and I thought we had the perfect solution. We would both pinch in low so he couldn't use that tremendous strength of his. At the snap I flew out only to find air as George had hurdled the two of us. We never touched him. Not only was George the strongest tackle we had

ever encountered but he was very quick and agile. He was the best I have ever seen.

After the first few weeks of practice, the coaches knew George was an outstanding player. They had seen him do amazing things on the practice field day after day. However, they kept coming back to the fact that he was only 17 years old and in their experience a player that young couldn't keep up the pace that college football demanded. They knew George had great potential and would be a great player some day but they couldn't believe that he could consistently play in the games at the same level he had shown in practice. It wasn't very long before they were convinced otherwise.

Since George consistently performed as he had, they couldn't deny him his rightful place on the team. Accordingly, they placed George on the second team going into the first game against Dartmouth. George not only got in the game but played an aggressive, flawless game against a strong Dartmouth team.

In his letters home, George did not comment much about his progress on the football field, but just prior to the second game his family in Chicago received a clipping from the *Worcester Telegram* from George. It was a picture of George in his football gear with a caption that read "Freshman may play Saturday." George had crossed out "may play" and wrote "will start."

In the week before the Crusaders' second game against Dusquesne, George became a starter when Jim Landrigan hurt his knee and was unable to play. Not only did George start, but he played an outstanding game. He seemed to be at the bottom of every pile on defense, out in front leading the interference on the Crusaders' runs and was consistently the first man down under punts. Ank Scanlon, Lud Wray and the other Holy Cross coaches were realizing that George was one of the best linemen they had ever seen. After two more games they were convinced George was exceptional.

The following games were of mixed success. Holy Cross lost to Dartmouth and Dusquesne, then won against a weak Fort Totten team 40 to 0. They lost the fourth game to Syracuse but the fifth game was the turning point. The Crusaders showed tremendous improvement as they upset a strong North Carolina State team by the score of 28-0. According to George:

> This was our first big win of the season against a very good team. It was a confidence builder for the team because in that game the team played the way we knew we were capable of playing. One thing that helped us that day was our end coach, Hughie Devore (later to coach at Notre Dame). He gave the pep talk before the game. I can't remember what he said but I do recall it was very inspirational.

The Crusaders then tied a strongly-favored Andy Kerr-coached Colgate team 6-6. A loss to Brown was discouraging but the Holy Cross team put it all together for a 13-0 win over Temple and a 28-0 victory over Manhattan. The Crusader defense limited Temple to a net gain of 36 yards rushing and Manhattan College to a mere 25. With George and his teammate Tom Alberghini leading the charge on defense, the Crusaders showed they were fast becoming one of the best defensive teams in the East.

After the Crusaders defeated Manhattan 28-0, the *New York Herald* reported:

> The 5,000 drizzle-drenched and half-frozen spectators not only watched the clicking Crusaders trample all over the Jaspers, but they also saw freshman George Connor deliver another All-American performance at tackle as he and his hard-hitting mates in the Holy Cross frontier smothered every Manhattan move. Standing head and shoulders above all the others was Connor, the 17-year-old stripling from Chicago. Big George spent most of the

afternoon in the Manhattan backfield breaking up plays, harrying passers and delivering tackles so robust that their echoes bounced around the rain-spattered stands. Mr. Connor was all tackle.

It wasn't only the Holy Cross defense that was coming together but also the offense. Scanlon's complicated, single-wing, unbalanced line offense was jelling – Bezemas, Sullivan, McAfee and the other backs were now comfortable with the various formations and were operating like a well-oiled machine. Holy Cross was a much better team than their 4-4-1 record indicated.

The final game was against their arch rival, Boston College. The BC team was undefeated, ranked number one in the country after outscoring their opponents 249-19, and was slated to play in the Sugar Bowl. Prior to the game there was the usual pre Holy Cross-BC game hype in the press. Much of it centered around George and how he would fare against the unbeaten Eagles. When Ank Scanlon was asked by the press who was the most improved player on his team, he replied, "I would have to say this freshman, George Connor, the tackle. I have found that Connor has become the sort of tackle spectators watch operating instead of watching the ball carrier...Now when you get a tackle like that you really have some-thing." When asked whether Connor was very green when he came out for football, Scanlon responded, "We thought so, but the boy changed colors very quickly."

George recalled the Boston College game this way:

I'll never forget preparing for the Boston College game. BC was undefeated, number one in the nation. They had an All-American fullback, Mike Holovak, an All-American tackle by the name of Gil Bouley, and at end, Don Currivan who later played with the Rams. The big thing about that game was the preparation. Our end coach Hughie Devore was a close friend of

Hunk Anderson the line coach for the Chicago Bears. The two met in a hotel in New York City. BC ran the T- Formation and not much was known about how to defend against it. Hunk, one of the best defensive strategists in the NFL, gave Hughie the defenses. When Hughie returned to Holy Cross to implement the plan, we knew we had something. On offense, we had the single wing brought in by Ank Scanlon. He used an unbalanced line with a lot of traps. It was a somewhat complicated system which took time to learn and perfect. By the time of the Boston College game we were ready. We started two or three freshmen, one senior (our captain, Eddie Murphy) a junior end and the rest were sophomores.

From their respective records, and from any perspective, it looked like the mismatch of the year. No football expert gave Holy Cross any chance at all of giving the great Boston College team a competitive game, let alone winning. The morning of the game, George saw his uncle, Father George. During the course of the conversation, the Monsignor inquired, "George, do you think the Holy Cross team can give BC any kind of game?"

Without hesitation George replied, "Father George, we're going to beat them today."

Stunned by George's reply, the Monsignor tried to ease what he thought would be a terrible disappointment for George. "You must realize they have the most devastating team in the country so I hope you do not get your hopes too high."

"I know they have a great team," replied George, "but so do we and we're going to win today."

Father George walked away, no doubt wondering what type of lunacy had befallen his nephew.

On the cover of the program that day was a picture of the Boston College captains, Fred Naumetz and Mike Holovak, wearing football jerseys (not their game jerseys) with the numbers 55 and 12. As fate would have it that was the final score of the historic game played at Fenway Park on November 28, 1942 – with Holy Cross the winner. The game stunned sports fans throughout the nation. This game was voted in 1950 by a panel of sportswriters as the upset of the half-century. Many of today's football historians and sportswriters still call it the greatest upset ever.

From the opening kickoff, Holy Cross dominated the game. The Crusaders did everything right and Boston College could never seem to get its vaunted offense and defense going. George, at 17 years old, became a star that day by his continued trapping of BC's All-American tackle, Gil Bouley. The Holy Cross backs – Ray "Cookie" Ball, John Grigas, Tom Sullivan, Reds McAfee and Johnny Bezemas – kept the BC team off balance the whole game with dazzling runs, sharp passes and unexpected plays. For example, John Grigas, who had never passed until that game, threw a touchdown pass. The Cross linemen, Captain Ed Murphy, George Connor, John DiGangi, George Titus, Tom Alberghini, Ted Strojny and Bill Swiacki devastated the Eagles blocking with their explosive backfield. On defense, they completely dominated the BC line which was considered the best in the country. Holy Cross not only beat the Eagles that day, the Crusaders totally destroyed and embarrassed them. In one of the newspaper columns after the game, it was reported that George said, "At the beginning of the game Bouley was ribbing me by saying, 'Well, so they have to send schoolboys to play against me.' After the game he came over to me and said, 'I take it all back, you're a real man.'"

George remembered:

> They got the opening kickoff and marched the length of the field but fumbled into the end zone and we got the ball on the 20 yard-line. We took the ball and marched down and scored. They came back and scored and then we scored and kept scoring. I'll never forget a game like that. In the fourth quarter, I

was so excited I couldn't add up the score on the scoreboard. It was just a marvelous feeling. None of us wanted the day to end...ever.

In the game, all we did on offense was take our fullback in the single-wing and set him as a flanker outside the end. That spread their line and then we ran our same plays. They were in a wide six-man line and I would pull and kept trapping their tackle, Gil Bouley.

In the third quarter, there was a chant in the stands, "Bouley made a tackle, Bouley made a tackle." I paid for it years later when Bouley was with the Rams and he got me pretty good one game. The Holy Cross – BC game was a great one. I'll never forget it.

In Chicago, Dad and Mother, Mary Ellen and I were listening to the football scores when we heard an announcer say Holy Cross was ahead of BC at the end of the first half. We couldn't believe it. Even the announcer said, "That doesn't seem right (the score). I'll have to check on that." By late afternoon it was confirmed. Holy Cross had indeed beaten the great BC eleven.

For reasons beyond football the game will long be remembered by many people in the Boston area. The *Worcester Telegram* reported that prior to the game the Boston College team, the projected winner, had been invited to attend a victory party at the Coconut Grove, a landmark Boston nightclub. When BC lost the game, the players declined to attend. That night there was a fire that consumed the whole nightclub. Hundreds of people died in the worst nightclub disaster in the nation's history. Although BC lost the game, the team and their families can be forever grateful that losing a game proved to be the stroke of luck that spared the BC team from being caught in that dreadful fire.

When the news of the fire was aired on radio news flashes, my parents, sister and I were anxious about the safety of Chuck (a sophomore at Holy Cross) and George. Because we had read the article in the *Worcester Telegram* we assumed that as the winners of the game, George, his teammates and other Holy Cross students would be at the Coconut Grove.

Dad immediately placed a call to Holy Cross in an attempt to ascertain the whereabouts of his two sons but couldn't reach anyone who could be of help. After numerous prayers, much floor pacing and nervous eating, the phone finally rang at about 1:30 a.m. Dad answered on the second ring expecting the caller would be someone returning his call but it was Chuck. Chuck sounded like he had been celebrating for awhile but Dad didn't mind. Chuck said he and George and their friends were safe and were celebrating the Holy Cross victory at a place some distance from the fire. With some prayers of gratitude and sighs of relief, the Connor family went to bed exhausted. It had been a long and emotion-filled day.

In recalling the game Reds McAfee says:

> We (Holy Cross) had some very good players. In the backfield Grigas and Bezemas were terrific runners, Sullivan and Ray Ball were excellent blockers. On the line Eddie Murphy, Swiacki and Alberghini were very good and George was the best, without a doubt. That day everything jelled for us, everything we tried worked – even Grigas throwing passes. We had a very good team and beat BC badly – it was no fluke."

For George, the Boston College game of 1942 had been an experience of a lifetime. He not only played in one of the greatest football games of all time but his team did the unbelievable – they defeated the number one ranked team in the nation and did so decisively. Further, he played the game which earned him national recognition. Participation in that game was one of George's cherished memories.

In looking back at the season George said,

> I had great coaches at Holy Cross. Hughie
> Devore was the end coach, Sheldon Beise of
> Minnesota the fullback coach, Vince McNally the
> backfield coach and Lud Wray was the line coach
> (People will remember him as the line coach at
> Pennsylvania under Bert Bell.) Wray was way ahead
> of the times. He was great on fundamentals and
> taught me the modern lineman stance with the
> knees more apart and the rump sort of high.
>
> The main challenge for the Holy Cross team was
> that Head Coach Ank Scanlon's system was the third
> different system in as many years. They went from
> the Notre Dame box formation, to the T-formation
> under Joe Sheeketski, to the current single-wing sys-
> tem with an unbalanced line. I played the running
> guard next to the center on the strong side which I
> loved. I pulled either way to lead interference or to
> trap. I enjoyed a lot of success. I was the first one
> down under punts and did a lot of things at Holy
> Cross. It was a great year for me and the team.
>
> During the season, I hung around with the four
> players Ank Scanlon brought with him from
> Philadelphia – Reds McAfee, who played at St. Joseph's
> for him, Tom Smith, an end who was later Chief of
> Police of Philadelphia, Joe Campbell from Northeast
> Catholic and Tom Kenny, who also played at St. Joe's.
> Most of the players from the East in those years went to
> prep school before entering college to hone their
> football skills and to show their talents for scouts in
> order to get scholarships to college. It was like a feeder
> system as many schools such as Boston College, Holy
> Cross, Fordham and Notre Dame tapped the prep

schools for football talent. Because of this, at 17, I was the youngest player on the squad but physically I was their equal. I found that I was equal or better than most as far as my football training, which I attribute to the great coaching in Chicago's Catholic League. The coaching in that league was so far ahead of the high schools and prep schools in the East that I was better trained in fundamentals than most of my fellow players.

When the post-season All-Eastern team was announced, George was named on the first team along with such notable players as Robin Olds the great Army tackle, Mike Holovak of Boston College, Bill Dutton from Pitt and Paul Governali of Columbia. George's selection marked the first time a freshman had ever been chosen for the first team and at 17, the youngest player who had ever gained a berth.

Father George, who originally had doubts that George would play very much at Holy Cross, was now completely convinced that George's father's assessment of him as a player was absolutely correct. No one was happier to be wrong than the Monsignor and there was no prouder uncle in all of New England.

During the 1992 football season, the surviving members of the 1942 Crusaders' team met in Worcester for the Holy Cross-Fordham game where they were honored at halftime. That evening at a local restaurant, the 1942 teammates enjoyed a gala reunion swapping stories and getting caught up on each other's lives. Even though George only played two years at Holy Cross, it surprised no one on the 1942 team that it was George who originated the idea for the reunion. They knew how much he loved Holy Cross and cherished his time with his Holy Cross teammates.

With his first year of college football over, George turned his attention to basketball. Holy Cross had discontinued its basketball program in the mid 1930s. When the legendary Moose Krause of

31

Notre Dame fame came to Holy Cross in 1938 as an assistant football coach, he re-instated the basketball program. Under Krause, who was an All-American basketball player at Notre Dame, the Holy Cross cagers developed into an above average team despite being handicapped by poor training facilities. Prior to the 1942 football season, Krause left Holy Cross to return to his alma mater to become an assistant line coach under Frank Leahy. Hop Riopel, Krause's assistant, took over the duties of head basketball at Holy Cross. Riopel had seen George play football but had no idea George could also play basketball. After a few practices, Riopel was amazed at George's agility, court savvy and scoring ability. Riopel made George one of his starters.

With very limited practice time the Holy Cross cagers opened their season in New York on January 6, 1943 against a crack Fordham team. The Crusaders lost 66-42 but surprised the crowd by giving the highly favored Ram team a close contest well into the second half. George made his college basketball debut that evening by scoring 19 points; he led all scorers. Because of the war, no home court and limited practice facilities, Holy Cross had an abbreviated basketball schedule. When the shortened season was over, George was high-point man on the team and had not only played extremely well but as one of the opposing coaches put it, "George Connor is as good a basketball player as he is a football player."

Between the opening game on January 6th and the second game against Brown on January 16th, George celebrated his 18th birthday. Like all men turning 18 in those days, George registered for the draft. On the same day he enlisted in the Navy's V-12 program. This program was designed to train future naval line officers and it also allowed those in the program to be eligible to complete the equivalent of two years of college studies.

With the basketball season over, George's thoughts turned to football. He was concerned that Holy Cross would not be able to field a football team for the 1943 season due to the war. All those in the Marine Corps and Army reserves were transferred to other schools or given other assignments and three senior starters, Ed Murphy,

Johnny Bezemas and John Grigas would also be missing from the team for the coming season.

One day George got word to report to Captain Davis who was in charge of the Navy program at Holy Cross. As a Navy V-12 student, Captain Davis was George's ultimate superior officer. With that in mind, George's first thought was, "What did I do now?"

When George arrived at the office, Captain Davis invited him to sit down. George figured he would take whatever punishment he might have coming, for whatever the problem, was standing up. George declined the offer to sit. The Captain said, "I have orders on my desk to transfer you to Notre Dame."

George replied, "Captain Davis, I have just one question. Are we going to field a team here this year?"

The Captain said, "We certainly are."

George said very firmly, "Captain, you can tear up the orders. I want to stay here at Holy Cross."

How and why George received such orders is open to speculation. It is obvious that someone with some powerful clout pulled some strings in Washington to effect the transfer. Whatever the case, it was done without George's knowledge. His reaction to the transfer orders substantiates this fact. Had George accepted the orders he could have played at Notre Dame for the 1943 season when the Irish won the National Championship. George's refusal of the transfer was born out of his love for Holy Cross. This act of loyalty to his school was characteristic of George. Loyalty to his family, his friends and to his schools is a virtue George displayed his entire life.

When the '43 season rolled around, the only starters for the Holy Cross football team remaining were George, Reds McAfee and George Titus who was elected captain. Tom Kenny, a reserve guard, was switched to quarterback, Bob Lawson, a reserve end, became a starter and the remaining players, other than George, were relatively small and inexperienced.

The Cross team did have some good fortune when Stan Koslowski transferred from Notre Dame. Stan was at Notre Dame for spring practice in 1943 and had all the makings of a future star. He had good size, and speed and was shifty but his best characteristic was that he was tough. The Notre Dame coach, Frank Leahy, liked what he saw and had great hopes for the young back. Stan loved to play football, but unfortunately for Stan, or maybe for Notre Dame, Stan also loved to play golf. He was almost a scratch player. One day Stan was missing from practice so Leahy sent the manager out to find him. The manager reported back to Leahy that Koslowski was on the golf course. This infuriated Leahy who could not understand why anyone would miss practice without a valid excuse. And to be playing golf, that was beyond comprehension. The next day at practice Leahy called the first and second teams together. He told them that he wanted to punish Koslowski so the players were to play as hard as they could. He then named a team of some reserve players to team with Stan. This team was on offense the whole time. Stan, playing halfback, carried the ball three out of four plays. The hitting was brutal. After about a half hour, the players on defense were feeling so sorry for Stan that after a tackle one of the players would whisper to him to just stay down and end the punishment. Stan would have no part in quitting. After about fifty minutes, Leahy called a halt to the drill. The players who were there cannot remember one single play on which Stan did not gain some yardage. At the end of the drill Stan took off his helmet and walked right up to Leahy and handed him his helmet saying, "Here, you need this more than I do." Stan exited the field and left the campus the next day.

Stan transferred to Holy Cross in time for the 1943 season. He not only made the team, but became the team's leading ground gainer. George related a story about Stan's toughness.

> During the Cornell game, Stan badly split his tongue and required several stitches. We only had about 14 players who could play, so we called three time-outs in a row so the doctor could stitch Stan's tongue together. Stan never left the field and con-

tinued to play a great game. He was one of the toughest players I ever saw.

Holy Cross opened the 1943 season at home against a highly favored Dartmouth team which was loaded with Navy V-12 and many Marine reserve transfer students. When the final whistle blew, Dartmouth was fortunate to escape with a 3-0 victory after being out-played by the determined Holy Cross eleven. And eleven it was, as the entire Crusader first team played all sixty minutes.

Earl Brown, the head coach of Dartmouth was not in a good mood after the game. "Connor? Connor?" moaned Brown in his post-game press conference. "Sure he's a great tackle. But can I ask you gentlemen a question? Is there a tackle in the world who can know – or act as though he knew – just where every Dartmouth play is going? Listen, some day...I'm going to unravel this mystery for you."

It wasn't a mystery for the sportswriters and fans who witnessed the game. Before each defensive play George and Frank Griffin, the other tackle, stood behind the line until Dartmouth called its signal. Then George took what he considered the threatened side, usually the strong side, and Griffin the other side. George was right about 90 percent of the time and completely wrecked the Dartmouth attack playing most of the game in their backfield.

By the following day Coach Brown had cooled off and said, "If there's a better tackle in the country than George Connor, I'd like to see him. Connor could make any team, pro or college, in the country." Dartmouth's Mel Downey who played the previous year with Holy Cross and was then a 247-pound tackle, said in the locker room after the game, "That Connor, gees! He's a one-man team. Couldn't even trap him. He hit me once in a trap play and I thought I'd never recover...and we used to be buddies."

Although young and inexperienced, the 1943 Holy Cross team compiled a 6-2 record with a season cut short due to the war including a canceled BC game. George continued his great play for the remainder of the season and if anything, got better as the season progressed. George's ability to guess opponents' point of attack became one of the minor legends of Eastern football. One rival coach commented, "All I want to know about Holy Cross is where George Connor is going to play – and I want to know it before we huddle instead of afterward."

His efforts earned George All-Eastern for the second straight year and All-American honors. George also was selected as the recipient of the George Bolger Lowe Award as the outstanding football player in the East. His coach, Lud Wray, said, "If he had a normal four-year college career, he would rank among the tackle greats of all time." One of George's teammates, Tom Alberghini, commented, "George is not only a great player but he is unaware how good he really is." All this for an 18-year-old sophomore.

Bob Lawson who was a starter at end on the 1943 Crusader team and saw a lot of action on the '42 team, recalls playing with George.

> It was such a pleasure to play on the team with George. With him next to me at tackle, I could roam all over because George took care of about half the field. I rarely had a back block me as George knocked down all the blockers in our area. The only bad part of being on the same team with George was the blocking drills in practice when he would knock our heads off in the two-on-one drills. He was a great teammate in every way. He was just as nice off the field as he was good on the field. It was a great pleasure to be with him in 1992 at our 50-year reunion of the 1942 team.

One aspect of George's two-year football stint at Holy Cross that bears mentioning is his iron-man durability. In the first game his freshman year he played the entire second half. From that time on he played 60 minutes of every game except for the final ten minutes of his last game when he was forced to leave the game because of an injury. George would demonstrate this iron-man quality in more dramatic fashion when he played for the Chicago Bears years later.

In 1944, George was elected Captain of the Crusader team. His uncle, Monsignor George Connor who played at Holy Cross in 1905, 1906, and 1907 under the legendary "Iron Major" Frank Cavanaugh, was one of the top ends in the East. The Monsignor was the first underclassman to be elected captain of a Holy Cross football team; a distinction which wasn't duplicated until George achieved the same honor 37 years later.

For the 1943-1944 Holy Cross basketball season George, who was elected captain, was joined by another Chicagoan, Bert Dolan. Dolan played his high school basketball at Loyola Academy on Chicago's north side. George was captain and center of the Holy Cross team, with Dolan a starting forward. The two played a major role in the fortunes of Crusader basketball in their again abbreviated season. George led all scorers with a 16-point average per game. George's role was best described by Roy Mumpton in his column in the *Worcester Telegram*:

> Connor appears just at home on a basketball court as he does on the football field. The 18-year old really moves around for such a big man. He can shoot too, especially from close up...Big George isn't merely a scorer; he's a good floor man too, an excellent feeder and a hard cager to handle when he's operating from the bucket...

After the basketball season, George received orders to report to the midshipman school at the University of Notre Dame. Before departing Holy Cross, George would participate in one more athletic contest. The Naval athletic officer scheduled a triangular inter-hall track meet for his Naval trainees. George was entered in the meet in the shot put, the 100-yard dash and the 220. When his good friend, Bert Dolan heard George was going to run the 100-yard dash he laughed because he too was entered in the 100. Bert, who ran track in high school, albeit the mile, thought he would leave George in his dust as they competed in the 100. Bert had no illusions about winning the 100 with some great athletes in the race but he did want to beat George.

As the gun cracked to signal the start of the 100, Bert got off to a fast start with George back in the pack. In describing the race Bert said:

> I was speeding down my lane when I started to hear a loud pounding noise, which kept getting louder. Out of the corner of my eye I spotted George. The next thing I knew he was even with me and then passed me. I couldn't believe that George could possibly run that fast.

When the meet was over the final tally showed that George had won the shot, finished second in the 220 with a 23.5 seconds performance and third in the 100 with a 10.6 effort. Bert did win the mile run with a time of 5:04. To this day Bert loves to tell the story of racing George in the 100 and hearing his heavy steps.

In looking back at his two years at Holy Cross, George said:

> My decision to attend Holy Cross was one of the best moves I ever made. It afforded me the opportunity to play in the unforgettable BC game, to play with some great guys and to make some friendships that would last a lifetime.

In one of life's pleasant duplications, there are two with the name of George Connor from the same family in the Holy Cross Sports Hall of Fame. Monsignor George S. L. Connor was inducted in 1957 because he was an outstanding end on the football teams of 1905, '06 and '07 and the star of the basketball team in the same years. His nephew George was inducted in 1974 because he was an outstanding tackle and he too was the star of the basketball teams. George received his honor despite the fact that he did not graduate from Holy Cross.

CHAPTER FOUR

The Navy

George received orders from the Navy to report for midshipman's training at Notre Dame in July. The midshipman program consisted of 90 days of intensive training designed to produce line officers for the Navy. Hence the nick name "90-Day Wonders" for its enrollees. Upon successful completion of the course of training the graduates would be commissioned ensigns in the U.S. Navy.

The head football coach of the Notre Dame football team for the 1944 season was Ed "Tex" McKeever. He had been an assistant to Frank Leahy at Boston College and continued with Leahy when he came to coach at Notre Dame in 1941. When Leahy joined the Navy in early 1944, Notre Dame named McKeever its head football coach.

As one of the best recruiters in college football, McKeever was well-versed on the top football players in the country which meant he was well aware of what George could do on the football field. McKeever sought out George on the Notre Dame campus and asked him to play for Notre Dame. As much as George loved to compete and play football, he was very conscious that he was no longer a civilian but rather a Navy Midshipman under orders to attend classes with no option of cutting classes. Without hesitation, he told McKeever he was in class from 8 a.m. to 5 p.m. and therefore had no time for practice. Amazingly, McKeever asked George if he would play in the games on Saturday without any practice during the week. He assured George that he could learn the offensive plays and would have no problem on defense. It took George about a second to decline the offer. As he put it, "There was no way I was going to play without the benefit of some practice time and besides it wouldn't have been fair to the guys who did practice every day."

George successfully passed the midshipman course in late October, 1944 and was commissioned an ensign. By coincidence, George and Chuck were commissioned ensigns within 48 hours of each other. (Chuck received his commission and wings as a naval aviator in Pensacola, Florida.) Further, they arrived at 7321 Indiana Avenue within two hours of each other, each with a 20-day leave. To make the coincidence even more unusual, the brothers were ordered to report to bases in the same area of Miami, Florida on the same day – Chuck to aviation school and George to the sub-chaser school.

Back at home, like all parents of sons and daughters in the military service, Mother and Dad proudly hung a blue emblem in the front window of our house with two white stars on it, signifying there were two from that house serving our country in the armed services. As you traveled throughout our neighborhood, similar emblems could be seen in homes and apartment buildings, sometimes three or four in a row but rarely none in any one block. What you hated to see, was a residence that displayed the emblem with a gold star on it. The gold star meant that someone from that family was killed in action.

As one who served in three branches of the service, the Marine Corps, The Navy and the Army, Dad was very proud of the fact that Chuck and George were serving their country and like all parents with sons serving, Mother and Dad worried about their safety. Dad followed the events of the war very closely on the radio newscasts and in the papers. When his boys finished their respective training and were assigned to the Pacific theater of operations, he purchased a large map of the Pacific so as to better follow where he thought Chuck and George would be. When the war against Japan ended, there were prayers of thanksgiving from the Connor house knowing Chuck and George had come through the war unharmed.

At the Naval Training Center (NTC) in Miami where George reported for duty, he was delighted to hear the Center had a basketball team. He learned that the previous year the NTC team had won the championship of the 16-team Navy basketball league. When the team assembled the coach was thrilled with the star-studded cast he had. There were such players as Leo Klier, the Notre Dame All-American; Bob Halstead from the 1942 Stanford NCAA championship team; Tom Thompson of Michigan; John Lujack of Notre Dame who was not only a star football player but had been a starter on the 1943 basketball team; Ernie Andres, an All-American from Indiana University; and George who had led the Holy Cross basketball team in scoring for two consecutive years. The NTC team won a second consecutive championship with George a starter and one of the high scorers. "The team was awesome with the talent we had. Every player was so good and able to score with a variety of shots," remembered George with delight.

Even more impressive than the team are the stories of what happened to the various members after the war. Ernie Andres played third base for the Boston Red Sox; John Lujack became the quarterback of the Notre Dame football team and led it to National Championships in 1946 and 1947 while winning the Heisman Trophy in 1947. George, of course, went on to a brilliant football career at Notre Dame and the Chicago Bears. It is interesting to note that as proficient as these men were in basketball, all three gained later fame in another sport.

Shortly after the basketball season ended, George completed his naval training and was ordered to report for sea duty. His orders were to report for sub-chaser duty on the *SC 1039*, then in dry dock for repairs at Guadalcanal. The *SC 1039* was a 110-foot-long, wooden-hull ship with a complement of three officers and 25 seamen. Shortly after George reported for duty, the then executive officer, Ralph Strayhorn, was made the skipper and George the second officer. Strayhorn had played in the line for the North Carolina Tar Heels before entering the Navy and would return to North Carolina after the war to captain the 1946 Tar Heel team.

At one point the *SC 1039* docked in Pearl Harbor. George was on deck when a command car parked nearby and a sailor emerged asking for an Ensign Connor. After George identified himself, the sailor told George he had been sent by Commander Leahy to bring George to the

Navy operations office as soon as possible. When George and Leahy met, the Notre Dame coach was most gracious in inquiring about George's family and congratulating him on his outstanding play at Holy Cross. Leahy told George he had wanted him to come to Notre Dame when he graduated from high school, and now he very much wanted him to attend Notre Dame after the war. He said, "George, I promise you two things if you come to Notre Dame. We will win the National Championship and you will be an All-American." Leahy fulfilled those promises in the 1946 football season.

The home base of George's ship was Ulithi Atoll, near Guam in the Yap Island chain in the South Pacific. Ulithi's lagoon is deeper than most which is why the Navy had its ships there. When his ship was in port, George would play in pick-up basketball games. One day, George played against a lanky naval officer by the name of Mickey Vernon. George didn't know the man's name at the time nor did he know that Vernon was the star first baseman for the Washington Senators. The two would meet again in early 1947 when both were honored by the Philadelphia Sports Writers' Association – George as College Lineman of the Year and Vernon as the American League batting champion.

George's favorite story about his duty aboard the *SC 1039* is about the time they had to refuel at sea. According to George,

> The tanker pulled alongside our ship and after the hoses from that ship to ours were connected, the tanker attempted to pump the fuel but nothing happened. Strayhorn, our skipper said, 'George go down to the engine room and see what you can do. The captain of the tanker is upset with us for throwing him off schedule.' In the engine room of the *1039* the chief petty officer was hollering at the crew but nobody seemed to know what to do – and neither did I.
>
> I don't know what made me say it but I asked, "Did you throw the switch?" The chief went to the

hose connection and pulled some switch that I had never seen before and all of a sudden the fuel started pumping through the hose. The chief looked at me with new-found respect and said, "Nice going, sir." I was somewhat of a hero on the ship for a while. I later told Strayhorn about how it had been a wild guess to ask about the switch and we had many laughs about my outstanding technical knowledge.

When the war in the Pacific ended, George and the crew of the *SC 1039* took the ship to San Francisco where it was de-commissioned. George was honorably discharged from the Navy in March, 1946.

CHAPTER FIVE

Notre Dame: The 1946 Season

When George was released from the Navy in late spring of 1946, our brother Chuck was already enrolled at Notre Dame. Chuck was a transfer student from Holy Cross where he completed two years before being called to active duty in the Navy Air Corps. Chuck had preceded George to Holy Cross but didn't play football there despite the fact that he was an outstanding player who had played alongside George at De La Salle. He passed on playing football at Holy Cross because his course of study was aeronautical engineering and that required his being in labs most afternoons.

Chuck was in the Navy V-5 program while at Holy Cross, a program designed for future naval aviators. In the spring of 1943, Chuck received his orders for active duty which eventually landed him at the University of Wisconsin. While stationed at Wisconsin, Chuck went out for the football team coached by Harry Stuhldreyer, one of the legendary Four Horsemen of Notre Dame. He soon became one of the starting guards. The week before Wisconsin's opening game of the 1943 season, Chuck received his orders to report to Iowa Pre-Flight as his next base. Chuck decided he would give up his leave before reporting to Pre-Flight in order to play in Wisconsin's opening game against Marquette. He was all over the field making tackles and was the star performer in a losing cause against a powerful Marquette team. After the game, in front of the rest of the squad, Coach Stuhldreyer told the players of Chuck's unselfish act. The coach said for that act of loyalty to Wisconsin, he would award Chuck his varsity "W" at the end of the season. True to his word, at the end of the season Chuck's letter and sweater arrived in the mail. It may have been the only time a football player at Wisconsin was awarded his monogram for playing in only one game.

Chuck played for Iowa Pre-Flight for the remainder of the 1943 season. He and George were reunited when, as new ensigns, they were assigned to nearby naval bases in Miami, Florida.

The big question for George was should he return to Holy Cross to complete his education and make use of his two years of football eligibility or should he transfer to Notre Dame to be near home? George had a deep love for Holy Cross which he displayed many times through the years. However, he had been away from home at Holy Cross and in the Navy for four long years and he longed to be near home. There was one other factor that weighed heavily on his decision to forego returning to Holy Cross in favor of entering Notre Dame. Dad had been ill for some time and that had put a big burden on Mother. George remembered it this way:

> While I was in the Navy, Dad had been ill. He had one eye that was sutured shut for 21 months with an opening for drops. He would return to the Mayo Clinic every three months to have the eye checked. He couldn't drive, he couldn't work and Mother had to go back to work to support the family. When I returned from service and saw all this, I knew if I went to Notre Dame he could see me play which he couldn't while I was at Holy Cross. The doctors told me that watching me play would be good for his health and his spirit so I made up my mind to attend Notre Dame. After I made the decision, Dad didn't chastise me for the decision even though he was worried what his brother, Monsignor Connor, would think. When Notre Dame played Army in 1946 and Monsignor Connor wanted four tickets to the game, I knew everything was all right.

George had enough credits from Holy Cross to be admitted to Notre Dame as a junior. However, because of the new rules concerning athletic eligibility, transfer students were required to have a certain number of credit hours at the new school before they were eligible to participate in inter-collegiate sports unless they were starting over as freshmen. Both George and Frank Kosikowski, as transfer students, were required to obtain the needed credits to be eligible to play football in the fall. There was no official summer school that year at Notre Dame so it was arranged for George and Kosikowski to join with some Brothers of the Holy Cross order in their summer program as a way of taking the courses they needed. Typical of George and his sense of humor, the day he reported to his first class, he gave the teacher his card and said, "Brother Orchid reporting for class."

When George entered Notre Dame he became the fourth St. Columbanus neighborhood lad to play for the Irish. Preceding him were Joe Locke (1927-1929), Carl Cronin (1929-1931), and George Benigni (1944). When I entered Notre Dame I became the fifth from our neighborhood to play at Notre Dame. All of us lived on Indiana Avenue within five blocks of each other.

Prior to the beginning of summer practice, George met with Coach Frank Leahy whom he had not seen since they met at Pearl Harbor during the war. During that meeting Leahy had assured George that if he would attend Notre Dame after the war he would be an All-American and that Notre Dame would win the National Championship. Now that Leahy actually had George at Notre Dame, he seemed to change his tune somewhat as he asked, "Oh George, with all the great players we have returning, do you think you can make the first team?" Without hesitating a moment, George replied, "Coach, I wouldn't have considered coming to Notre Dame unless I was positive I would be your starting left tackle." Leahy didn't say a word but merely nodded, smiled and walked away. Inwardly, Leahy was no doubt saying to himself, "I can't wait to see that lad prove that statement."

The official summer practice was due to start August 15th but

Leahy had the squad report about a week early under the pretense that a documentary movie about Notre Dame football was going to be filmed. The players who reported that early day in August, 1946 were the largest contingent Leahy ever had report for summer practice. Among the ones who were there were players from his first team and players from each year's team on through the previous season's team. In addition, there were the many outstanding players Leahy had recruited while he was in the Navy during the war.

Leahy's assignment as a Lieutenant Commander in the Navy was to install and supervise the recreational facilities of the major submarine bases in the Pacific area. Leahy, I am sure, did an outstanding job as he conscientiously carried out his assignment. However, with Notre Dame football never far from his thoughts, Leahy made it a point to note which players he encountered who would make excellent candidates to play at Notre Dame after the war. In reality, Leahy went further than merely noting which players he wanted. He made it his mission to recruit these players whenever possible. Leahy's wartime recruiting paid dividends as he brought to Notre Dame such players as Frank Kosikowski, George Strohmeyer and George.

Leahy put together the coaching staff he wanted. Back from the pre-war days were Joe McArdle, Johnnie Druze and Moose Krause. McArdle and Druze had been with him at Boston College in 1939 and 1940. He rounded out his staff by adding Wally Ziemba to coach the centers and Bernie Crimmins and Bill Earley as backfield coaches. It is interesting to note that with the exception of Krause, all the other coaches played under Leahy either at Fordham or at Notre Dame.

Leahy conducted a spirited spring practice that year but it wasn't until summer practice started that all the players were back from service and the new freshmen were available. There were 46 players returning who had won a monogram on one of the previous teams; more than a dozen of them had won two or more monograms (a monogram winner under Leahy had to accumulate a total of sixty minutes playing time during a season). The list of returning players included future Hall of Famers John Lujack, Emil Sitko, Bill Fischer and Ziggie Czarobski. In addition to the players who had previous experience playing at Notre Dame and his wartime recruits, Leahy also had some outstanding players coming to Notre Dame as freshmen. Included in this group were such players as Leon Hart (Heisman winner), Jim Martin (Hall of Fame), Mike Swistowicz, Larry Coutre, Frank Spaniel, Bob Lally, and Ralph McGehee, all of whom became starters on the Notre Dame teams during the next four years.

When the squad met that early August, it was the most talented group of football players ever assembled as one unit in the history of Notre Dame and arguably the most talented ever assembled at any college. Leahy's task was twofold. First, he had to determine who from this amazing group of players would become his first and second teams. Second, he had to find a way to mold these diverse players ranging in age from 17 to 25, into a cohesive unit. Leahy wasted no time in getting to work. He was well aware that opening day against the University of Illinois was less than six weeks away.

From the first team meeting Leahy made several points clear to his squad. He stressed that no one, regardless of previous experience, had a lock on a starting job. He would determine who of the group were the toughest players and they would start even if he had to switch some positions. He promised that the team would be the best conditioned college football team in the country and he warned that no player could be late or miss a practice session without prior approval. There was no question in any of the players' minds that Leahy meant what he said. It promised to be a brutal summer practice. It was.

Summer practice usually has two sessions, a morning and after-noon. Leahy added a third. It was his belief that the veterans returning from service during the war would have problems getting their legs in shape. Accordingly, he had the squad up early to run the lakes between Moreau Seminary and the main campus before break-fast. The team managers kept track of attendance while the assistant coaches supervised the run. Needless to say, no one missed these runs. Out on the field the morning of the team's first day of practice,

Leahy put the squad through the usual calisthenics and then the hitting started in earnest. At the conclusion of that session of practice, he ordered the squad to run a relay race. Ten captains were named who then took turns selecting their team man by man from the approximately 100 players on the field. Each player would have to run with a football the distance of the field, then around one of the coaches and back to where he started, at which point he would hand the ball to a member of his team. George described it this way:

> The captains started to select players for their relay team. About the eighth man chosen for our squad was a big blubbery guy and I thought, "There goes our chance of winning." The winning team would not have to run the wind sprints and laps and I wanted our team to win. When this fat guy got the ball he passed up backs and ends and gave us a lead. Our team won thanks to this guy. I went up to him and said, "You don't know me and I won't tell you what I thought about you but my name is George Connor and I want to be on your team." It was Bill Fischer and we played along side of each other for two years.

In those early days of practice, not many of the Notre Dame players knew George or what he could do on the football field. They were soon to learn. When the squad lined up for their first scrimmage, Leahy put George at defensive left tackle. Thinking back on that day George said,

> I always hated it when a linebacker put his hands on my back. It was a trap play on offense and as the play unfolded, our linebacker – I think it was Jim Mello – pushed me. I hit Bob Hanlon on his thigh and he stepped on my left hand. Bob was almost knocked out. It was the day of the College All-Star game and I went

to Chicago to attend the game with my hand in a splint. It kept getting bigger so I went back to school to find I had a broken hand. The doctor put my hand in a cast and I wondered what I would do. I knew Leahy would move on without me if I couldn't practice. Between our trainer Hughie Burns, and Doctor Green they devised a cast that went over the fingers on up to the elbow. It had wire running through it – it must have weighed over ten pounds. When I came on the practice field and the squad saw the size of the cast for the first time, several of them hollered, "I want to be on your side." I never missed a moment of practice with my new cast protecting my hand.

Meanwhile back in Chicago at the Connor home, Dad was hearing reports, mainly from me, of how well George was doing at Notre Dame. His spirits rose on hearing these reports and so did his desire to watch George play in his first game for the Irish team. With that in mind, Dad and Mother traveled to the Mayo Clinic to have the doctors examine Dad's eye. When Dad told the doctors he could discern more than a cloudy image from the small peep hole in his stitched eye lid, they took the stitches out and examined his eye. To the delight of Dad and Mother the doctors told them his eye condition had improved to the point he could he could resume his normal activities. One has to wonder how much Dad's uplifted spirits played a part in his physical recovery.

I was able to give our Dad a first-hand account of how well George was doing on the football field at Notre Dame because I was there. I had received an athletic scholarship from Notre Dame while at De La Salle Institute and reported to football practice for summer practice. It marked the first time George and I had ever been on a football field at the same time. I had my first direct experience with George as a football player early on my first day of practice. Along with other freshmen backs, I was assigned to that fiendish drill called, "murderers' row." My first task was to attempt to run against a line of guards, all 16 of them, spaced about seven yards apart. When I somehow survived that line I was ordered to run against the row of 16 tackles with George the first one in line. If I had any thought that brotherly love might influence George to go easy, it was quickly dispelled. When I approached George carrying the ball he hit me so hard I landed on my back about five yards from the point of impact with George on top of me. I learned the hard way that George didn't tackle a person, he tried to run right through a ball carrier. I also learned it hurts but it's possible to survive being hit by what seemed like a freight train.

I fortunately didn't directly encounter George again until about a week before the team's first game of the season against Illinois. I was the first-team halfback on the scout team that was to run the Illinois plays against the first and second teams for the next five days. On about the third play of our first scrimmage, I first made a counter move to the left and then carried the ball off tackle to our right. George was on defense at left tackle. As I ran toward the line I was greeted by two bodies crashing into me that caused me to land in a heap of bodies about seven yards behind the line of scrimmage. It seems that George had hit the two scout-team players who tried to block him and hurled them into me. There were many more plays like this during the course of scrimmaging against George and the first team. When I would tell Dad how George was doing on the practice field at Notre Dame I was able to paint a first-hand picture.

As the Irish team prepared for their opener against a very talented Illinois team, George was firmly entrenched as the starting left tackle. He was also slated to kick off. It was not until the week before the game that Dr. Green took the huge cast off George's hand. Prior to the game, Dr. Green and Hughie Burns devised a cast with some light-weight material that they encased in rubber, and then taped the hand. To disguise which hand was the broken one, they taped the other hand too. Up to this time all Notre Dame linemen taped their wrists but not their hands. This was the custom throughout college football. George continued to tape both hands and by mid-season all Notre

Dame linemen did the same. By the end of the season, almost all college linemen did likewise. George, it appears, was responsible for this new custom.

Ordinarily there would have been an election of a team captain prior to the first game of the season. More often than not this was done at the conclusion of the previous year's season but because of the war, there was no election at that time. Leahy and his coaching staff debated whether to appoint one or hold a team meeting to elect a captain. Leahy told his staff that he was of the opinion that to hold an election or to name a captain would run the risk of causing friction among the players. Bernie Crimmins, then an assistant coach, later explained Leahy's reasoning. He said,

> Leahy had players who he had coached before the war, players who played during the war when Leahy was in the Navy, players who were freshmen out of high school and players who were recruited from the service teams. Added to that, some of the players were military vets and some non-vets. With that kind of mix of players Leahy thought that to have an election might cause the players to split into factions. He wanted to avoid this at all costs.

Leahy's solution to what could have been a thorny problem was to name a captain or co-captains for each game. This was the first time in the history of Notre Dame football that the Irish football team did not have a regular captain. As it turned out, Leahy's decision proved to be wise as the team never was divided. On the contrary, the team had as much togetherness and team spirit as any Notre Dame team ever had.

The opening game of the 1946 football season was an important one for the team and for many of the individuals involved. It was Frank Leahy's first game back as coach since the 1943 season. It was also the first game since the 1942 season for players Bob Livingstone and Jack Zilly; the first time since the 1943 season for John Lujack, Jim Mello and Ziggie Czarobski. It was the first time in a Notre Dame uniform for George, Jim Martin, Emil Sitko and George Strohmeyer. The only starters who had played the previous season wearing a Notre Dame uniform were Bill Fischer and Fred Rovai. It was a new era – the post-war era – and everyone both on the Illinois team and the Notre Dame team was anxious for the season to begin to see how good they were.

In practice the week before the game, George had been booming his kickoffs into the end zone. Now it was for real, the opening game. With his adrenaline flowing George had every reason to believe he would nail the kickoff into the end zone. It didn't happen. George kicked a line drive that traveled about five feet above the ground and was fielded by the short man for Illinois, Ruck Steger, a big fullback. Steger took about two steps when he was hit by a devastating tackle by George, who no doubt was embarrassed by his poor kickoff and took his frustration out on Steger. Years after their playing days George and Ruck became very good friends. Occasionally, Ruck would remind George that he had hit him on his thigh on that opening kickoff in the 1946 game. Ruck claimed the thigh caused him difficulty for some time. George didn't remember the particular tackle and thought Ruck was putting him on. One day, long after Leahy was out of coaching, he came to Chicago. George, Ziggie Czarobski and some other Notre Dame players were to meet Leahy for lunch. George also invited Steger to come to the lunch. When Leahy was introduced to Steger he said, "Oh Ruck, I remember the opening kickoff in the '46 Illinois game when George hit you with a hard tackle that caused a contusion on your right thigh." Ruck broke in and said to George, "See, that's what I've been telling you."

That tackle by George set the tone for the way the Irish team would play that day. Notre Dame, before a packed house of 75,000 people in Champaign, defeated a Rose Bowl bound Illinois team, 26-6. That game marked the beginning of "The Golden Years" of Notre Dame football which would see the Irish team go undefeated for four seasons.

With his easy-going manner, George always made friends easily. He was getting to know his Notre Dame teammates and they him. One thing his teammates observed was that George could be one of the nicest guys on the team when he was on campus and even in the locker room. But, once he was on the practice field and put a helmet on, everyone on the team knew George was all business. Following his daily routine, George would leave the home dressing room in the stadium, walk across the street to the entrance of Cartier Field, and check in with the team manager. Once inside the practice area, he would jog to where the helmets were, don his helmet and become a warrior. Even his expression changed when the helmet was on – his eyes narrowed with a look that seemed to convey the message – "Don't get in my way. I'm here to punish anyone who does."

I can personally attest to that "look" and the intensity that was behind it. As a member of the "B" team at that time, we scrimmaged the varsity almost every day which meant that I was in many scrimmages against my brother. Fortunately, I never played directly opposite him but unfortunately, I did get hit by him several times. George didn't see faces of the opponents, rather when he saw a player with a different colored jersey, he hit that player with everything he had, his brother included.

The only time on the practice field that the "look" seemed to soften was when he and his cohort Ziggie would have some fun with Freddie Miller. Miller was Frank Leahy's teammate on the 1929 Notre Dame team and was also the owner of Miller Brewing in Milwaukee. Coach Miller, as the team was instructed to call him, flew his own plane to practice several times a week. He would don his coach's garb and spend his time on the practice field with Moose Krause (the tackle coach), George, Ziggie and the rest of the tackles since he had played tackle in his day. What George and Ziggie would do when Miller was at practice was to ask him questions about technique for playing tackle. Miller was flattered. To the consternation of Leahy and Krause, Miller would spend several minutes on each question thus eating up precious practice time, time that could have been spent on the constant contact drills that went on on Cartier Field. Of course, that's exactly why George and Ziggie went through their routine – to get a breather from the constant hitting. That prompted the guards, who were closest to the tackles on the practice field and killing each other, to label those question and answer sessions, "The Tackle Tea Parties."

One can't write about George's football career at Notre Dame, or about his life for that matter, without writing about his fun-loving sidekick, Ziggie Czarobski. In physical appearance, personality, approach to situations and even their style of play on the football field, the two were mirror opposites. George was tall, well-proportioned and had the look of a well-trained athlete. Ziggie was shorter, somewhat rotund, and looked slightly out of shape. On the field, George used his speed, strength and agility as a hard charger who liked to play in the opponent's backfield. Ziggie never charged across the line of scrimmage, but rather waited in the line where he used his powerful arms and legs to ward off blockers. Off the field George was outgoing and friendly with a delightful sense of humor. However, compared to Ziggie, George seemed quiet and reserved. Ziggie was more than outgoing. He was an event. He would come on a scene like an explosion. One knew when Ziggie was there.

Though they were opposites in so many ways or possibly because they were opposites, George and Ziggie were magnetically drawn to one another. They were also very much alike in other ways, perhaps the most important ways. Both had a passionate love of people; both loved the University of Notre Dame and their teammates in a special way; both had a strong desire to help other people, particularly the less fortunate; and both loved to have a good laugh and have fun. The friendship they formed as teammates during the 1946 football season grew stronger as the years passed. They shared a lifetime of experiences together and their love for each other was such that when Ziggie died in 1984, George was so devastated that he went into a depression that lasted many months.

On the way to the climactic game with Army, the Irish beat Pitt 33-0, Purdue 49-6, Iowa 41-6 and Navy 28-0. During those games, Ziggie continually entertained his teammates with his quick wit and antics on the field, in the locker room and at the noon meetings. In a much-told story, Coach Leahy saw Ziggie taking a shower before practice one day and inquired, "Oh, Zygmont, why are you taking a shower before practice?" Ziggie replied, "Coach, it gets too damn crowded after practice." And it was Ziggie at one of the noon meetings who broke the tension during one of Leahy's talks.

Leahy was not pleased with the way the team was performing and told them, "We are going back to the basic fundamentals." Leahy then held up a football and said, "Lads, this is a football." Ziggie, sitting in the front row immediately called out, "Hold it Coach. You're going too fast. I'm trying to take notes."

The 1946 Army-Notre Dame game that resulted in a 0-0 tie has received as much publicity through the years as any Notre Dame game in history. The game is most remembered as a defensive classic that pitted two of the best teams ever assembled against each other. From the Notre Dame side, this game has been second guessed more than any other Notre Dame game. What would have happened if Leahy had put Ratterman in at quarterback? Would Notre Dame have scored if Panelli or Cowhig had carried the ball when Notre Dame was near Army's goal line? Should the Irish have kicked a field goal when they were so close to the end zone? The list goes on. John Lujack, who made a famous game-saving tackle of Doc Blanchard in that game, makes a good point when he said a few years ago, "Here it is over 50 years since we played the game and people still talk about it. That wouldn't happen if we had scored, so maybe a tie isn't all bad."

Because of that game, sports fans have one of sports' best trivia questions: How many future Heisman and Outland winners participated in that game? The answer is seven: Glenn Davis and Doc Blanchard of Army, and John Lujack and Leon Hart of Notre Dame all won the Heisman Trophy; George Connor and Bill Fischer from Notre Dame and Joe Steffy of Army were all Outland Trophy recipients.

Following the Army game, the 1946 Irish team breezed through the final three games defeating Northwestern 27-0, Tulane 41-0 and

Southern Cal 26-6. George, who was outstanding all year was named "Lineman of the Week" by the Associated Press after the Tulane game.

The 1946 Notre Dame football team ended the season as the number one team in the country in total offense and in defense and was the winner of the National Championship. It is the defensive numbers that are so amazing. During the season Notre Dame allowed the opposition a total of only 24 points. There were no extra points, no field goals and no team scored more than six points. This is a modern record at Notre Dame which may never be broken given the way the game is played today.

It had been a very exciting and fulfilling football season for George. He was the outstanding lineman on a Notre Dame team that won a National Championship. George was rewarded for his play during the season by being selected as the consensus All-American at left tackle and the first recipient of the Outland Trophy for the best interior lineman in the country. The Philadelphia Sportswriters' Association voted George the College Football Lineman of the Year. As with the Outland Trophy, George was the first recipient of this award.

To cap off this great year for George, he was voted captain for the 1947 football season by his Notre Dame teammates.

Spring Practice

George had never participated in a spring practice during his high school days or while he played at Holy Cross College before his military service. There was always a "legitimate" reason. In the spring of 1946, the last spring practice before he would graduate, George did not see any reason to start playing in the spring at this late date. It had not hurt his ability to play so far. George reasoned, why do it now? The question was how to get out of practice, particularly in view of the fact that he was the captain-elect for the 1947 football season.

As George told it,

> I had a growth on my left hip so I went to see my uncle, Dr. John L. Keeley, a prominent Chicago surgeon. Dr. Keeley advised that the growth be removed. This was done at Mercy Hospital in Chicago just prior to the start of spring practice. The growth turned out to be a benign cyst, but it was larger than expected. This required Dr. Keeley to put in some gauze packing, with the end sticking out to act as a drain.
>
> I told Hughie Burns, the team trainer, about the surgery and the fact that I would not be able to participate in spring practice. The truth of the matter is that I could have played in about a week or so, but with an excuse like this to miss the grueling and hated spring practice, I was going to take advantage of it.
>
> As expected, Leahy asked to see me in his office the next day to hear first-hand why I had missed the first day of practice and was reportedly going to miss the entire spring practice. I was prepared for the meeting with my plan of attack firmly set in my mind.

George described his meeting as follows:

> When I went into his office I said, "Hi, Coach. I understand you wanted to see me." "Oh George," he said, "I hear you have had some kind of minor surgery. What is the problem, lad?" I told him about the lump and what Dr. Keeley had done. I told him that Dr. Keeley said that I was not to participate in any athletics for several months. Leahy, always the skeptic when it came to injuries or anyone missing practice asked, "George, do you mind if I see the wound?"

I thought he might do this so I said, "Coach, I'll be happy to show it to you."

What followed is not easily described without getting too graphic. George rigged the bandages and drain such that Leahy ended up with blood on his white, Palm Beach suit. In a shaky voice Leahy said, "Oh my God, George, put that drain back." Leahy's face was ashen. He tried to compose himself and said, "George, George, don't go near the practice field. You take care of yourself and I'll see you at summer practice." George exited the office a happy man. He had avoided the dreaded spring practice once again.

Years later George told Leahy that he had deceived him regarding the seriousness of his injury. After hearing George's version of what happened, Leahy still did not believe him. He said, "Oh no, George, you had a serious hip problem, and had you not sat out the spring practice you might have been forced to miss part of the season. That would have cost us at least two victories and the National Championship."

In May, 1946, after spring practice had ended, Jerry Groom, who would later gain stardom at Notre Dame as an All-American center and linebacker, came to Notre Dame at Frank Leahy's invitation for a recruiting visit. Since John Lujack was away from school on a speaking engagement, Groom was assigned to stay in his room. While in the room, Groom wanted to make some notes concerning his visit so he innocently opened the desk drawer in search of some paper and a pencil and was shocked to see a drawer with a lot of loose cash in it. Lujack and George were both excellent speakers and, as stars on the 1946 National Championship team, were much in demand as speakers at various functions. It was customary and accepted practice to get paid for these speaking engagements, usually anywhere from 50 to 100 dollars. Lujack never had any extra money until this time and probably didn't even have a bank account, so he just put the cash in his desk drawer. Leaving loose cash in a desk drawer in a student room in that era was almost as safe as depositing it in a bank.

The following day, Groom met with the center coach, Wally Ziemba who was with George and Moose Krause. This was the first time George and Groom met and the two would form a life-long friendship. Groom quickly learned about George's playful nature when, after relating to the group about opening Lujack's desk drawer and finding all that cash, George said, "Jerry, Lujack is only a quarterback. Can you imagine how much more money there would have been from speaking engagements if he were a tackle or a center?"

CHAPTER SIX

Notre Dame: The 1947 Season

Summer Practice

When the team reported for summer practice Ziggie was already in hot water. He had received a telegram from Coach Leahy during the summer months informing him that he was aware Ziggie was grossly overweight. Further, Leahy wanted him to report for practice weighing no more than 225 pounds. In Leahy's words, "I don't want any fat, funny men on my team."

Ziggie, who weighed about 270 when he received the ultimatum telegram, immediately went on a strict diet. But when he reported to summer practice, he was still 20 pounds over Leahy's limit. In a quandary as to what he should do, he sought out his pal, George. George advised Ziggie that his only course of action was to confront the matter head on and request an extension of the time limit from Coach Leahy. Ziggie did just that and was granted a two-week reprieve. Those two weeks were pure hell for Ziggie as he practiced in near 100-degree heat wearing a rubber suit under his football gear.

When weigh-in day arrived Ziggie, although he looked great, was still seven pounds over his limit. In typical Ziggie style, he bribed the stadium caretaker to rig the locker room scale to be off by seven pounds. To the delight of his teammates and Coach Leahy, Ziggie made the weight limit imposed upon him. The irony of the day was that every player on the squad had to weigh in daily. With the scale rigged, Leahy learned when he checked the weight chart that evening that the team as a whole had lost 640 pounds since the previous day.

A couple of days before summer practice ended, the football team moved from Sorin Hall where we had been housed. For the coming school year George and I would be roommates in Alumni Hall. The previous year both of us had lived in Alumni but with other room-mates. Sharing a room with George would not be new as we shared a room, along with our brother Chuck, growing up on Indiana Avenue in Chicago. The nice part about this arrangement was that Chuck would be across the hall in a single room.

Since the three of us got along so well, the room arrangement was ideal, particularly for me. For the four years prior to coming to Notre Dame I had little contact with Chuck and George because they were at Holy Cross and then in the Navy. When they had left home, I was 14-years-old. Now 18, I was old enough to have a different kind of relationship with them and I loved it.

Almost always in good humor, George was very easy to live with. We enjoyed each other's friends and seemed to find something each day to laugh about. For instance, one day George decided we should re-arrange the furniture in our room. We had two beds, two desks with chairs, two lockers, two easy-chairs and a couch. The day in question, we moved the various furniture around then George said, "You go outside, then come in the room like it's your first time and see how it hits you." When I came into the room, I looked around and said, "No, it doesn't look right." We followed the same routine for about an hour with the same result when, after yet another arrange-ment, I asked George to go outside, come in the room and give his evaluation.

George came in the room and pronounced, "That's it." We plopped on our respective beds proud of our moving day. As we surveyed our handiwork, it hit us both at the same time – the furniture was arranged exactly the same way as when we had started over an hour before. I don't remember how long we laughed but, however long, it was enough to put the incident in our memories forever.

The squad that assembled for the 1947 summer practice was a seasoned group. From the previous year's national championship team only three starters had graduated, Jack Zilly at right end, John Mastrangelo at right guard and Jim Mello at fullback. Replacing Zilly was Leon Hart, who would be named to the All-American team that year. The replacements at guard and fullback were Marty Wendell and John Panelli, both outstanding veteran players. If anything, the three positions were upgraded, which added to the overall strength of the team.

At one of the practice sessions, before any of the players were on the field, Frank Leahy was talking to Jim Costin, the sports editor of the *South Bend Tribune*. "Look at that," Leahy said. "See who the first player to come on the field is? It's the same all the time. Your great competitors, great athletes are the fellows who come out first, work hardest and leave last."

He pointed to George who had just come through the Cartier Field gates to the practice area, the first player to put in an appearance for that session. A minute later John Lujack came on the field. "You'd think I arranged it that way," Leahy observed. Later, George's view of practice as "You play on Saturday as you practice during the week" would pay huge dividends for the Notre Dame team.

The expectations for the team were indeed high, so high that most writers predicted another National Championship for the Irish gridders. However, there was one problem. Leahy must have believed what the press was saying about his team because he completely changed the way the team prepared for the coming season. What happened can best be described by George.

> One of the first practices of the '47 season was probably the worst practice session I ever participated in at Notre Dame. We did our calisthenics and then started running plays like it was the end of the season. Warren Brown, the noted sportswriter of the *Chicago American*, was at practice. I knew he was going to have dinner with Coach Leahy so I waited until he came out of the coaches' room after practice. I said, "Mr. Brown, will you do me and the team a favor? (I think one of the reasons I was elected captain was because I hadn't been at Notre Dame as a young player so I wasn't under

Leahy's influence. I would speak up when needed.) As Mr. Brown and I walked to the dining hall, I said, "Mr. Brown, you watched practice and it was pretty bad wasn't it?" He admitted it was bad and asked what was the problem.

"The coach forgot the drills – the blocking, the tackling and all the drills we practiced every day that made us so good," I replied.

I know Mr. Brown must have talked to Leahy because the next day Leahy said to the team, "Lads, I made the most grievous error I have ever made in my coaching career. I had you running plays like it was the last game of the season. Now we are going back to fundamentals; we will have the drills we always had, the blocking, tackling and individual drills we always had. We are going to build on that." And that's exactly what he did. We did win the championship that year.

The Games

Two weeks before the opening game with Pittsburgh, George suffered an injury in practice. At the hospital in South Bend his injury was diagnosed as a severely sprained ankle. George refused to stay in the hospital or the student infirmary on campus, so they brought him back to our room in Alumni Hall. When I was satisfied that George was resting as well as he could, I walked the short distance to the cafeteria to call our parents. (There were no phones in student dorms in those days.) Dad, in his medical practice, had treated many football injuries. I wanted some advice on what I could do to help George.

Dad gave me some detailed instructions as to how I should prepare George for the night ahead which Dad knew would be a painful one. I was to put a heating pad on a pillow, put a towel over it and cradle George's bad foot in it before I wrapped an ace bandage around the outside of the pillow to secure everything in place.

Armed with Dad's instructions, I returned to our room with the needed supplies which I had scrounged along the way. At about 10:15 p.m., I began my medical role of getting George prepared for the night. At first everything went well. I gently placed George's leg in the pillows, making sure the heating pad was in the proper place. I was almost finished when George said, "Oh no, the angle isn't right – that hurts. You better start over."

So I started over, and again part-way through George said, "I don't think that's going to work that way. It's throbbing too much." Again I retraced the steps of the procedure and after a few more times with George telling me to change something or other about the pillow arrangement, he was finally satisfied. By now it was about five minutes to 11. I was exhausted from the long day of practice and from playing nurse, and very ready to get to my bed to get what I hoped would be a good night's sleep. I undressed, turned out the light and gratefully crawled in bed.

About two bliss-filled minutes passed before I was startled from my half-asleep state to hear laughter coming from George across the room. He was laughing so hard I couldn't imagine what was wrong. "What's wrong?" I shouted as I stumbled out of bed in the darkness.

Gasping for breath between his peals of laughter, he finally blurted out, "We have to be the dumbest guys in the world – all that work for nothing. The electricity is off."

He was right. In our effort to get Dad's instructions right about the heating pad, we completely forgot that the main current to all student rooms was automatically cut off at 11 p.m. every night. All that work getting the heating pad set for the night had been for nothing. I crawled back into bed and must have laughed myself to sleep.

There was no doubt George would miss the first game and the worry was that he might be out of action for much of the season. He did miss the game against Pitt but his pal Ziggie, knowing George was missing, played the game of his life making tackles all over the field as the Irish won 40-6.

The Notre Dame team and George in particular were very fortunate to have the premier trainer in college football, Hughie Burns. He personally supervised George's rehabilitation which was painful but effective. In practice before the second game against Purdue and only two weeks from the day George was injured, Leahy noticed that George was tentative in some of the drills. Always the master psychologist, Leahy devised a drill to allow George to regain his confidence. He had the second-team backfield, and only the right side of the line including the center, in a live scrimmage with George as the sole defender. They ran off-tackle plays, traps, quick openers, all at George. The drill lasted for 30 minutes and the offensive team never gained more than a yard or two.

Years later Leahy told his nephew Jack Leahy about that day in 1947. He said, "Jack, in all my years of playing and coaching football, it was the greatest exhibition of defensive tackle play I have ever seen."

By the third game of the season, with George again playing outstanding football, Leahy came up with a brilliant, albeit short-lived, plan to stifle the opponents' offense. (However brilliant, the idea wasn't original as Ank Scanlon and Lud Wray had devised a similar scheme for George during the 1943 Holy Cross season.) Leahy was aware that the other teams were running their plays away from George's side. This was a logical strategy since the opposing teams knew from either past years experience or from watching film of Notre Dame games that it was virtually impossible to gain much yardage running against George. The opponents' strategy was to run away from George at left tackle. Leahy reasoned that most teams ran to their strong side, which varied depending on the formation they were in. Leahy's plan had George and the right tackle, Ziggie, stand behind the line of scrimmage while they were on defense as if they were linebackers. When the other team broke from its huddle and got into its formation George had the option of selecting which side he would play and Ziggie would play the other. To be in their proper defensive positions before the ball was snapped meant both George and Ziggie had to move quickly to make it in time. After doing this successfully for about a half a quarter, Ziggie was perspiring profusely and somewhat out of breath while George wasn't even breathing hard. In between plays Ziggie said to George, "Moose (as he usually called George), I know you are getting very tired running back and forth, so why don't you just stay at left tackle and I'll play right tackle." That ended Leahy's new defensive strategy.

"One of the things that made the practice sessions more bearable," commented George, "was having Ziggie there."

He was the one who started the cheers on the practice field as a way of breaking the tension. He would imitate a bugle call and then give a cheer and we would all join in. For example, in practice before the Purdue game when Ziggie gave the bugle call and then called out, 'We want to eat. We want to eat.' Leahy who was standing nearby almost had apoplexy at the thought that his players were asking to eat in the middle of a scrimmage. He looked over at us and asked, 'What did you say?' In a heartbeat, Ziggie called out, 'We want to eat (pause) Purdue.' Leahy got that quizzical look on his face but let it go. Ziggie did things like that all the time. Maybe not so bold as the Purdue cheer but his cheers were always good for the team.

With the team living up to the pre-season predictions by playing outstanding football, the Irish handily defeated Purdue, Nebraska, Iowa, Navy and Tulane. Only Northwestern gave them a battle on the way to their last game of the season against a strong Southern Cal team.

It had been 17 years since a Notre Dame team had finished a season unbeaten and untied. The last to accomplish this feat was Knute Rockne's 1930 team, the last he would ever coach. Rockne also won back-to-back National Championships in 1929 and 1930. A victory for Leahy's 1947 players in this final game would put them in the history books as one of Notre Dame's greatest teams. Leahy did not need a special pep talk to get his players ready for this game.

George reflected the attitude of the team when he was interviewed prior to the game:

> When you play at Notre Dame there's only one time and place you can win a football game – that's Saturday afternoon on the field. Every Saturday we meet teams that are fired up for us and ready to shoot the works just like Southern Cal will be. Well, we can shoot the works too, because it's our last game. They won't be any more eager to win than we are. We feel like nothing can stop us from winning this game because all of us want to have the honor of having played on two successive National Championship teams for Notre Dame.

The attitude of the team was evident on the field as the Irish soundly defeated the Trojans 38-7 to win coveted back-to-back National Championships. George played his finest game while at Notre Dame. Warren Brown wrote in his column:

> If this Chicago boy [George], playing his final game for Notre Dame, was not an All-American there isn't any such thing. From the opening seconds of the game he recovered a Trojan fumble, to give Notre Dame possession, and start them off to the first three of their ultimate 38 points. Connor was here, there and everywhere on offense and defense. When Emil Sitko was on the way to his 76-yard touchdown run, he needed one block. That was all. Connor was there to give it, and on went Sitko unimpeded.

After the game, Frank Leahy echoed Brown's assessment of

George's play, saying, "I never saw a greater tackle. I doubt if there ever was one as great as George was against the Trojans." In a post-game interview George said, "It was the greatest thrill of my life to captain a Notre Dame football team, and the high point of it all came when we beat Southern Cal."

It was a great year for George and the 1947 Notre Dame football team. When the post-season honors were announced, George was again consensus All-American, as was John Lujack, who capped his story-book college football career by being named winner of the Heisman Trophy. Some of George's fellow All-Americans that year who would later go on to star in pro football were Bobby Layne (Texas), Doak Walker (Southern Methodist), Chuck Bednarik (Penn) and Bill Swiacki (Columbia), a Holy Cross teammate of George's in 1942.

The 1947 team set a record that still stands at the College Hall of Fame. Seven of the 11 starters on that team have been inducted into the College Hall of Fame. They are Bill Fischer at guard, John Lujack at quarterback, Emil Sitko at halfback, Leon Hart and Jim Martin at ends, and George and Ziggie, both tackles.

Commenting on the success of the 1946 and 1947 Notre Dame teams, George said,

> We had great players and the best coaching staff in college football. Our team was the best conditioned and most fundamentally sound team in football with a great team spirit. There were no egos, no prima donnas. We played as a team with every player giving it everything he had for the good of the team. There was one other factor about our team that might have made us different from the teams we played. Our team was loose and we had fun. Most of the players were service vets and mature guys. They had seen too much to get up-tight. And, we had Ziggie to keep us loose. He was not only the team comedian but he was a very good football player. He started on three Notre Dame

National Championship teams (1943, '46, '47); you have to be a good player to do that.

I played tackle between two great players – Jim Martin at end and Bill Fischer at guard. With those two on either side of me, I had the freedom to play with reckless abandon. Bob Livingstone was one of the best broken-field runners I ever played with. Red Sitko was a great back and John Lujack was great both on offense and on defense. If we were a passing team, John would have set all kinds of records.

We had so many excellent players on the squad. Our scrimmages during the week were some of the toughest opponents I played against all year. One of the things about my two years that is rarely mentioned is that we really had two teams. The first team would play the first quarter and the so-called second team would start the second quarter and play most of that quarter. The first team would start after the half and play as long as needed. This alternating of teams gave us an advantage. It would tire the opponents and allow our team to be well-rested. I can't ever remember being tired in a game at Notre Dame.

I loved my two years playing for Notre Dame and it was a great honor to be the captain of the 1947 team. Frank Leahy was a great coach. He knew all facets of the game and was a great teacher. One aspect of his coaching that often goes unnoticed is the superb job he did in blending a diverse age group into a cohesive unit. It was a particular pleasure to play under our tackle coach, Moose Krause, whom I became very close to in the years that followed my playing days.

I love my teammates from those days. They were not only tremendously talented football players but were and are men of great character. If one had two or three teammates who were exceptional men, you would consider yourself very fortunate. I was blessed to have a whole team full of such men. Where can you find such men as John Lujack, Pete Ashbaugh, Bob Livingstone, Cornie Clatt, Joe Signaigo, Jerry Cowhig, Marty Wendell, Ziggie Czarobski, Zeke O'Connor, Art Statuto, Paul Limont, and the list goes on, all on one team?

Once a year during a weekend of a home Notre Dame football game, the teammates from those teams meet. We have been gathering like this for almost 30 years. It is such a joy for me to see these guys and ones from other years, such as Creighton Miller and Jerry Groom. We have a close bond that is hard to describe. Let me just say, I consider myself very fortunate to have played when I did under great coaches and with such marvelous and talented guys.

Senior Thesis

George was due to graduate in the 1948 January class. But before he graduated he had to write a senior thesis for his Sociology major. With the approval of Father Raymond Murray, the Dean of the department, George selected as his subject the "Psychology of Salesmanship." George worked diligently on his thesis because he knew that Father Murray could be very critical of work not done to his satisfaction. When the paper was completed, George submitted his work.

It was common knowledge among students who took classes in Sociology that Father Murray did not like football and barely tolerated football players. Father Murray also was known to frown on football students who went on to play professional football after graduation. Hence, George was very apprehensive about his upcoming meeting with him. At the meeting, Father Murray told George his thesis paper was unacceptable and that it should be completely redone. When George looked at the paper it was filled with Father Murray's red marks and critical comments.

As George left the meeting, he knew the talk about Father Murray and his dislike of football players was indeed true. George pondered what to do. He knew his thesis was good but he also knew there was no way to get it approved by Father Murray unless he could devise a new approach. After some thought, George came up with a solution whose cunning would have made his pal Ziggie proud.

Aware that Father Murray was an avid reader of the local newspaper, the *South Bend Tribune*. George contacted his good friend Jim Costin, the sports editor of the *Tribune,* and asked for a favor. He asked Costin to write a short article to appear in the *Tribune* that would report that George was going to pass on playing pro football in order to work in the U.S. Penal System. To add credibility to the article, George suggested it not be on the front page.

Costin wrote a short article to the effect that George Connor, the All- American tackle at Notre Dame, had opted to make working in the penal system his life's work thus forsaking the opportunity to play professional football. The article appeared on the third page of the *Tribune* several days later. George had his thesis retyped without changing one word from the previously rejected paper. Several days later George met again with Father Murray. This time a smiling Father praised George's excellent paper and congratulated him on his decision to work in the penal system rather than play pro ball. George received an "A" on his thesis. It would seem George really did understand his subject, "The Psychology of Salesmanship."

East-West Shrine Game

Before he graduated in January, 1948, George played in one more football game as a representative of Notre Dame. He, along with teammates John Lujack and Ziggie Czarobski, were selected to play on the East squad in the annual East-West Shrine All-Star Game in San Francisco's Kezar Stadium on New Year's Day. George, John Lujack and Ziggie arrived in San Francisco about ten days prior to the game. The other twenty-three members of the East squad were in for a treat when they met Ziggie for the first time. He immediately corralled his new teammates and led them to a local bar where they started a party that seemed to last until game time. Each day Ziggie found a new bar to entertain the group in. The squad was so enamored with Ziggie that they elected him their captain. It was the first time in the history of the Shrine Game that a player was elected unanimously. Ziggie, of course, voted for himself.

One of the coaches of the East squad was Bernie Bierman who was the very successful coach at the University of Minnesota, an ex-Marine and known to be a strict disciplinarian. Maintaining discipline proved to be difficult with Ziggie on the field. Several times during the practice sessions Ziggie liked to lead cheers and generally disrupt the serious mood Bierman attempted to set. Bierman, aware of Ziggie leading the squad to the bars in the evening, held a bed check one night. Finding the players missing, Bierman ordered a special team meeting the following day. In the middle of Bierman's tirade Ziggie interrupted and said, "Coach, the joke's on you. We knew you were going to have a bed check so we were on the floor above having a pillow fight." Bierman's face turned red and he stormed out of the meeting. In his pre-game talk to the team, Bierman told them they were the worst conditioned and most poorly-prepared team he ever saw, and that it would be a miracle if they could just not totally embarrass themselves during the game.

After returning the opening kickoff to the 30-yard-line, the West team marched down the field to score. After the extra point, Ziggie hollered, "Everyone assemble on the 50-yard-line." Lujack thought Ziggie would chew the team out for the sloppy play. Instead, Ziggie said, "Wasn't that a magnificent drive the West team had? Let's give them a cheer." The fans, and particularly Bierman, couldn't believe what they were witnessing when the 11-man East squad huddled at midfield and shouted with loud voices: "Who's a Team? They're a Team. They're a Great Team. The West Team. The West Team. The West Team."

The East team, with marvelously talented players, then settled down and proceeded to completely dominate the West team. The East won the game, 40-9, to the surprise of most of the fans and to the utter amazement of Bierman. At the time, it was the most points scored by one team in the history of the Shrine Game.

After the Shrine Game, George, Lujack and Ziggie returned to the Notre Dame campus – George in time to graduate in the January, 1948 class and Lujack and Ziggie in the June class. Thanks to Ziggie's antics, George and Lujack added to their portfolio of Ziggie stories, which helped make them a big hit on the post-season banquet circuit. As for Ziggie, he continued to entertain all around him. After graduation, he commented, "I would have been Phi Beta Kappa if it wasn't for my grades."

Comments from George's Notre Dame teammates.

Joe Signaigo

"I first met George, who had transferred from Holy Cross, in Frank Leahy's office upon my return to Notre Dame after the war. I was assigned to take him under my wing and show him the campus. George was very impressive at that time being close to 6 feet 4 inches tall. George was the most respected player on the 1946 and 1947 National Championship teams. He was our leader. He, along with Coach Leahy, helped instill in us the desire to win. It has been an honor and privilege to be a teammate of George, as well as a friend. I look forward to sitting with him at our yearly reunions and reminiscing about how it used to be. Most of the time we conclude that at our best we could play with today's players and still be national champs."

Bill Walsh

"George was the epitome of a teammate to me. I was third string and George always treated me as an equal. It meant a lot to me as I had been the starting center the year before. You always knew he would help you if you needed it. He and Ziggie were the best two tackles in the country for two years. It was a pleasure to be a middle linebacker behind those two great players. They sort of made it easier."

"He was always there when needed, picking up our morale by his leadership and consistent effort at practice. All my thoughts of George are what a great teammate and player he was and that it was a tremendous thrill to be his teammate for two years. He was a great one."

Jim Martin – Hall of Fame (Deceased)

"When people ask me who was the best player I ever played with, I don't hesitate to tell them George Connor. Playing alongside him was a delight. George was so good. He took care of everything that came our way, which gave me the opportunity to play recklessly. He was a great leader – one that the whole team looked up to. It was an honor to be his teammate."

Art Statuto

"There are many events I could relate about George's character and ability, but one that stands out is the time after a particularly exhausting practice session, George made the rounds of all the 'hamburgers' (reserves) and did his best to buoy up the spirits of all who participated. His own fanny had to be dragging as much, if not more, than the rest of us but his leadership determined that the 'troops' needed comfort and solace before he could take care of his needs. To me, his leadership qualities were even better than his great playing ability and he was the best as a player."

Bill "Moose" Fischer – Hall of Fame and Outland Winner

"George was the fastest and most agile lineman I ever saw or played against in college or pro ball. Playing alongside him for two years at Notre Dame was remarkable. We were so in tune with each other that we would change blocking assignments without the coaches' permission. George was immediately accepted at Notre Dame when he came in as a transfer student because he was truly a wonderful man and great player. George led by example and by his natural leadership qualities. I never saw any of our players or any opponents get the best of George. He was so fast that there might have been one or two backs who could beat him in a 100-yard dash but it would have been only by a step or two."

"His Chicago Bear line coach, Hunk Anderson,

once told me that George was the smartest linebacker he ever coached and the most efficient. He was Hunk's pride and joy and according to Hunk, his best overall player. In my opinion, George was the greatest, the very best and more, in both college and pro ball."

Frank Tripucka

"I first heard of George Connor when I was in high school. One of our players at Bloomfield High, Frank Muehlhauser, was several years ahead of me. Frank was a terrific player, 6 feet 2, about 230 pounds and fast. I talked to him after he had played fullback for Andy Kerr at Colgate. Frank told me that when Colgate played Holy Cross there was a player, George Connor, on the Holy Cross team that threw him around like he was a paper doll. After the war, at Notre Dame, I encountered George. He threw the players on the Notre Dame team around the way Muehlhauser had described. George Connor was the best tackle I ever played with or against. When they moved him to linebacker with the Bears, it made it worse. Instead of being at one position, he could now roam the field. He was all over the place making tackles, rushing the passer and knocking down passes. He was the best. As a person, they don't come any better than George. He's always the same George – greets you with that big smile and that friendly way he has."

CHAPTER SEVEN

The Chicago Bears

Despite his student status in 1946 with another year of eligibility remaining, George was the first-round draft choice of the New York Giants. Following the draft the owner of the Giants, Wellington Mara, made a trip to Chicago to meet with George at our south side home. Both George and Dad were very impressed with Mara and his sincerity as he told them how much the Giants would like George to play for them. George told Mara he planned on returning to Notre Dame for another season. He also told Mara that he had played in the east for two years in college and did not want to play in New York. Mara seemed to understand and later traded the rights to George to the Boston Yanks in return for Paul Governali, the Columbia All-American quarterback.

Ted Collins, the manager of vocalist Kate Smith, was the owner of the Yanks. Collins called George to make arrangements to sign him. In introducing himself to George, he made a point of the fact that he was a good friend of Father John Cavanaugh, the President of the University of Notre Dame. "I told him I didn't want to play for the Boston Yanks," recalls George. "He tried to threaten me by saying he would call Father Cavanaugh to use his influence. I told him to go ahead and call. My mother was also a good friend of Father Cavanaugh." Later, Collins received a call from George Halas, owner and coach of the Chicago Bears. This resulted in George's rights being traded to the Bears in return for a big tackle, Mike Jarmoluk who played for the Bears in 1946 and 1947.

That year top college prospects, like George, had the benefit of dealing with two teams, one from the NFL and one from the newly formed American Football Conference. In the new league, George was first the property of the San Francisco Forty-Niners until they traded his rights to the Cleveland Browns. Creighton Miller, the star halfback on the '43 Notre Dame team, was hired in 1944 by Art McBride, Sr. to scout prospects for the newly formed Cleveland Browns' team. Miller recalls that when he first met Paul Brown in 1944, the appointed team coach, Brown told him that George Connor was at the top of his list of players he wanted for the team.

George met several times with Art McBride, the new owner of the Browns and one of George's fellow students at Notre Dame. Later Bob Voights, the former Northwestern coach who was on the staff of the Browns, met with George several times. "I liked both Art and Bob Voights and our talks were always very friendly," recalled George, "but I told them I wanted to play in Chicago."

Prior to the Boston Yank and Chicago Bears' trade, George paid a visit to the Chicago Cardinal camp in Waukesha, Wisconsin to talk to Jimmy Conzleman, the coach of the Cardinals. He told Conzleman and some Cardinal front office people that he was interested in playing for them. As a Chicago south sider George was a Cardinal fan. The Cardinal officials told George they were all set at tackle and therefore weren't interested.

George then called George Halas and told him he was interested in playing for the Bears. The two set a date to meet at the Bear office several days later. George told Halas of his desire to play in Chicago and that he was currently the property of the Boston Yanks. He also related how he had offered his services to the Cardinals. Halas said, "It's a good thing you didn't go with them. You just hang tough with Boston and maybe we can work something out." Shortly after their meeting, Halas made the trade with Boston to acquire the rights to George.

In January, 1948 much was written in the Chicago papers about the upcoming press conference to announce the signing of John Lujack, the Heisman Trophy winning quarterback from Notre Dame. However no date was set. Lujack was the Bears' number one draft choice and with Sid Luckman nearing the end of his career the signing of Lujack was big news for Chicago Bears' fans. What was unknown to the press is that George would sign with the Bears the same day as Lujack. According to George here is how the signing came about:

> After the trade, Halas and I met several times to work out the financial arrangements of the contract. He told me to meet him in his office the morning of January 25th. I didn't know the Bears had a press conference scheduled that afternoon to announce the signing of Lujack. When Halas and I met and he gave me the contract to sign I said, "Coach, before I sign this I would like my lawyer to look at it." He asked, "Who's your lawyer?" I said, "Judge Cornelius J. Harrington of the Circuit Court." Halas said, "If you think you have to, then go see him." Judge Harrington went through the contract and crossed out three clauses and wrote in another to the effect that if I was injured the Bears would still have to pay me. The parts he crossed out had to do with trading and releasing me. The upshot of this was to make it a non-release contract. Judge Harrington and I went back to Halas' office to learn that we held up the press conference for almost three hours.

The announcement that the Bears had signed the number one college quarterback (Lujack) and the number one lineman (George) on the same day made the front page of the sports sections of all the Chicago papers the following day.

Bear Camp – A Marked Man

Before George reported at Bear camp in Rensselaer, Indiana he was already a "marked" man. George recalled what happened:

> One of the tellers or someone at the bank told Ray Bray and Chuck Drulis (Bear players who used the same bank as I did) what my bonus was. Now they knew my bonus was as much as they were making as Bear players. At the Bear camp word spread to Bulldog Turner, Fred Davis and other veterans. Given this, they were really gunning for me when I reported to camp. On top of that, many of the pro players at the time had an intense dislike for Notre Dame players, "The Gold Domers" they used to call us.
>
> In the scrimmages, Drulis, Bray and Turner were so intent on getting me that many times they tipped the play. I held my own on the field despite the continual attempts of some of the veterans to get me. It was obvious they didn't want to associate with me so I hung around with Don Kindt, Lujack and some of the other rookies. When camp ended and the coaches cut the squad down to 31 players, Bulldog Turner, the Bear captain, came up to me and said, "Kid, we didn't like you when you came in and I'm not sure we like you now but you're a helluva football player. Welcome to the team."

George's "huge" bonus was $6,000. In today's market, several players have received bonuses of 8 to 15 million.

Hunk Anderson

George's line coach while he was a player with the Bears was Heartly "Hunk" Anderson. Hunk played his college football under Knute Rockne and later became his line coach. After Rockne tragically died in an airplane crash in 1931, Hunk was named Notre Dame's head football coach. Hunk eventually teamed up with George Halas to become a well-known and respected Bears' line coach.

To say that George loved Hunk is an understatement. The two developed a relationship over the years that was more like father and son than coach and player. Yet, this was not always the case. As a matter of fact, for the first several weeks George was at Bear camp, Hunk treated him as someone he didn't like at all.

Following his habit, George was the first one on the practice field each day and, more often than not, the last to leave. His work ethic on the field was exemplary. In the evenings, after the team meetings, many players slipped into town for a few beers but George passed on such outings. Given his excellent behavior on and off the field, George couldn't understand why Hunk barely spoke to him. Hunk was a fellow Notre Dame man, George reasoned. "I haven't done anything wrong; so what's the problem?" George asked himself.

The Bears first exhibition game was in Memphis, Tennessee against the New York Giants. George and his roommate, John Lujack, were in poor spirits. George, because he wasn't making any headway in his relationship with Hunk no matter how hard he tried, and Lujack because he had a chipped bone in his ankle which happened in the All-Star Game that still bothered him. The two decided to break their strict training regimen and have a few beers. They soon joined up with some other players and had a party.

The next day at game time the temperature in Crump Stadium climbed into the upper 90s. With the oppressive heat, all the players were showing signs of its effects. At halftime the Bear team lay on the grass in the end zone since the locker room was too hot to use. George, who had played the second quarter, was stretched out on the turf perspiring profusely. Hunk approached George and in that gruff voice said, "Connor, were you drinking last night?"

George thought, the one time since the beginning of camp I go out and Hunk catches me. He replied, "Yes, I was."

"What were you drinking?" asked Hunk.

"Beer," George replied.

"How much did you drink?"

"About a case," George answered.

Hunk smiled and said, "Thatta boy. You start the second half."

George played the entire second half. As it turned out, Hunk thought George was a prude, a goodie-goodie. Once Hunk learned that George had had some beers, he concluded he was a regular guy. From that day on, the two were great friends.

In their second exhibition game the Bears played the Washington Redskins in Baltimore. It was George's first encounter with the legendary quarterback Sammy Baugh. George described what happened:

> He was the greatest quarterback I ever played against. He was about six feet four, had a great stiff-arm and was tough. One play I beat my man and headed for Baugh who was fading back to pass. Sammy tripped as I hit him a real hard shot and we both went down hard. He jumped up, helped me up and said, "Nice tackle, George Connor." I couldn't believe he knew my name. He was the best passer I ever saw. He had very few of his passes intercepted because he could put the ball exactly where he wanted so the defender couldn't get it. He was the best and he was tough.

In that same game against the Redskins, George's dental bridge came out and appeared lost. He told the official he thought he knew where it was and got down on his hands and knees and began to look for it. The officials and players from both teams soon were on their hands and knees looking for George's bridge, which eventually turned up. Bert Bell, the NFL commissioner was monitoring the game on radio. He heard the announcer say, "There's a time out on the field. The Bears, Redskins and the officials are all on their hands and knees looking for something. I think the official lost his whistle." Later the official told George, "You got me in deep trouble with the commissioner looking for your teeth."

The 1948 Rookie Bear Season

The players and coaches were optimistic about their chances to win the championship that year. In the past seven years they had been champs four times, the latest in 1946. The previous year, the 1947 season, they had finished second with an 8-4 record. On the plus side for the coming season: Most of the key players were returning, including Sid Luckman, George McAfee, Ed Sprinkle, Ken Kavanaugh, Jim Keane, Chuck Drulis, Ray Bray, Bulldog Turner and Fred Davis. The latter four had been selected to the All-Pro team the previous year. On the negative side: Several of these players were nearing the end of their careers, in particular Luckman and McAfee. To counter this, the Bears signed Lujack as heir apparent to succeed Luckman at the quarterback position and J. R. Boone, a promising running back from the University of Tulsa. In addition, to bolster the line the Bears signed George, Paul Stenn (a tackle from Villanova who had previous pro experience with the Redskins and Giants) and Washington Serini (a guard from Kentucky University).

With the exhibition games behind them, the Bears began their quest for a championship with impressive wins against the Green Bay Packers, their arch-rival, and the 1947 NFL champs, the Chicago Cardinals. To run their streak to four straight victories the Bears soundly defeated the Los Angeles Rams and the New York Giants. The road to the championship was temporarily sidetracked by a 12-7 loss to the always tough Philadelphia Eagles. However, the Bears got right back on track by winning six games in a row. This brought their record to 10-1. The Bears and the Cards had identical 10-1 records going into the final game which would be for the division championship.

Before a packed house at Wrigley Field the Bears dominated the first half, holding the Cardinal "Dream Backfield" of Paul Christman, Elmer Angsman, Charlie Trippi and Pat Harder to a mere 21 yards rushing. To begin the second half, the Bears opted to try an onside kick. This proved to be their downfall. The Cards recovered the kick-off and rallied to win the game by a score of 24 to 21, thus thwarting the championship bid of the Bears. The Cardinals played the Eagles for the NFL championship game and lost 7-0.

The 1948 season ushered in the two-platoon rules which allowed unlimited substitution. Prior to that time, the rule was "limited substitution" which meant that the majority of players played both ways (offense and defense). With unlimited substitution, the era of specialization came into being. Even with this, many of the interior linemen (centers, guards and tackles) continued to play both ways.

George had a very good year, playing both ways dividing the time with Fred Davis, one of the meanest players in the league. Hunk Anderson was so comfortable with playing either George or Fred Davis at left tackle that he allowed them to freely substitute for each other. George learned the hard way to keep an eye on Davis before he went in the game for him. After he played for about six minutes, Davis would raise his hand which was the signal for George to take his place. On the first play after he entered the game, the player opposite George would belt him with a fist in the face. (George wore no facemask, although Davis did.) After this happened a few times, George watched Davis closely. He saw Davis raise his hand for George to come in the game, on the next play slug the player opposite him, and then leave the game. A much wiser George said, "from then on I announced in a loud voice when I entered the game, 'Connor in for Davis,' but I also ducked." That ended George being greeted on the first play after he entered with a fist in the face.

George's roommate on road trips was John Lujack, who had a sensational rookie year playing full time on defense and spelling Luckman on offense. For his great play on defense, Lujack was named All-League on the defensive team, a rare accomplishment for a rookie.

The 1948 season marked the first time since 1946 that George and Lujack played football without their fun-loving friend, Ziggie. Czarobski had signed a contract with the Chicago Rockets from the American Football Conference. Without the discipline of coach Frank Leahy to keep him in condition, Ziggie's weight ballooned out of control. From the reports heard in Chicago, Ziggie was not having a good year. I encountered Ziggie just prior to the end of the season and asked how things were going. Ziggie replied, "Great" which surprised me. He explained:

> The guy who films our games is not nearly as good as the one we had at Notre Dame. Remember how his films covered almost the width of the field? Well, the Rockets guy's film only covers about eight yards. Once I figured that out, I make sure I am always more than eight yards from the ball. When the coaches review the films, they can't find me.

Ziggie wasn't the only Rocket player who didn't play well that year. The team lost thirteen games while winning only one.

Tarzan

In 1948, Hollywood movie moguls decided that it was time to replace Johnny Weissmuller as Tarzan. George, who had no acting experience at all, was among the many actors and athletes on the list of candidates to be considered as a potential new Tarzan.

While on the west coast with the Bears, George had his screen test. George likes to kid that the reason he didn't make the grade as

Tarzan was that he had trouble with the line – "Me Tarzan, you Jane." According to reports what really happened is that the producer, when viewing George's test and saw his size, reportedly said, "If George was playing Tarzan and was in a fight with a lion, the lion would be the underdog." George did not get the job.

Although George's screen test was a minor event, it received a lot of press in the Chicago papers. There was a picture of George in a loin cloth with an elephant in the background in one of the Chicago newspapers. George took some good-natured kidding about his short-lived Tarzan role. Once George and I went to one of the neighborhood bars where many of George's friends were known to gather. As we walked in, we spotted a group we knew at the bar. As we approached the group, Bob Walsh, one of George's good friends, walked right by us without saying a word. By the look on George's face you could tell he was perplexed as to why his good friend would ignore him. In less than a minute Bob returned and greeted George, "Sorry I didn't stop to say hello. I had to go outside to give your elephant a drink."

The 1949 Bear Season

Assessing the 1948 season Halas said,

> Johnny Lujack gave one of the best all-around performances I ever saw in our final game against the Cardinals. He easily could have completed 12 or 13 passes in a row if our ends had held onto the ball. We are fortunate to have him back with such other great second-year men as George Connor, Joe Abbey, Paul Stenn and J. R. Boone. The record shows how much they meant to us this past year...and how much they will mean to us in this coming season.

To the men already on the squad, the Bears added several good rookie prospects. The best of them were John Hoffman, a back from Arkansas University, and George Blanda, a quarterback from the University of Kentucky. Blanda would make his mark in pro ball by playing 27 years, an all-time record, as is his total of 2002 points scored. His storied career earned him induction into the NFL Hall of Fame.

One of the big names from the 1948 team, Bobby Layne, would be missing from the 1949 squad. During the summer Halas sold Layne's contract to the New York Bulldogs in what seemed like a minor deal at the time. However, as sports fans know, Layne would go on in future years to lead the Detroit Lions to two NFL championships and have a Hall of Fame career as one of the NFL's greatest quarterbacks. As it turned out, the sale of Layne would be one of Halas' biggest blunders, especially when considering that both Luckman and Lujack would be out of pro football in a matter of a few years.

The Bears opened the 1949 season against the Packers in Green Bay. Although Lujack was knocked out in the second quarter when he was involved in a violent collision with one of the Packer players, he recovered to lead the Bears to a 17-0 victory. Lujack not only was involved in all the Bear points with a 16-yard field goal, two touchdown passes and two extra points but he also intercepted three Packer passes. One of the astounding aspects of the Bears' victory is that their defenders, Lujack, McAfee and Bill DeCorrevont did not allow the famed Packer aerial attack to complete a single pass the entire game.

On the intense rivalry between the Bears and Packers, George recalled:

> The rivalry was so heated that when we would go to Green Bay they used to hire bands to play outside our hotel rooms all night to prevent us from getting a good night's sleep. There used to be two or three thousand Packer fans meeting us at the train station

just to look at the hated Bears. One time after we beat the Packers, a fan walked up to Halas at the station and punched him in the face.

In the 1948 game, right before the half ended, "Indian Jack" Jacobs kicked me in the chin and opened up a cut that required 13 stitches to close. In those days we didn't have a team doctor who would travel with the team so I had to go out of the stadium to a little shack where the doctor Halas hired sewed me up. Then the trainer had to apply some protective padding for my chin. By then, the team was already on the field.

When I tried to get back in the stadium there was a Packer fan manning the gate and he wouldn't let me in. "But I have to play," I told him. "Tough" he said. There were a couple of Bear fans who came down from the stands and started a fight with this guy and I got in. As I ran to the inner fence, the Packer fans started beating me over the head with programs, lunch bags, anything they could get their hands on. I finally jumped the inner fence and ran across the field to our side. When I got there Halas said, "You're late. That will cost you 25 bucks." Later, when he found out what happened, he canceled the fine.

George was a little peeved, to put it mildly, about the way he had been treated by the Packer fans. But this gave him an incentive to hit especially hard the second half.

In their second game, the Bears defeated the "Big Red," the Chicago Cardinals, the 1948 Western Conference Champs, 17-7. The Bears lost their next game to the Rams by a score of 31-16 as Bob Waterfield and Elroy "Crazylegs" Hirsch put on an offensive display to the dismay of the fans at Wrigley Field. The fourth game of the season was against the 1948 NFL champions, the Philadelphia Eagles. The game would prove to be of historical significance in the annals of pro football because it was a game in which the nature of the linebacking position was forever changed.

The Eagles had a powerful running game led by Steve Van Buren, who was first in the league that year with 1,146 rushing yards and 11 touchdowns. Van Buren was a 225-pound back who had speed. He was a punishing runner who could go around people, but he also had the strength and desire to go through would-be tacklers. His most productive yardage was gained on a sweep around end, usually to his right. Pete Pihos, the Hall of Fame right end, would flank wide and block back as Van Buren would start his sweep, led by a hoard of blockers including Joe Muha, the fullback, the pulling guards, Bucko Kilroy and Mario Giannelli, and the right halfback, Bosh Pritchard. To the opposing end and linebacker it looked like a heard of wild buffalos coming at them. To counter this play, Hunk Anderson, the wily defensive coach of the Bears, came up with a unique solution. He asked George to switch from his tackle position on defense and play left linebacker. He instructed George that his job was to strip the interference whenever Van Buren started on his famous sweep. George's key was to watch Pihos blocking back and the Eagle's right guard. When he pulled out to his right, George would use his speed to get across the line quickly and his power, size and tenacity to crash into any opposing players in front of Van Buren.

The first time the Eagles ran the sweep, George sprinted across the line of scrimmage and knocked down two blockers about five yards behind the line. The backfield was so congested with bodies that Van Buren also went down. The strategy was successful beyond even Anderson's imagination. George repeatedly knocked down Van Buren's interference, leaving Van Buren open to be tackled by the other Bears. On many of the plays, George did his job so well that in addition to stripping the blockers, he also managed to get Van Buren for a substantial loss.

Without their bread-and-butter play to rely on, the Eagles went down in defeat for their only loss of the season. That day George became the first of the big, fast, mobile linebackers. He became the prototype of the modern linebacker. Hunk's innovation of having a big, agile tackle play the linebacker position changed the nature of linebacking from that day on. After that game George became a full time linebacker while he continued to play tackle on offense.

Although the Bears had lost to the Rams, they had defeated the two teams who had played for the NFL championship the previous year. They also had beaten their arch rival, the Packers. With four games under their belts, they were very happy to be 3 and 1 at this stage of the season. But their high spirits were short-lived as the Bears were defeated in New York in their next game by an inspired NY Giant team, 35-28. The Bears were as inept on defense as they had been sensational against the Eagles the week before. The 35 points scored by the Giants represented the highest total ever scored by the Giants against the Bears in their 34-game rivalry that stretched back to 1925.

Even in defeat, the Bears looked great at times on offense, especially when Lujack was passing to Jim Keane who set an NFL record that day as he caught 14 passes for 193 yards. The Bears spotted the Giants 21 points before they began to roll and eventually tied the score 28-28 in the fourth quarter. However, two plays later, Charlie Conerly tossed a screen pass to Gene Roberts, who went 85 yards for the winning touchdown. The defeat was a crushing blow for the Bears, virtually knocking them out of the championship race. It was a particularly bitter loss since many of the Bear players felt they could have won if Halas had started Lujack instead of Sid Luckman. George told the inside story of what happened:

> During the summer before the season started, Luckman had thyroid surgery. He was used sparingly the first few games as he recovered from his surgery. Lujack played most of the time. For some reason, Halas decided that Luckman would start in New York

as sort of a homecoming for him since he was from New York and attended Columbia. The papers ran the story with sub-headlines, "Luckman Gets Green Light." One of the Bear players hung a green light in his locker.

Luckman at this time was past his prime. This, coupled with the fact he hadn't played much prior to this game, caused our defeat. He couldn't get the offense moving. We were down 21 to 0 at halftime. When Lujack came in the game he was red hot. So was Jim Keane, who set a receiving record that day. It's my opinion, shared by many of the Bear players, that if Lujack had started the game we would have won easily.

A demoralized Bear team had to face the unbeaten Rams in Los Angeles in their next game. Lujack threw for 315 yards in the Giants game, an incredible accomplishment since he did not enter the game until just before halftime. He was now leading the league in passing, ahead of such greats as Sammy Baugh, Bob Waterfield and Tommy Thompson. A record 86,080 fans watched the game in the Memorial Coliseum as a pass interference call in the last five minutes allowed the Rams a touchdown to defeat the Bears 27-24. After the game Halas complained bitterly about the officiating which he said gave the Rams two touchdowns. The Bears were almost mathematically out of contention with a 3-3 record. However, they refused to quit and won their next five games against the Packers, Lions, Redskins, Lions and Steelers. During this stretch of games, George, who usually split offensive left tackle duties with Fred Davis, was getting more and more playing time in recognition of his superb blocking skills. He continued to play full time on defense as a linebacker, both as a middle linebacker and outside linebacker.

Going into the last game of the season against the Cardinals, the Bears still had a chance for a division title if the Rams lost to the

Redskins and the Bears beat the Cardinals.

The Bears did defeat the Cardinals 52-21 before 50,101 cheering fans in Wrigley Field. Lujack was brilliant as he passed for 468 yards and six touchdowns, breaking the NFL record for yards gained in a single game. Lujack's six touchdown passes fell one short of the record set by his teammate, Sid Luckman, against the Giants in 1943. Lujack came within two yards of surpassing Luckman's record, as on two of Lujack's completed passes, the receiver was downed on the one-yard-line. Of Lujack's 24 pass completions, three were tackle-eligible passes, with Paul Stenn catching two for 11 yards and George one for 25.

The Rams, however, also won their game and ended the season with an 8-2-2 record and the undisputed claim to first place. As the Bears reflected on the season, they knew the loss to the Giants had cost them a division title.

But George had had a great season. As a second-year player he gained recognition as one of the best blocking tackles in the league on offense and a linebacker who played equally well on the run and on pass defense. His play earned him second team honors on the NFL All-Pro team. His teammate, Lujack, was rewarded for his great season by being named to the first team on the All-Pro team.

The 1950 Season

Before the 1950 season commenced there was a major event in pro football – namely the collapse of the All-American Football Conference which had started after the war in 1946. The main reason for the collapse was the domination of the conference by the Cleveland Browns under the leadership of Paul Brown. To adjust to the influx of players coming into the NFL from the defunct conference, the league held a supplemental draft and re-aligned the teams. From the All-American Conference, the NFL added the two best teams, the Cleveland Browns and the San Francisco Forty-Niners as new members.

To accommodate the new teams, the new NFL Commissioner,

Bert Bell, put Cleveland in the former Eastern Division (temporarily called the American Conference) along with regulars: Philadelphia, Pittsburgh, the New York Giants and Washington. He added the Chicago Cardinals from the West and switched the New York Yanks (formerly the New York Bulldogs) to the Western Division (temporarily called the National Conference). In the new National Conference were the LA Rams, Chicago Bears, Detroit, Green Bay, San Francisco and the NY Yanks. There were now six teams to a division as opposed to the former five-team divisions.

As the Bears gathered at summer camp, the coaches and players were optimistic about their chances to win the division title. Since George had joined the Bears in 1948 the team had gone 10-2 in '48 and 9-3 in '49. They lost the title in both years by only one game. To add to their feeling of optimism, they had a seasoned team plus the addition of the aging but still agile Alf Bauman and some outstanding rookies.

Heading into his third season with the Bears, George was considered one of the veterans of the team along with Ken Kavanagh, Jim Keane, Ed Sprinkle, Fred Davis, Paul Stenn, Wash Serini, Bulldog Turner, Chuck Drulis, Ray Bray, Sid Luckman, George Blanda, John Lujack, George Gulyanics, Don Kindt and J.R. Boone. Since George's first year, players such as Bill Wightkin, Wayne Hansen, Curly Morrison, Bones Weatherly, Fred Negus, Stu Clarkson, Julie Rykovich and Frank Dempsey had joined the team.

Frank Dempsey played his college ball at Florida. When he reported to the Bear camp in August, 1950 at St. Joseph's College in Rensselaer, Indiana, there were about 95 players, including the veterans, who were in camp. Dempsey was 6´ 4˝ and weighed about 230 and was very fast for a man his size. According to Dempsey:

> The veterans tested the rookies at every opportunity to see if we had the guts to withstand the punishment they handed out. Added to that, all the veterans except three, George Connor, Ken Kavanaugh and Sid Luckman never spoke to us off

the field. George seemed to sense how worried I was about making the cut as he would make it a point to see me after practice and say, "Don't worry Dempse, keep playing hard and you'll make it." I really appreciated that.

On the last day of camp when the squad had to be trimmed to the league limit, Halas told Dempsey he was switching him to guard to take the place of the veteran Chuck Drulis who had been traded to the Green Bay Packers. Dempsey was thrilled to make the team, since making an NFL roster in those days was extremely difficult. With six teams in each division and each team permitted to carry only 32 active players for a total of 384 active players in the league, it was difficult to make a roster. To put this in perspective, today there are 31 teams with an active roster of 45 players for a total of 1,395 active players. This means that today more than a thousand more men play pro football than in 1950.

George's teammate, Don Kindt, was a first-round draft choice from the University of Wisconsin the year before George joined the Bears. He was George's closest friend on the Bears' team. Neither believed in harassing rookies but they did believe in having some fun with them. They would target some wide-eyed rookie and wait until they were with him in the trainers' room. Then George would ask Kindt how his back was holding up; how his old wound from WW II was faring. Kindt would reply, "It's holding up pretty well but sometimes the memories haunt me." If the rookie didn't bite and ask what the war wound was, George would coax Kindt to tell the rookie the story. Kindt would relay the following:

> I was in an Army ski patrol in the Italian Alps when I was separated from my unit. I saw a German ski patrol in the distance and knew my only chance of survival was to hide in the snow and hope my white outfit would blend in so I wouldn't be spotted

since they were headed in my direction. As I lay in the snow I could hear the Germans coming and then I could feel their skis on my back as they went right over me single file. That's why I have these scars on my back. Thank God for the precision of the Germans or I would have many scars on my back.

The rookie would be astounded as he listened to Kindt's tale. George and Kindt would nod to each other with a look that implied, "We suckered another one." In fact, Kindt's scars were from back surgery performed years before he joined the Bears and the scars from the surgery were two parallel lines across his lower back. They pulled their act at least twice in every training camp and never failed to fool some gullible rookie.

The Bears fared very well in the exhibition season, winning four out of the six games played. The only teams with a better pre-season record were the Browns and Redskins who were undefeated. The Bears' best win was against the champion Philadelphia team. As one of the sportswriters put it,

> A couple of Notre Dame graduates and a former Northwestern Wildcat gave the veteran Eagle line a lesson in rushing that will not soon be forgotten – neither by the Eagles or the 30,000 fans who watched the game. The two Irish battlers were end, Bill Wightkin, a rookie and George Connor. The Northwestern Player was Alf Bauman.

In an exhibition game against the Cleveland Browns played in Cleveland, George had an encounter with the great Otto Graham. George told what happened:

> Graham fumbled near the line of scrimmage and I scooped up the ball and started to run. There was

no one in front of me. I had visions of a touchdown. I had to run on the infield part of the field still there from the baseball season. As I was running over the pitcher's mound, I was clobbered from behind. I was hit with such force that I was seeing stars. I had never been knocked out but this was close. As I laid on the ground, I turned to see a big number 60 on the guy on the ground next to me. I said, "Otto, what are you doing hitting a guy like that?" Graham said, "George, there was no way I was going to let a lineman score on my fumble."

In talking about Otto Graham, George went on to say that in his opinion Graham was one of the greatest quarterbacks who ever played. He said he would put him on a par with Sammy Baugh. George said Graham was an outstanding passer and a superb field general. He was tough, as George found out when Graham almost knocked him out with that bone-crushing tackle.

To open the regular season the Bears traveled to the west coast for a two-week stay to play the Rams and San Francisco on successive Sundays. The Rams, who had defeated the Bears twice the previous season, posed one of the biggest obstacles for a championship season. The Rams had two great quarterbacks, Bob Waterfield and Norm Van Brocklin plus a veteran team. They had a secret weapon, Elroy "Crazylegs" Hirsch, who would make his surprise debut as a flanker.

In the trainer's room before the game, George was talking to his teammate and pal, Don Kindt, when the veteran Bear fullback, George Gulyanics came in. Gulyanics told Kindt and George that he had a sore back and didn't know whether he could play that day. George knew they needed Gulyanics against a tough Ram team so he improvised a solution for Gulyanics' back problem. George describes it this way:

I said to Gulyanics, "You know my Dad is a doctor. Well, I was telling him about your back problem and he came up with a solution for you." I then cut some strips of tape and asked Gulyanics where it hurt the worst. When he told me, I put aspirin on strips of adhesive tape and applied the tape to the areas Gulyanics indicated. I told Gulyanics that as he began to perspire, the aspirin would melt and be absorbed directly to the sore areas and ease his pain.

Gulyanics must have believed George because he gained about 140 yards that day and had a great game. The Bears edged out the Rams 24-20 in a tough defensive battle. Despite the fact that Waterfield and Van Brocklin out-passed Luckman and Lujack 263 yards to 148 and Hirsch caught three passes, one for a touchdown from his new flanker position, the Bears gained 214 yards on the ground compared to the Rams' 92. They also played stellar defense when it counted. Commenting on the defense after the game, Hunk Anderson said of George:

He was great. The Rams had the ball, fourth down, close to our goal line. Waterfield faked a handoff and kept the ball on a bootleg play. He had three blockers in front of him when he started running but Connor at defensive linebacker, blasted through all three of them and made the tackle. Later he hit Van Brocklin so hard he ruined a pass. Weatherly intercepted and ran for a touchdown. That means Connor gave us one touchdown and kept the Rams from scoring one. What more can a tackle do in one game?

George played an outstanding game to be sure. The fact that he did so, given his physical condition prior to the game, is quite a story. George suffered a hip pointer in the prior game. As those familiar with football injuries know, a hip pointer is a very debilitating injury. The injury is such that any body movement causes severe pain and it usually continues for several weeks. George spent the first few days after the injury at home in bed until he had to board the train for the trip to the west coast. He had to spend his time on the two-day train trip flat on his back while Ed Rozy, the Bears' trainer, gave him periodic hot-pack treatments.

By game time, George was considerably better but still in no condition to play. But despite this, George decided to dress for the game. Prior to suiting up, Ed Rozy sprayed George's hip with ethyl chloride which deadened the hip area and then taped the hip. George talked with Halas before the game and told him he didn't think he could play but would be available in an emergency.

Little did George know that the emergency would come on the first play – the kickoff. Frank Dempsey was George's replacement and suffered a severe neck injury on the kickoff. George went to Halas and said, "Let me go in for Frank. I don't know how long I'll last but let me try." Halas gave his permission.

According to George,

> Once I got in the game, the adrenaline started to flow and the hip, although a little painful, didn't bother me enough to hinder my play. I even intercepted a pass and ran pretty well. At halftime, Rozy again sprayed my hip and I played the entire game. When the game was over my hip felt better than it had before I played. I don't know if it was due to adrenaline, body heat or just running it out, but for some reason I was able to play and the hip didn't bother me the rest of the season.

The next test for the Bears were the Forty-Niners, the second best team in the All-American Conference. San Francisco featured Frankie Albert, the left-handed passing quarterback, who many thought was the best passer in the pro ranks. During the week the Bears, in a complicated trade involving six men, traded with Baltimore for Dick Barwegen, the former Purdue player who was considered one of the best blocking linemen in pro football. With this addition, the Bears boasted of having the best blocking left side of the line in the NFL with Bill Wightkin, George and Barwegen.

Since San Francisco was new to the league, George had never seen them play. He tried to make up for his lack of first-hand knowledge of how they operated by watching many hours of 49er game film. As the middle linebacker, he didn't worry so much about plays up the middle, those he could handle. His area of study was the swing passes and backs who ran wide where his diagnosis of the play direction would have to be virtually instantaneous for him to be effective. He paid particular attention to Joe "the Jet" Perry, a speedy back who rightfully earned his nickname. What George saw in the film was Perry, after a toss from the quarterback, Frankie Albert, speed around the end as fast as George had ever seen. He knew he could not hope to run from his middle linebacker position to get to the sidelines to meet Perry – he was just too fast. From his study of the film, George saw that Perry would sprint to the sidelines and when the defense was pursuing him, he would cut sharply back toward the center of the field – cut back against the grain as it's called. This maneuver often resulted in a long run for Perry.

The plan for Perry that George designed was simple but effective. Rather than attempt to race Perry to the sidelines, George would drift in that direction to a point that would intersect Perry's angle of his cutback. In the 49er game, the first time Perry ran his sweep, George waited until he made his cut back and hit him with a jarring tackle. Perry went down in a heap. George told what happened:

> I watched Perry from my middle linebacker's
> spot. He started left and Albert flipped the ball out to
> him. He was so fast that I couldn't catch him. I waited
> for the cut back, and when he did, I nailed him. I said

to him, "why don't you go back and tell Albert to give you the ball again." I knew he was up to something. On the next play Perry swung out in the flat on what looked like a pass play. I ran up to cut the angle. Perry wasn't even looking for a pass. He was going to lower the boom on me. Before he was ready for me, I nailed him and knocked him out with a big hit right in front of the 49er bench. I heard later they changed Perry's contract such that he had to finish a game to get his full pay.

Another 49er player George often played against was Gordie Soltau. For a tight end, he was very fast. George observed the technique Soltau used to gain big yardage on passes to him. He would sprint right to the opposing linebacker and make contact with him. Then he would push off from the defender and before his opponent could recover, Soltau would go out to the flat and was usually open for a pass. To offset Soltau's maneuver, George decided to play him soft and not allow Soltau to get to his body to push off. George and Soltau became good friends and later, Soltau said to George, "You SOB, you hurt my game. Everyone started to play me the way you did."

The Bears rallied in the second half to defeat the 49ers, 32-20. Nine of the Bear points came from the toe of George Blanda who kicked three field goals.

In the third game, the Bears lost to their arch rival the Green Bay Packers, 31-21. Although the Bears won the statistical battle, the Packers capitalized on every Bear mistake. It was a bitter loss for the Bears but they got their revenge two weeks later when they beat the Packers, 28-14; after they had defeated the Cardinals, 27-6.

But the Bears were derailed on their quest for a championship when, in New York, the Yanks defeated them, 38-27. The loss dropped the Bears to third place. Early in the game, with George Ratterman at quarterback for the Yanks, George was playing middle linebacker on defense. George recalled:

> When the Yanks set at the line of scrimmage, Ratterman scanned the defense and looked at me and said, 'Hi, George.' I thought how nice it was that an opponent was so friendly and relaxed a little. With that, the ball was snapped and a quick handoff to the fullback got 15 yards right through my position. I don't think I ever talked to an opposing quarterback again.

After the loss to the Yanks, the Bears came back and won four in a row, defeating the Lions, the NY Yanks at Wrigley Field, the 49ers and the Rams.

Again they gained the lead in the division standings. With two games to go, the Bears had to win them both to clinch the division crown or split the games to ensure at least a tie. Although the Bears had bested the Cardinals at Comiskey Park, they knew it would be a tough battle as the Cards had a habit of knocking off the Bears in crucial games. To add to their worries, George and Paul Stenn would miss the game because of injuries.

The Bears looked anything but sharp as the Cards beat their cross-town rival, 20-10. Commentating on the game, Warren Brown, the noted Chicago sportswriter wrote:

> For everyone who maintained stoutly that the Bears looked bad because the Cardinals made them... My own opinion...is that the difference between the Bears who seemed to look so non-plussed at Comiskey Park was the presence of George Connor with the one and his absence from the other. Connor is all football player, in the professional field as he was in college. He is not the hot and cold performer so many of his associates and his opponents seem to be. He is not sensationally "up" for one game and dis-

tressingly "down" for another. I sometimes have my doubts of the inspirational values of professional football, but if there is any player in the whole league who has inspirational value it is Connor. In college when he couldn't lead'em; he dragged'em. He plays his football for Halas the same way.

Sometime later George revealed the part our mother played in his missing the game:

I had a severe leg injury and had not practiced all week. The only time I left the house was to be driven to Wrigley Field to get a treatment from our trainer. Despite this, I had every intention of playing that Sunday. Mother, in no uncertain terms, said, "If you play I will personally go down on the field to take you out of the game like I did to your brother (Chuck) when he was in high school." Knowing my mother, I missed my only game that year.

Mother was not only responsible for George missing his only game that season, but she was also responsible for Ed Sprinkle, the so-called meanest man in pro football, missing practice - a first for Sprinkle.

George usually drove to Bear practice at Wrigley Field from our home on the south side. One day, for whatever reason, his teammate Ed Sprinkle was picking him up. Mother opened the door to greet him and when she saw how he looked she said, "Ed, what's wrong? You look terrible." Sprinkle told her he had a sore throat and didn't feel well. She had him sit down and called Dad to take a look at him.

Dr. Connor examined Sprinkle's throat and took his temperature. It registered over 102 degrees. Dad explained that the throat looked infected and that Ed should be in bed. With that, Mother said, "Ed, you go to the back bedroom and get in bed. You're not going to practice today."

"I can't miss practice," he protested. "Halas will fine me big time."

"Don't worry about Halas, " Mother countered rising to all of her 5´1˝ stature. "I'll take care of him." With that she went to the phone and called Halas at the Bears office. When she returned she said, "Ed, you're excused from practice and there will be no fine."

I guess the moral of the story is that even strong men like Ed Sprinkle and George Halas are no match for a determined mother.

◆

◆

◆

The Bears gained a tie for the division lead and the right to play the Rams in a playoff game by defeating the Lions 6-3. Blanda, who had been traded to Baltimore in the Barwegen deal and later reclaimed by the Bears, was the hero for kicking two field goals.

In the playoff game at the Los Angeles Coliseum before 90,000 fans, the Bears went down in defeat 24-20. It was a bitter defeat for the Bears who had lost out for the division championship for three straight years in the last game of the season.

During the Ram game, George demonstrated a technique he used while playing linebacker. Rather than watching the ball, George keyed on the movement of the line and the backs. With third down on the Bear six-yard-line, the Rams' fullback, Dick Hoerner, went in motion to the right. George, backing up the left side of the Bear line, moved out a few steps to cover Hoerner (just far enough to keep him a blur in my left eye, commented George). Hirsch, the Rams right end, sprinted straight ahead, then broke right in the end zone. Scenting a pass, George turned to cover the blur which was the fullback Hoerner.

"Then," George recalls, "something strange happened. Hoerner cut back toward me. Naturally, I waited to pick him up and suddenly, out of nowhere, two other Ram blockers popped into sight running behind Hoerner. In a spot like that, you don't look at faces, but I guess they were the Rams' right guard and left half. Anyway, they had to be running interference." Whereupon George plowed into Hoerne; Hoerner bounced backward into the two following interferers, and all four players crashed resoundingly to the turf. Then, Don Kindt, the Bears safety, tackled the Rams' quarterback Bob Waterfield, who was attempting to sneak through left tackle on an artfully concealed maneuver.

"Connor smashed that play," Halas commented later, "without ever seeing the ball carrier. What's more," Halas added admiringly, "Connor threw himself right into the meat grinder to do it and he has been doing that his entire career."

During the 1950 season, George and I were roommates in an apartment on the south side of Chicago. I had graduated from Notre Dame in June and was attending Law School. As a Marine reservist, I had just received orders to report for active duty for officers training at Quantico, Virginia. A short time later I had an amazing talk with George Halas, the owner and coach of the Chicago Bears.

One evening, when George returned to our apartment he told me he received a message that I should call Frances Osborne, George Halas' secretary to arrange a meeting with Halas. I was flabbergasted, and so was George. We could not imagine why Halas wanted to see me. I called Miss Osborne as instructed and a meeting with Mr. Halas was set. At the agreed upon time, I went to Halas' office where he greeted me warmly. He said he heard I was going on active duty with the Marine Corps and wanted to know why. I was somewhat taken aback by his question but replied that all eligible men, which included most of my pals, were now being drafted to serve in the armed services because of the Korean War. I felt it was my duty to also serve.

Halas said, "Jack, if I thought this was a real war I would ask all my players to join the armed services with me and I would personally lead them in battle. This isn't a real war. Don't go in the Marines and run the risk of getting killed."

I didn't know what to say so Halas went on to tell me he was a captain in the Navy Reserve and still had a lot of influence with the Navy. (He sponsored the annual Armed Services Charity Game with the proceeds going to the Navy, so I knew his statement to be true.) He said all I had to do was to give him the word and he would see to it that I was put in the Navy and assigned to the Great Lakes Training Center in nearby Waukegan as a physical instructor.

Still a little stunned by his offer, I replied, "Thank you for your concern and the offer. I have no doubt you could do what you say, but I feel I should proceed on the path I'm on."

He nodded his understanding, shook my hand, wished me luck and told me if I changed my mind to call him.

In the season, George had a sensational year on both offense and defense. For his play, he, along with Johnny Lujack and Dick Barwegen, were selected to the All-Pro team along with such players as Tom Fears-Rams, Dan Edwards-NY Yanks, Arnie Weinmeister-Giants, Joe Signaigo-NY Yanks, Chuck Bednarik-Eagles, Joe Geri-Steelers, Doak Walker-Lions and Marion Motley-Browns. This was the last year in which the All-Pro team was selected as one unit without separate offensive and defensive teams.

After the season, the NFL made plans for their first Pro-Bowl Game. George was selected for the National Conference, along with Bear teammates Fred Davis, Ed Sprinkle, Johnny Lujack, Dick Barwegen and Ray Bray. In a passing duel between Otto Graham of the American Conference and Bob Waterfield of the National Conference, Paul Brown's American team defeated the Nationals, 28-27, in the inaugural Pro-Bowl Game of modern football played on January 14, 1951 in Los Angeles.

The 1951 Season

At age 26, George was beginning his fourth year as a pro. He was now recognized as one of the best blocking tackles in the league, but of more importance, he was considered one of the best, if not the best, linebacker in all football. He was also one of the leaders of the Bear team. Rookies and veterans alike looked to him for leadership.

At this stage in his life, George was not only a veteran Bear player but also a veteran corrugated box salesman. From the time he first joined the Bears, George wanted to have a business career. He had received very valuable advice from a fellow Lake Shore Club member and dear friend, Gene McNeil, an older, successful businessman who George greatly admired. McNeil told George, "Kid, don't be like a lot of professional athletes and rely only on the money you earn playing football. Find a business career where you can learn the business and do well. You should learn to live on your income from your business career and save the money you earn from playing football." George did just that.

George joined a corrugated box company with headquarters in Terre Haute, Indiana, where he spent months receiving his training to prepare him to be a salesman. Eventually George joined the sales force of Hoerner Boxes of Keokuk, Iowa, that employed him for the next twenty-five years. George worked as diligently selling boxes as he did playing football. Within a few years he was one of Hoerner's leading salesmen.

◆

◆

◆

Missing from the Bear camp for the upcoming season would be three of the Bears' greatest players, Ken Kavanaugh, a superb pass receiver, Sid Luckman, one of the all-time great quarterbacks and George McAfee, a sensational open-field runner. They retired after brilliant careers. The latter two would later be inducted into the Pro Hall of Fame in Canton, Ohio, Luckman in 1960 and McAfee in 1966. Luckman became the NFL's first, great, T-formation quarterback. During his 12-year career with the Bears he won four NFL championships. His greatest day passing was in 1943 at the Polo Grounds when he passed for a record seven touchdowns.

McAfee from Duke University joined the Bears in 1940 to become one of the best game-breakers in pro football. He was a speedy runner, a dangerous pass receiver, an excellent pass defender and one of the game's best kick-return specialists. His 12.8 average on 112 punt returns still stands as a record. George recalled McAfee's special aptitude for returning punts.

> One of the seldom mentioned aspects of McAfee's astonishing punt returns is that he rarely caught the ball while standing still. He had great speed and sure hands but what made him unique among punt returners is that he caught the ball on the run. He would play unusually deep as he prepared to catch a punt. As he judged where the ball would come down he would start running and by the time he caught the ball he was in full stride. With his speed and already with a full head of steam he usually ran right by the defenders. He was always a threat to take it all the way for a touchdown. I've never seen anyone catch a punt on the run since McAfee.

Like George, John Lujack was also beginning his fourth year as a Bear. Early in the 1950 season, Lujack hurt his throwing shoulder which caused him problems the entire season. The pain was so severe at times that it caused him to throw with a semi-side-armed delivery. As Lujack was quoted at the time, "if you can't throw with an overhand motion, you can't be as accurate as you would like to be." Despite these throwing problems Lujack managed to be fourth in the league in passing with 121 completions and in total yardage with 1,731 yards. He carried the ball 63 times for a total of 397 yards for a league-leading 6.3 average per carry. He was the second leading scorer with 11 touchdowns, three field goals and 34 extra points totaling 109 points. These accomplishments again earned him selection as All-League. The question going into the 1951 season was, would his shoulder allow him to play at his best level?

Prior to going to camp, George had signed a new two-year contract with the Bears. Negotiating a contract with George Halas was never a pleasant experience, as all Bear players knew only too well. Halas was known to use every devious ploy he could think of in his contract talks with his players.

George, aware of Halas' reputation in contract sessions, prepared himself to do battle as he entered Halas' office to talk about his contract. He was greeted warmly by Halas who immediately congratulated George on his outstanding season – not what George expected. George described the rest of the meeting this way:

> As I was seated across the desk from Halas he said, "Well Kid, what did you have in mind?" I told him I thought I had a good year and gave him my figure for a new contract which was considerably larger than what I had been making. He said, "George, you did have a good year but your figure is high and besides you did make some mistakes." With that he reached in a drawer and pulled out a sheet of paper and began to read how in one of the games I got knocked down and the other team scored. Then he read from another sheet of paper he pulled out about some other mistake I supposedly made. I asked, "Who wrote those things?" Halas said, "Oh, some fans." (I suspected he wrote them himself.)
>
> He continued, "I don't think I can give you that kind of money," and selected a pencil from his desk and began to write figures on a pad of paper. We sat there in total silence as the minutes ticked by as he waited for me to cave in. Finally, I said, "Coach, can I borrow your pencil?" He gave me his pencil and I began to doodle on a pad I had and again we sat in silence for several minutes. He broke the silence and

asked, "What do you think?" I said, "No matter how I figure it, I deserve the raise I'm asking for." He hesitated for a moment and said, "Okay kid, that's what it will be," and we shook hands.

As George left the office, he spotted teammate Bill Wightkin waiting his turn to have a contract discussion. George liked Wightkin and wanted to give him the benefit of what he had just learned in his meeting with the boss. George explained in detail Halas' strategy of first the compliments, then the negative letters, his silence and writing figures on his notepad. George emphasized to Wightkin that the trick to a successful negotiation was borrowing Halas' pencil. George said, "Once you do that, you've got him."

Later George saw Wightkin and asked him, "How did it go?"

A dejected Wightkin replied, "Not too well. I didn't get a raise."

George asked, "Did you borrow his pencil?"

"Yeah, I borrowed his pencil like you told me," replied Wightkin, "but he borrowed it back and I didn't know what to do."

The Bears showed a combination of veterans and rookies as they opened regular season play with an impressive win over the Packers, 30-21 in Green Bay. The rookies were represented by Whizzer White, a fancy runner from Arizona State (not the Whizzer White who later became a Supreme Court Justice) and John "Kayo" Dottley, the big back and tough runner from Ole Miss. The two backs scored on runs as did veteran Julie Rykovich and sophomore Chuck Hunsinger. During the course of the game, Johnny Lujack completed 12 of 18 passes for 160 yards which helped eliminate fears that his bad shoulder would hinder his passing accuracy.

The Bears were upset in the second game by their cross-town rivals, the Chicago Cardinals, 28-14. They needed a winning streak if they hoped to realize their goal of a championship season. The Bears got their winning streak as they won the next four games against the NY Yanks, 49ers, Lions and Redskins. These wins put them in the lead in their division.

These games put them in the lead but they also put them to the test. In the Yank game the Bears were leading 24-0 with only three minutes to play. The Yanks, to the surprise of everyone including themselves, mounted a rally and scored three touchdowns to make the final score, 24-21. Likewise in the 49er game, the Bears almost blew a 13-0 lead when San Francisco put on a rally in the fourth quarter only to fall short with a final score of 13-7. In the Lion game, with the Bears leading 28-23, the Lions had the ball on the Bears' 30-yard-line when Don Kindt ended the comeback try by intercepting a Bobby Layne pass. In addition, both Whizzer White, the fleet-footed rookie, and Johnny Lujack were carried off the field in the 49er game. White injured his knee and Lujack sustained a severe ankle sprain which would cause him to miss the next two games. Filling in for the injured Lujack was Steve Romanik who acquitted himself well.

The Bears' quest for a championship suffered a setback when the Detroit Lions defeated them 41-28, before a full house in Chicago. The Lions were led by the former Bear, Bobby Layne, who threw for four touchdowns. The loss put the Bears in a tie for the division lead with the Rams.

A come-from-behind victory over the Packers 24-13 put the Bears back on track for a division title. Trailing 13-10 in the third period with the Packers on the move at the Bears' 15, the turning point of the game came when George, from his linebacker's position, jarred Tobin Rote so hard he lost the ball. It was recovered by the Bears at their 11. In 15 plays, the Bears scored with great running by Dottley, Gulyanics and Rykovich. Dottley scored the clinching touchdown late in the fourth quarter. With this win, their sixth in eight games, the Bears moved into a tie for the Western Division lead with the Rams.

In 1922, Ernie Nevers, playing for the Chicago Cardinals, set a league record when he scored all the Cardinal points in defeating the Bears, 40-6. In Cleveland, for the Bears' ninth game, it was William (Dub) Jones, the 6-foot-4 veteran back for the Browns who almost duplicated the feat of Nevers. Jones ran for six touchdowns as the

Browns defeated the Bears, 42-21. Unlike Nevers, Jones had Lou "The Toe" Groza to kick the extra points. The defeat dropped the Bears into a second place tie with Rams behind the 6-2-1 Lions.

The Bears went down in defeat, 42-17, in their crucial game with the Rams before the largest crowd of the season (50,286) at Wrigley Field. It all but ended their chance to win their division. The Bears still had a chance for a tie for the lead with the Rams if they won their last two games against the Yanks and the Cards while the Rams lost their final game with the Packers.

The Bears' next game was against the New York Yanks at Yankee Stadium in New York. After a somber trip to New York following their devastating loss to the Rams, the Bears settled into their hotel, the Concourse Plaza, not too far from Yankee Stadium. Hunk Anderson, the wily Bear line coach, privately huddled with several of the veterans on the team and told them, "You guys were so tight going into the Ram game that the Little Sisters of the Poor could have fielded a team and beat you." He added, "I'm taking bed check tonight and I don't want to see any of you in your room. Go out and have a few beers, maybe that will loosen you up so you can play Bear football."

At this time, I was a Marine lieutenant assigned in Quantico, Virginia. I had been in touch with George and told him I would come to New York to see him. He told me to meet him at Toots Shor's restaurant late Friday afternoon which I did. George came in with Johnny Lujack, Don Kindt and a few other Bear players. Upon seeing George and his teammates, Toots Shor joined our group. It was the first time I met the famous restaurateur. After about an hour of visiting, George said they had to return to the hotel for a team meeting but would be back in about two hours. Toots (as everyone called him) asked me what I was going to do in the meantime. I told him I would have some dinner and wait for George. He asked me if I would like to have dinner with him. Naturally, I was thrilled with the offer and gladly accepted.

Much to my surprise we had dinner in Toots' private office. Toots told me how he got started in the business as a bouncer with Sherman

Billingsly, the then-owner of the Copacabana, the famous New York nightclub. After many fascinating stories about his career, he talked about George. He told me he had met, mingled with and was friends with hundreds of sports figures. He said of all the men from the various sports that had come in his place through the years, George stood out as the model of clean living and how a professional athlete should conduct himself. He added that George is among the few athletes who have been invited to his apartment. He concluded by telling me that George was the type of person he would like to have marry his daughter.

Later George returned to the restaurant and told Toots and me about Hunk Anderson's advice about staying out. Both George and Johnny Lujack who came with him, agreed that Hunk was right and that they intended to stay out and have a good time. By this time we were joined by Chuck Comiskey, the owner of the Chicago White Sox baseball team, who was in town for a league meeting. Toots told George he had better leave his place because there would be too many people who recognized Lujack and him. He said it wouldn't be good for them to be seen in a bar the night before a game. He said he would call a pal of his who owned a bar where we could go in relative obscurity. After hours in the bar Toots had recommended, I remember sitting on the curb at 57th and Madison in the wee hours of the morning. I told George and the others that I was very tired and had to get some sleep. I went back to the Concourse Plaza Hotel where I had a cot in George's room. I awoke about 6 o'clock when George and Lujack came in the room. As dawn was breaking about a half hour later, I looked out the window and recognized Bulldog Turner walking down the sidewalk to the hotel entrance. George and Lujack had already been to mass and had breakfast. They had about an hour to shower and get dressed before attending a team meeting. When they left the room, it was the last time I saw them until after the game.

As I settled into my seat at Yankee Stadium I felt miserable – too much to drink and too little sleep. I couldn't imagine how George, Lujack, Turner and the others who stayed out all night must have felt getting ready to play football. I found out later that the whole Bear team, with the exception of John Hoffman, who was ill, had stayed out late. I honestly didn't know what to expect as I waited for the kickoff.

As I feared, the Bears looked very sluggish the first quarter. They managed only three points on a George Blanda field goal. Then to my surprise and perhaps theirs, the Bears scored three times in the second quarter and led 24-7 at the half, and 35-14 going into the final quarter.

Meanwhile, Chuck Comiskey, who had stayed out with George and Lujack and was feeling the effects of the late night, was in a baseball meeting in one of the New York hotels. He asked one of the bellhops to check the Bears' score. When it was reported to him that the Bears were leading at halftime, 24-7, he couldn't believe it. He thought for sure they would get trounced, given the drinking and late hour of the previous evening.

George described the game this way:

> As we were getting dressed for the game, Lujack discovered that he had left his contact lenses and play book back at the hotel. Once the game and the hitting started, it brought us back to life. However, several times during the game Lujack couldn't remember the name of the play he wanted to call. Fortunately, we were on the infield part of the field. Like in a sandlot game, he drew the play in the dirt and it went for a touchdown. I think Lujack threw four touchdown passes that day. On one play, John Hoffman, one of the ends, was wide open and Lujack threw a perfect pass to him which would have been a sure touchdown but he dropped the ball. Oddly, Hoffman had a cold and was the only Bear player who did not go out the night before.

Incredibly, the Bears went on to win the game with the Yanks by a score of 45-21. It's all the more astounding when one considers that Lujack was without his contact lenses and couldn't see very well. Perhaps it was the adrenaline surge of a game that brought the Bear players to life or maybe it was the fear that Halas would find out about their late-night doings that inspired them to play so well. Whatever the reason, the Bears won a must game that kept their mathematical hopes for a tie for the division lead alive.

In the Bears' final game and for the fourth time in five years the Cardinals sabotaged their playoff ambitions by defeating the Bears, 24-14, at frigid Wrigley Field. Charlie Trippi in a spread formation had his greatest day as a pro as he ran 13 times for 165 yards, scored two touchdowns, and passed for the other one in completing nine out of 20 tosses for 106 yards. To add to Trippi's day, he leveled Ed Sprinkle with a terrific right to the jaw near the end of the game. He was ejected from the game for his misdeed but he had already caused enough damage to the Bears.

Looking back on the Bears' season, it was apparent that Lujack's injuries, which had caused him to miss several games and severely hampered his ability to throw the ball in the other games, resulted in the Bears' inability to sustain a consistent offense. Without a dynamic quarterback to power the offense, the Bears could not keep pace with the Rams,who had Waterfield and Van Brocklin to throw to the likes of Elroy Hirsch, or with the Browns, who had Otto Graham throwing to great ends, Dante Lavelle and Mac Speedie.

When the All-Pro teams were selected after the season, George again was on the first team. There were two recognized services selecting the teams – UP (United Press) and AP Associated Press). That year was the first time both an offensive team and a defensive team were named. On the AP team George was selected as one of the two offensive tackles (the other was Lou Creekmur of the Lions). On the UP team George was selected as a linebacker along with Bednarik of the Eagles. No other player in all of pro ball was named to both the offensive team and the defensive team. This was the start of an incredible string of two-way honors for George.

For the second straight year George, John Lujack and Dick Barwegen were selected to play in the Pro-Bowl Game, now in its second year. The game was billed as a rematch between Paul Brown, of the Cleveland Browns as coach of the American Conference (Eastern) stars against Joe Stydahar of the Rams for the National Conference (Western) all-stars.

George played almost the entire game. On offense he was superb in his blocking both for runs and in pass blocking. However, it was on defense as a linebacker that he stole the show. One series of plays in which George starred is still regarded as one of the classic examples of outstanding linebacker play. Late in the game, with Otto Graham attempting to rally his team behind, the American Conference stars tried an end sweep to the right. George reacted to the play from his linebacking position and knocked down two blockers to throw the ball carrier for a loss. On the next play George bolted through the line and sacked Graham for a huge loss. On the third play George moved to his right to crash through several blockers to foil an attempted screen pass. On fourth down George raced 30 yards downfield to knock down Graham's pass near the far sidelines. After the game, Joe Stydahar called that series of plays by George the greatest exhibition of linebacking he had ever witnessed.

When they totaled the ballots for the most valuable player after the game, there was a tie between George and Dan Towler who had a great game on offense. A second ballot awarded the honor to Towler but to those who witnessed the game, it will always be remembered as the game when George put on a unbelievable exhibition of linebacking.

Game Day

Like most professional athletes, George had a game-day routine. It really started the evening before when he would have a steak dinner with a baked potato and vegetables, then attend an early movie near the house. He was usually home before 10 p.m. Up until this time he was loose and talkative. Then he would have a snack, usually some cake with a couple of glasses of milk (George didn't drink coffee or tea). As he had his snack, his mood changed from fun-loving to one of quiet reflection. I once asked him about this. He said it was then that he started to concentrate on the upcoming game and what he wanted to do in the game. Once he was mentally prepared, he seemed to relax and was ready for a good night's sleep.

From the time he was up on the morning of the game, he had his game face on. He didn't want to talk as he ate a good meal before departing for Wrigley Field. When George got "the look," he was a different person. He became a warrior. I can remember thinking as I saw him leave that I felt sorry for players on the other team who would have the misfortune of crossing his path during the game.

The next time I would see George was after the game when he was back to his old self. He had the ability to play as hard as possible during the game and then leave the warrior mentality on the field. The game was over. He did his best; now was the time to relax and enjoy life.

John Lujack

Because of his multiple injuries, but most particularly a bad shoulder and recent knee surgery, Lujack retired from pro football. He was still a premier defensive back but he couldn't throw as accurately as he once could and his bad knee restricted his mobility. He might have continued with his pro career but the high standards he set for himself wouldn't permit him to continue to play if he couldn't play at top form.

Lujack had an impressive but short-lived career with the Bears. Because his playing days with the Bears only numbered four years and because it was so long ago, football fans and even some sportswriters seem to forget his accomplishments. In 1948, with Luckman still the starting quarterback, Lujack was kept busy by playing full time on defense. He also spelled Luckman on offense where he completed 36 of 66 attempted passes for six touchdowns. In addition, he kicked 44 extra points and scored one touchdown for a total of 50 points. Because of his outstanding play on defense where he intercepted eight passes, Lujack made All-League on defense, an extraordinary accomplishment for a rookie.

It was in his second year, 1949, that Lujack, now playing full time on offense, came into his own with a career year. He led the league in completed passes with 162, in total yardage with 2,658 yards and in touchdown passes with 23. Against some stiff competition from Sammy Baugh, Tommy Thompson and Bob Waterfield, Lujack was named as the All-League quarterback.

In his third season, Lujack hurt his shoulder. Despite this injury which hampered his throwing ability, he managed to throw for 1,731 yards. In addition he was the second-leading scorer with 109 points and led the league with a 6.3 rushing average per carry. His efforts earned him first-team All-Pro selection. In his fourth year, Lujack again hurt his shoulder, and suffered a severe ankle sprain which caused him to miss several games. Even with his injuries he completed 85 passes for 1,295 yards and eight touchdowns and scored 50 points on seven touchdowns and 10 extra points. His play earned him second team All-Pro honors.

It is George's opinion that had Lujack not been injured, he may well have gone down in professional football history as one of the all-time great quarterbacks. As it was, George claims that John Lujack was the best all-around football player he ever played with or against.

The 1952 Season

As the Bears embarked on the '52 season, some familiar names from past teams were missing. Players such as Johnny Lujack, Fred Davis, Ray Bray, Paul Stenn, Jim Keane and Stu Clarkson were gone. The departure of Lujack meant that for the first time since 1940, the

Bears would enter a season without an experienced quarterback. Added to the passing difficulties was the absence of league-leading receivers of past years, Ken Kavanaugh and Jim Keane.

To offset these losses the Bears had Bob Williams, the All-American from Notre Dame at quarterback, along with veterans George Blanda and Steve Romanik. Bill George from Wake Forest, who would become an all-time great and a future Hall of Famer, was added to the team as well as Jim Dooley, Jack Hoffman, Bill McColl, Fred Williams, Bill Bishop and Herman Clark.

Without Fred Davis to spell him on offense, George would be on the field more than ever before. He was already playing full time at his linebacking position but now he would also play full time on offense. Thus he became the only full time, two-way player on the team.

After a good training camp and exhibition season the Bears opened the regular season by defeating their long-time rival the Green Bay Packers, 24-14. A surprise for Green Bay and the fans was the switch of perennial all-pro center, Bulldog Turner, to right offensive tackle. The Bears' passing attack was more than enough as Williams completed 12 of 22 for two touchdowns. Romanik hit on five of 11 for 106 yards. Although a 13-point favorite against the Cardinals in their second game, the Bears went down in defeat at Comiskey Park, 21-10. Ollie Matson, the Olympic speedster, returned a kickoff 100 yards to spur the Cards on to victory.

In the third game of the season, the Bears beat a hapless Dallas Texan team, 38-20. Then the wheels seemed to come off as they lost the next two games to the 49ers and the Rams. They did come back and defeat the 49ers in a re-match, 20-17, only to lose the following two games to the Packers and the Rams.

In the ninth game of the season, an incredible incident occurred during the Bear-Detroit Lion game. Some background to the incident: the first black player to survive the cut and make the regular Bear roster was Eddie Macon from the College of the Pacific. He wasn't the first black player in the league by any means, as several notable blacks had made their mark with other clubs in previous years. Such players as Kenny Washington, the great UCLA back who played for the Rams, Bill Willis and Marion Motley of Cleveland Browns fame had played years before the 1952 season. However, many teams still did not have a black player on their roster. Macon was an easy-going guy who got along well with his Bear teammates but in some of the games the opposing players gave Macon a hard time with their crude, racial remarks. George liked Macon, but more than that George, as captain, felt a responsibility for each teammate. George recalled:

> When we played the Lions, they were taunting Macon with some pretty nasty racial remarks. After a while I had enough. I called to Macon and said, "Eddie, come with me." I grabbed him by the arm and we walked right into the Lions' offensive huddle. I said, "Some of you know me, my name is George Connor and this is my teammate, Eddie Macon. Eddie is a great guy and we like him. I don't appreciate the names you're calling him so I'm here to tell you to knock it off.

One can only imagine the shock of the Lion team when two opponents marched into their huddle, especially when one of them was an all-pro and known to be a very tough player. Whether it was fear of George retaliating if they kept up their taunts or whether he appealed to their sense of fair play is anybody's guess, but whatever the rationale for their actions, the Lions ceased their verbal abuse of Macon.

The Bears almost lost this game but in the last nine seconds George Blanda lobbed a pass to an unlikely receiver. Ed Sprinkle, who usually played defensive end, was in the game at offensive end. He caught Blanda's pass for the winning score of 24-23.

In what was to become a pattern that season, after winning a game the Bears lost the next two away games to Dallas and the Lions before defeating the Cardinals at home, 10-7, to end their season.

The only item of note about the last three games was the bizarre game against Dallas. Earlier in the season the Dallas Texans ran out of money and were being subsidized by the league. As a result they couldn't pay the rent for their home field and had to play their home games wherever they could negotiate a deal. For the game against the Bears, the Texans arranged to play in Akron, Ohio. Even then, the only time they could get was on a Thursday.

In a story that has been told over the years by many of the Dallas players, Jim Phelan, the Dallas coach, told his players before the game that there would not be many fans in the stands and that perhaps they would outnumber those in attendance. Instead of the team being introduced, he suggested the players go up in the stands and introduce themselves to the fans. The official count showed there were 3,000 in attendance although many suspect that figure was exaggerated. This is in contrast to 58,000 at the Bear-49er game in San Francisco or the 50,000 in Detroit for the Bear game the following week.

The Texans had not won a game that year. Even though the Texans had many talented players who would form the nucleus of the Baltimore Colts the following year such as Artie Donovan, Buddy Young, George Taliaferro and Gino Marchetti, there was no reason to suspect they could beat the Bears. They did, 27-23. The victory was the only win of their 1 and 11 season.

It was a disappointing year for the Bears, as they ended with a 5 and 7 record. Although the team did not fare too well, several Bear players had outstanding seasons. Named to the Pro-Bowl team were: Ed Sprinkle, Gene Schroeder, Dick Barwegen, Fred Williams and George. About playing in the Pro-Bowl Game, George said:

> The players love the Game and hope and pray for an invitation to play in it. It's more than the prestige they get out of playing. They get to know and play with men they have faced across the scrimmage line. Sometimes they've built up hatreds only to discover on the same practice field that the other fellow is really a nice guy. It has helped build a wonderful new and powerful morale in the whole league. In addition, I developed some lifetime friendships with some of the players such as Gordie Soltau of the 49ers and Arnie Weinmeister of the Giants.

George's West team defeated the East, 27-7. Defensive back Don Doll of Detroit was named the outstanding performer. He credited his linebackers, Ed Henke, Tank Younger and George when he said, "They hardly ever let a receiver get into my territory and this saved me plenty of headaches."

George at age 13 years old in Eagle Lake, Wisconsin.

George (#3) and his varsity basketball teammates sophomore year at Holy Cross 1942.

*Monsignor George Connor
and Holy Cross student,
George Connor.*

*In his junior year at Notre
Dame in 1946, George plays
varsity basketball.*

Chuck, Jack, Esther, Mary Ellen, Dr. Charles and George. (Chuck and George were home on leave from the service.)

1947 Notre Dame football coach, Frank Leahy (left), describes a play to team captain, George (center) and tackle coach, Moose Krause (right).

At Notre Dame, Ziggie Czarobski demonstrates advanced mathematics to George.

The Notre Dame 1947 National Championship football team: Leon Hart, Ziggie Czarobski, Marty Wendell, Bill Walsh, Bill Fischer, George Connor, Jim Martin, Emil Sitko, John Panelli, Johnny Lujack and Terry Brennan.

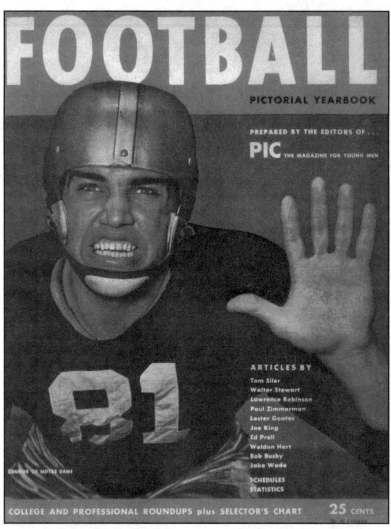

A 1947 cover of Football magazine features an intense George.

George at Cartier Field, Notre Dame.

George honored as Captain of the All-American team,
drawn by Joanne Gallagher.

Life magazine depicts George dwarfing Notre Dame's golden dome.

The first Outland Trophy, for superior performance by a lineman, is presented to George at Notre Dame.

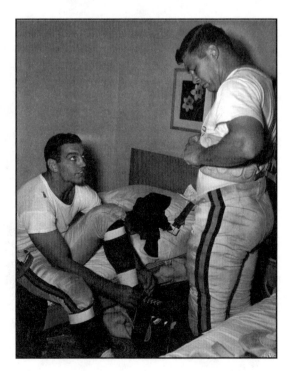

George and Chicago Bears teammate Dick Barwegan suit up.

George in action with the Bears.

George in Chicago Bears traditional publicity pose.

Interception.

In a game against the L.A. Rams,
George intercepts and stiff-arms a player off his feet.

A 1953 Bears shot, now as #71.

George dons a White Sox uniform and hits a few at Comiskey Park at the urging of Sox friends. He stuck with football.

Mayor Richard J. Daley asks George to be the Grand Marshal of Chicago's St. Patrick's Day Parade.

*George and his pal Mayor Daley are loose and laughing
at the party the Mayor threw for George.*

*Then a broadcaster for CBS, George interviews Commissioner of Football
Pete Roselle with broadcaster, Pat Somerall, assisting.*

In a 1962 visit to the south side, "Uncle George" poses with nephew Kevin and niece Terri, and had to duck his head coming into the front door of their home at 10609 S. Fairfield Avenue.

"Papa Bear" George Halas presents George at the Pro Football Hall of Fame induction ceremony.

Professional Football Hall of Fame induction class of 1975:
Roosevelt Brown, George Connor, Dante Lavelli and Lenny Moore.

The official George Connor Hall of Fame keepsake card illustrated by Mike Gardner.

George and Sue Connor, May 31, 1986.

George, Jr., Al and their dad in Florida.

In Moose Krause's booth at Notre Dame stadium, George, Moose and Jack.

Esther Connor's four sons: George, Ziggy Czarobski, Chuck and Jack.

*George, George, Jr. and Al enjoy a family party
at their friend Butch McGuire's pub.*

George, sister Mary Ellen and Jack.

Buddy O'Brien, George Jr. and George.

Charlie Carey and George always had a good time.

*At home at the microphone, George entertains the crowd of
Leahy's Lads gathered at Ridge Country Club.*

*Bob Williams, John Lujack, Johnny Druze and George receive Frank Leahy
replica sculptures for their dedication to the Leahy's Lads scholarship program.*

George accepts his Outland Trophy at a Notre Dame halftime wearing his tacky but treasured blue and gold Ziggy pants, with son, Al and ND President, Fr. Monk Malloy looking on.

Monsignor Ignatius "Fr. Mac" McDermott catches up with George at the Frank Leahy sculpture unveiling in 1997.

*Life-long friends George and Ed McCaskey
at Soldier Field for a Bears game.*

*A grateful city honors George's many accomplishments
by naming the corner of Walton and DeWitt in his honor.*

With George behind the wheel, a bus load of family and friends head to Canton, Ohio in 2000 for the 25th anniversary of George's induction into the Pro Football Hall of Fame.

On his 78th birthday, Angela and George, Jr. and Al celebrate with their dad.

Kaye and Tony Golden present George with the "81 is 78" birthday cake.

A resolution

adopted by The City Council
of the City of Chicago, Illinois

Presented by __ALDERMAN BURTON F. NATARUS__ on __NOVEMBER 28, 2001__

Whereas, George Connor is a lifelong resident of Chicago and has resided at 233 East Walton Place for over thirty years; and

WHEREAS, George Connor attended De La Salle Institute at 35th and Wabash where he was an All-City basketball player and All-State football player; George was also in the charter class of De La Salle's Sports Hall of Fame; and

WHEREAS, George Connor attended Holy Cross College for two years then served his country as an Ensign in the U.S. Navy in the Pacific Theater of Operations during World War II, from which he was honorably discharged in 1946; and

WHEREAS, George Connor attended the University of Notre Dame in 1946, earning a two-time consensus All-American on two National Championship teams, Lineman of the Year and Captain of the 1947 Notre Dame Football Team; became the first-time recipient of the Outland Trophy and was inducted into the College Hall of Fame in 1963; and

WHEREAS, George Connor played both offensively and defensively throughout his entire eight-year professional career as a Chicago Bear, winning All-Pro seven times, and has the distinction of being the only inductee into the Pro Hall of Fame to make the All-Pro team on both the offensive and defensive teams in the same year and for three consecutive years; George has also been selected for the All-Time Two-Way team by the Pro Hall of Fame; and

WHEREAS, George Connor has endowed a scholarship fund for De La Salle Institute to enable young, deserving athletes to further their educations; as a broadcaster and box salesman, he consistently devoted time to the community by giving numerous talks to educational, business and civic groups and he served on committees for the late Richard J. Daley; and

WHEREAS, George Connor is one of the founders of the Chicagoland Sports Hall of Fame and is now President Emeritus of the organization; now, therefore,

BE IT RESOLVED, That the Mayor and Members of the City Council of the City of Chicago do hereby congratulate George Connor on celebrating his 25th anniversary in the Professional Football Hall of Fame as a Chicago Bear Linebacker and for his honorary naming of a street sign at the southwest corner of the intersection of East Walton Place and North DeWitt Place; and

BE IT FURTHER RESOLVED, That a suitable copy of the resolution be prepared and presented to George Connor.

MAYOR

CITY CLERK

George, who played almost the entire game, was praised by Buddy Parker, the coach of the West team when he singled out Ed Henke of San Francisco and George for special commendation.

George was the lone Bear selected to the All-Pro team. It was the third year in a row that he was named to the All-Pro team. In 1950, his selection was as an offensive tackle. This year marked the second straight year George was selected on the first team by the AP(Associated Press) as an offensive tackle and first team linebacker on defense by the UP (United Press). No other player in pro ball consistently played offense and defense, let alone made All-Pro on both teams in the same year. George would again be named to both the offensive and defensive teams the following year, to make it an unbelievable three years in a row. This is a feat no other pro player has accomplished to this day.

The 1953 – 1954 Seasons

George was now beginning his sixth season with the Chicago Bears. When asked by a reporter if he thought he was an improved player after five years as a pro, George said, "I think I have improved tremendously. Experience teaches you to analyze plays faster and to figure your blocking angles faster. And you learn how to conserve your energy so you'll be able to use it when you need it most."

He was a three-time All-Pro. He participated in the inaugural Pro-Bowl Game in 1951, and in the 1952 game played one of his greatest games, which is still considered a classic example of how a linebacker should play. In contrast to most players in the league, George was playing both ways on a full time basis – tackle on offense and linebacker on defense. He had replaced Bulldog Turner as captain of the Bears. From an individual point of view it is hard to imagine anyone having a better career than George was having with the Bears. However, as with any dedicated player, George wanted his team to win a championship. The Bears had come close but could not win the coveted prize. In the 1953 season the Bears did not even come close to their goal as they suffered through a 3-8-1 season. As disheartening as this was for George, it was one of his best years as a pro.

It is worth noting that at this stage of George's career he enjoyed celebrity status, particularly in Chicago. He was well-respected by the sportswriters of the time, men such as Warren Brown, John Carmichael, George Strickler and many more. As an All-Pro player and captain of the Bears, George's photo was often in the papers, as well as favorable articles about him. In one of his well-known, year-end articles John Carmichael defined several words. For the word "Class," Carmichael defined it by writing simply "George Connor."

◆

◆

◆

Before the regular season got underway, Bill George was labeled by one of the sportswriters as the "Golden Greek." "I'm not a Greek, I'm Syrian," protested Bill to his teammates. George told of having some fun with Bill George about being Greek.

> The Bears were playing an exhibition game in Little Rock, Arkansas. The day before the game I called Bill's room and said, "Hey Greek, what are you doing for dinner?" Bill didn't have any plans so I said, "Come on with me. I want to teach you a lesson." We caught a cab and I told the driver to take us to the finest Greek restaurant in town. At the restaurant we ordered two beers and I casually asked the bartender where the owner was. He said the owner was in the kitchen and very busy. I said, "You tell him that Bill George, the Golden Greek with the Chicago Bears, is here." The owner almost sprinted out of the kitchen with apron on to greet us. When I introduced him to the "Golden Greek" he started hugging and kissing Bill and said, "I'm going to personally cook for you – you have never had a meal like the one I am going to prepare for you." After a great meal I went to pay and the owner said, "No, no, when Bill George, the Golden Greek, is in my place, it's on me."

After that Bill George didn't mind being called the Golden Greek.

In every city the Bears played for the rest of the season, George and Bill George pulled the same stunt in Greek restaurants. George and Bill ate very well that season.

The Bears opened the season against the new Colt team (the former Dallas Texans) in Baltimore. The hero of the Colts' inaugural was Bert Rechichar, an alumnus of Tennessee, who kicked a 55-yard field goal, the longest in National Football League history, one second before the half time. The previous record had been set by Glenn Presnell of Detroit in 1934. Baltimore won, 13-9, with the Bears' lone touchdown being scored on a run by Billy Stone behind the blocks of George and Kline Gilbert.

In their second game, the Bears squeaked out a victory over Green Bay when George Blanda hit Jim Dooley with a 16-yard pass in the final minutes of the game for a 17-13 win. In their third game, the Bears were again defeated by the Colts. This began a streak of four consecutive losses before a 21-21 tie with the Packers. Of their five games remaining, the Bears could only manage to win against the Skins and the Rams. It was a dismal 3-8-1 season, the worst while George was a Bear.

As bad as the season was for the Bears, it was an outstanding individual season for George. The league records show that he averaged 54 minutes a game playing both offense and defense. His average minutes per game exceeded any player in the league by a wide margin. It was an unusual sight to watch a Bear game and see one player who rarely left the field. As with today's game, when the ball changed hands, eleven men trotted off the field to be replaced by eleven teammates on the offensive or defensive unit depending on the circumstances. In all of professional football there was one exception to the eleven-man exchange. That was the Chicago Bears and George. George was the only player in the league who continued to play both on offense and on defense on a regular basis. Thus, in a Bear game, when the ball changed hands ten Chicago Bears left the field plus eleven from the other team leaving George standing alone as the only player on the field. This weird sight prompted many a new fan to ask, "Why is that one player standing alone out there?"

That standing alone and playing both ways was not a one game or one season thing for George. It lasted for three years. George was the only player in professional football ever to do so for so long. Chuck

Bednarik, the great All-Pro center from the Philadelphia Eagles, played both ways during the 1960 season and was called, "The Iron Man." George played both ways for six seasons, five of the seasons after the free substitution rules came into effect. Not only did George play both ways during those years but for three of the years he was named All-Pro on both the offensive team and the defensive team, an unbelievable accomplishment. This feat is all the more remarkable because George played three different positions – offensive tackle, defensive tackle and linebacker. Added to this display of versatility, George played all three linebacker positions. He played a lot at middle linebacker and helped to define how that position should be played. The records show that George was the only player in the history of professional football who was inducted into the NFL Hall of Fame to be named All-Pro on both the offensive team and the defensive team in the same year. He did it for three consecutive years. I venture to say that this record is one that will stand forever.

At the end of the '53 season, George was selected to play in his fourth Pro-Bowl.

The 1954 Season

The Bears added two very productive offensive players to the roster for the 1954 season: Harlon Hill, a lanky end from North Alabama College drafted in the 15th round, and Zeke Bratkowski, a quarterback from Georgia, who was their number two draft choice.

In an exhibition game against the Cardinals, George sustained an injury to his knee. The diagnosis at the time was that he had a bad sprain. George had to miss the remainder of the exhibition games to rest the knee in hopes it would heal sufficiently for him to be ready for the regular season. Despite the rest and the therapy, George was unable to push off on his bad leg. This restricted not only his mobility but also his ability to sustain a block. George knew he couldn't contribute to the team as a player but he had an idea of how to help the team. The biggest problem, as he saw it, was on offense at his left tackle spot. He felt that the linebacking was in good shape, particularly with Bill George and Joe Fortunato playing well. George went to Halas with an idea about the offensive left tackle position.

130

Bill Wightkin was an end but I knew he had the size, strength and blocking technique to make a very good offensive tackle. He would need a lot of tutoring and encouragement which I knew I could give him. I went to Halas and said, "You give me Bill Wightkin to work with and I'll make him an All-Pro offensive tackle." "Are you serious?" Halas asked. I told him I was very serious and he told me to go ahead with my plan.

Bill and I worked every day on his blocking. I would go one-on-one with him. Even with my bad leg, I could give him a good workout. The one thing I knew with Bill is that I had to get him mad. I would use every trick I knew to get him riled up. Once he was motivated, I was able to teach him the various techniques necessary to be an effective blocker in the pros. He learned well and became an excellent tackle. He was a big help to the Bears that year and was an All-Pro at tackle the following year.

As the regular season progressed, George tried his best to play some offense but was unable to play effectively. Orthopedic specialists advised him to forego playing football for the remainder of the season. At that time, a decision on surgery would need to be made. In mid-season, owner-coach George Halas announced that George would be placed on the injured reserve list. His spot on the roster was filled by Herman Clark who had recently been discharged from the Army.

To be inactive for the season was a bitter pill for George to swallow. Although he had sustained many injuries during the course of his football career, he had only missed one game due to injury in his six years of professional football . . . and that was because his mother made him!

After attempting various forms of therapy, the doctors advised George to have surgery. In January, 1955, Dr. John Claridge removed an internal cartilage and about a dozen pieces of bone. After the surgery, Dr. Claridge commented that he was amazed George could even attempt to play football given the condition of his knee.

George was not going to let a knee injury, albeit a very serious one, end his football career. With his fierce determination, he embarked on a vigorous therapy program immediately after the surgery which he maintained through the winter, spring and summer months. He was determined to have the knee ready for Bear camp in mid-August in preparation for the 1955 football season.

The Bears won their last four games of the 1954 season against the Colts, Rams, Cardinals and Lions to finish with a respectable 8 and 4 record. Bratkowski was the third leading passer in the league, throwing for 1,087 yards. The rookie, Harlon Hill, astounded the league with his speed and pass-catching ability. He led the league with a 25-yard average per catch and scored 12 touchdowns, also the best in the league. His play earned him All-Pro honors.

After one game had been played in the 1954 NFL season, Halas made one of the most bizarre trades in the history of the NFL. He traded his long-time defensive coach, Hunk Anderson to the Washington Redskins for tackle, Paul Lipscomb (not to be confused with "Big Daddy Lipscomb). George claims it was one of Halas' worst moves as owner/coach of the Bears. Anderson was one of the best defensive minds in the NFL and a coach who had the full respect of his players. As George's fellow Bear tackle and great friend, Fred Davis, used to tell George about Anderson, "Hunk never put us in a bad position."

CHAPTER EIGHT

The 1955 Season

Going to camp in 1955 was different from the previous seven for George. This time he was coming off major knee surgery and although his rehabilitation had gone well, he wasn't at all sure how the knee would hold up to the pounding that all players are subjected to in professional football. One thing he did know – he wasn't quite ready for contact work. Fortunately, Halas agreed with this. He suggested George stay out of contact drills until he felt the knee could withstand the many hits that go along with playing linebacker.

1955 was Doug Atkins' first year with the Bears after being traded from the Cleveland Browns. He and George were both recuperating from major knee surgery so their first weeks in summer camp at St. Joseph's College in Rensselaer, Indiana consisted mainly of running laps. George decided this would be a good opportunity to get to know his new teammate and to learn first-hand what motivated Doug as a player. Each day George would ask Doug one question and then let Doug do most of the talking. The first question was, what was his opinion of Paul Brown, the coach of the Cleveland Browns. Doug talked the entire running session about how he disliked Brown with his regimented practices and precise way of doing everything. The next day George asked Doug his opinion of the assistant coaches of the Browns and Doug again expounded. This questioning by George went on day after day until he had a good handle on the way Doug thought.

George also learned all about Atkins from Lindsey Nelson, the sportscaster who, like Atkins, was a University of Tennessee graduate. George learned that Atkins came to Tennessee on a basketball scholarship and also was an accomplished high jumper. As the story goes, one day General Bob Neyland, the legendary football coach at Tennessee, was walking through the gym when he saw this mammoth youth shooting baskets. "What's your name young man?" inquired the general.

"Doug Atkins," he replied.

"Atkins, how tall are you and what do you weigh?" asked the general.

"I'm six-feet-eight and 250 pounds."

The general, looking up at the huge Atkins, queried "What brought you to the University of Tennessee?"

Atkins told him he was on a basketball scholarship.

"Not any more. You're now a football player."

George felt he had a complete book on his new teammate. When the Bears took the field that fall on defense, George was the right-side linebacker with Atkins the right end. George was also the captain of the team and called the defensive signals. Before the first game, George approached Atkins and said, "Doug, you're a big man and need your rest. There is no need for you to go in the defensive huddle. You wait on the line and after I tell the rest of the team what defense we'll be in, I'll tell you. I'll also tell you whether I am playing outside of you or inside of you."

As George told the story,

Doug liked that but I noticed every once in a while he would look over his shoulder to make sure I was where I said I would be. After a couple quarters when I had won his confidence, I would tell him I would be on his outside. Before the ball was snapped, I would shift inside. I knew Doug could handle the whole right side by himself. This gave us a potent defense with the linebackers over-shifted left and Doug handling the right side.

George went on to say,

> Doug sort of put his game on cruise on some
> plays. I never said anything to him because even on
> cruise he was terrific. I saved my urging of Doug to
> play harder until we definitely needed it, like the time
> against the Baltimore Colts, when it was third and
> long. We knew Unitas was going to pass and we badly
> needed a sack. I went up to Doug and said, 'Doug, did
> you know that Parker (the Colts big tackle) said you
> were nothing but a hillbilly and he didn't say very
> nice things about your mother either.' Doug dug in
> his cleats, blew off the line, picked Parker up and
> slammed dunked him on the way to sacking Unitas.
> When Doug Atkins got mad, there was no one in the
> league who could stop him. I loved playing with
> Doug. Atkins was inducted into the Pro-Hall of Fame
> in 1982.

Zeke Bratkowski, the Bears' quarterback from the 1954 season, was called into the Army. This allowed second-year man, Ed Brown, from the University of San Francisco, and veteran George Blanda to have their chance directing the team. Both Brown and Blanda had spelled Bratkowski on occasion the previous season and now both of them would have the opportunity to see more action. They would have some great ends to throw to including the phenomenal Harlon Hill, Bill McColl, a second year-man from Stanford, and the veteran, Gene Schroeder. Not since the days of Kavanaugh and Keane, the great Bear ends of the past, did a Bear quarterback have such outstanding receivers.

Added on the Bear roster for the season was Joe Fortunato, an outstanding linebacker from Mississippi State, and Stan Jones, a guard from Maryland. Bill George was coming into his own as a great defensive player and newly acquired Doug Atkins would bolster the defense. Stan Jones, Bill George and Doug Atkins would eventually be inducted into the NFL Hall of Fame. Coming off an 8-4 record the previous year, the Bears were optimistic about their chances for a championship.

The Bears opened their season in Baltimore against a very good Colt team. A 79-yard touchdown run by Alan Ameche, a rookie back from Wisconsin, on the second play of the game set the stage for a 23-17 victory for the Colts. Oddly enough, it was Ameche's first carry in a regular season NFL game. George wasn't in the game at the time. Halas was not playing George full time because he apparently had some reservations about George's knee and how that would affect his play. Hill scored on a pass from Blanda and Bobby Watkins scored on a short run for the Bears. Later Blanda kicked a field goal for the Bears, bringing the score to Baltimore 23, Bears 17. Near the end of the game, the Bears tried a trick play with Bill McColl on a reverse from his end position. He completed a 59-yard pass to Harlon Hill which took them to the 20-yard line when the game ended.

The Packers upset the Bears at Green Bay in the second game 24-3. Nothing seemed to work for the Bears, as the only score they could muster was a Blanda field goal. Even the usually tough Bear defense had a bad day, allowing the Packer backs to gain yardage in huge chunks. This opened up the passing game for the Packer quarterback, Tobin Rote. George, who was now playing only defense and not full time, played his usual linebacker position and by objective standards acquitted himself well. But he knew he was not playing to the level he was accustomed to playing. He wasn't consciously favoring his bad knee, yet there seemed to be some hesitancy in his play compared to his trademark all-out style of play.

Zero and 2 was not where the Bears had planned to be after their first two games. Nor was 0 and 3 after their third consecutive loss, but that is where the Bears found themselves after losing to the 49ers at home, 20-19. It was a particularly frustrating loss as the Bears came up empty handed on the San Francisco one-yard line on the last play of the first half and on the three-yard line in the last minute of the game without a score either time. To add to their disappointment, Harlon Hill, the league's outstanding pass receiver, dropped a perfect pass from Ed Brown on the 10-yard line behind the 49er secondary in the third period and George Blanda twice missed open receivers on the goal line. Notwithstanding the loss, one very good aspect of the game, which augured well for the Bears' future, was the return of George to his pre-injury form. Here's what George said happened:

> As I watched our offense, I saw that the 49er defensive end, Charlie Powell, was killing us. I went to Halas and said, "Let me go in at tackle. I can handle that guy." On the first play, Powell put on a hard charge. I faked like I was going to meet him directly, then hit him low with a body block. He went down in a heap. The next time, instead of waiting for him on a pass block, I fired out and flattened him. From then on I owned him. It got so bad they took him out of the game. I was so intent on blocking him, I forgot all about my knee and played all-out for the first time since I was injured.

This was George's "breakout" game. Freed from consciously or unconsciously thinking about his knee, he once again was all over the field making tackles. With George playing like his old self, the Bears were now a team to be reckoned with, particularly on defense. This new vigor showed in their fourth game as the Bears manhandled the Colts in a return engagement played in Chicago. The final score was 38-10 but the score did not reflect the way the Bears dominated the game. As George Strickler wrote in the *Chicago Tribune*, "...at no time was there a question of Bear supremacy as the Colts found their vaunted passing attack rushed to distraction and their running game reduced to a periodic annoyance." At one point, George blitzed from his linebacker position and slammed into the Colts' quarterback, George Shaw, so hard that Shaw had to be carried from the field. Years later, Artie Donovan, a Hall of Fame tackle who played in that game, was interviewed by David Letterman on national TV. He was asked if he could name the hardest hit he ever saw on a football field, "That's easy," replied Donovan. "It was the time George Connor of the Chicago Bears hit our quarterback, George Shaw." Donovan went on to relate how George came through the line and hit Shaw hard against his face mask as Shaw tried to duck out of the way. Donovan continued, "Shaw went down in a heap with blood spurting all over the place. They carted him off the field and when he came to, he sat next to me on the bench. Still groggy, he turned to me and asked, 'How are my front teeth?' I looked at his mouth and said, "What teeth? They're gone."

Gary Kerkorian replaced Shaw and the Colt attack collapsed completely.

On their annual west coast swing, the Bears defeated both the 49ers and the Rams. In the final minute of the second period of the 49er game, Bob Toneff of the 49ers punched his former Notre Dame teammate, Bob Williams, on the chin. This seemed to ignite the Bears as they roared back in the second half and soundly defeated the 49ers, 34-23. A week later the Bears won in Los Angeles against the Rams 31-20 before a crowd of 69,587.

With three wins in a row, the Bears were now only a game off the pace for the lead in their division. The next hurdle was a rematch against the Packers at Wrigley Field. The Bears desperately wanted a fourth win particularly against their long-time rival, a team that had defeated the Bears in Green Bay earlier in the season.

Before a packed house of 48,890 fans at Wrigley Field, the Bears beat the Packers, 52-31. There were many stars on offense for the Bears including, Chick Jagade, Bobby Watkins, Harlon Hill and Bill McColl. On defense, the whole team played an outstanding game but none better than George who had his finest day as a Bear. As George Strickler wrote in the *Chicago Tribune*:

Ringleader in the battering and bruising was

George Connor, the 240 pound handsome, but calloused veteran of eight rigorous National League campaigns, who twice rattled the rafters of Wrigley Field with tackles that separated Packers from the ball on kickoff returns. It was the old Notre Dame star's greatest day in pro football and he left the game in the waning minutes to a standing ovation.

The Hit

The Packer game featured one of the most astounding yet violent plays in NFL history.

At the time I was home in Chicago on leave from the FBI. I had just completed my training in Washington D.C. as a special agent and was assigned to the Miami office. With our parents then living in St. Paul, I stayed at George's apartment. The night before the game, George and I went to dinner. During the course of our conversation, he told me it was possible that the 1955 season might be his last as a player. He went on to say, "Since you're leaving for Miami Monday morning, this might be the last time you will ever see me play. I don't know what it will be, but sometime in the game I'll do something special. I want you to know it's for you."

As I sat in my seat the next day at Wrigley Field, I was very conscious of the fact that I could very well be watching George play for the last time. As a result, I never took my eyes off George the entire game. After a Bear score, I was shocked to see George line up on the kickoff team. As any fan knows, it is rare to see a first-string player, let alone an All-Pro, on the kickoff team. With my binoculars trained on George, I watched him sprint down the field. My first thought, other than why in the world was he on the kickoff team, was that he hadn't lost any of his speed because of the knee surgery. I watched as he flattened first one blocker, then another and met the ball carrier with a ferocious tackle that caused the football to fly out of the ball carrier's hands. The fumble was recovered by the Bears and quickly led to a Bear touchdown. The next time George was on the field and each time thereafter, he played with a reckless abandon that caused havoc for the Packer offense.

In the second half, after a Bear score, George again sprinted down the field on the kickoff team. This time he headed straight for the middle of the wedge that the Packer team had formed at about the twenty-yard line. Veryl Switzer, a speedy back who had a 26-yard average in returning kickoffs, caught the ball at about the five-yard-line and headed straight up field behind the wedge. As he approached the wedge, George was running full tilt when I saw him bend a little at the waist and with his fists on his chest spread his elbows out as far as they would go. It was obvious that he intended to crash into the middle of the four-man wedge and take as many of them down as he could. For some inexplicable reason (perhaps it was because nobody wanted to take on a charging George Connor) the wedge parted and George and Switzer both running full speed, met head on without ever seeing each other. George's right shoulder caught Switzer in the middle of his chest and Switzer rocketed backward on his back while George never broke stride and kept running toward the goal line.

The sound of the two bodies colliding was thunderous. I have never heard anything like it before or since on a football field. At the moment of the collision, everyone in the stadium saw a helmet flying through the air and the ball also flying in the air. There was a very audible gasp from the crowd because between the violence of the collision and flight of the helmet and the ball, it looked as though Switzer had been decapitated. With bodies running around trying to recover the fumble that had resulted from George's hit, it was several seconds before Switzer's prone body came into view. Eventually there was a collective sigh from the crowd as it became apparent Switzer did indeed still have his head on.

While the unconscious Switzer was being attended to, George, who had run to the end zone, circled back to the Bear bench and was having his completely numb shoulder attended to. After several minutes, there was a loud applause from the fans. George, who had not been looking at the field, asked one of his teammates what the applause was for. The player told George that Switzer was conscious and being helped off the field. George commented, "I must be losing my touch."

George continued to play until the waning minutes of the game, when Halas sent in a substitute for him. As George came off the field, he received a standing ovation which lasted several minutes from the fans who knew they had just witnessed an unbelievable performance by one of their favorite players. Halas, never known to show affection, greeted George at the sidelines with a hug. Recently, Ed McCaskey, the Chairman Emeritus of the Bears and Halas' son-in law, told me that the only other person he ever knew Halas to hug was Vince Lombardi.

After the game, for the first time, I was admitted to the Bear locker room. The scene was one of wild jubilation with players congratulating each other. Amid the celebration, with George the center of attention, Bulldog Turner, the great Bear center who had retired several years earlier, came up to George, shook his hand and said, "George, in all my years playing and watching football, I have never seen anyone get hit as hard as you hit Switzer. I thought you killed him."

Bob Skoronski, who played 11 years with the Packers and was a mainstay, along with Forrest Gregg at offensive tackle on Vince Lombardi's great championship Packer teams, says:

> I didn't join the Packers until the following season so I didn't see the hit George put on Veryl Switzer in person. But, I saw it on television and watched the movies of that game many times. It was, without a doubt, the hardest hit I have ever seen to this day. Anybody who saw the hit and who doesn't say it was the hardest hit they ever saw is lying. I got to know Switzer. He told me he spit up blood every day for

almost a year as a result of George's hit. After a stint in the service, Switzer returned to the Packers to play. The Packers cut him. Switzer told me that he just didn't have the desire to play saying he didn't want to take the chance of ever being hit like that again.

Jerry Groom, who at the time was an All-Pro lineman with the Chicago Cardinals, was at the game. The Cardinals had played a Saturday night game which allowed Groom to be able to attend the Bear-Packer game on Sunday. He was seated with Jack Vanisi, the general manager of the Packers.

I was watching George on the kickoff team and saw his sprint downfield. When he was near the wedge, he dipped as if to break up the wedge and the wedge parted. George hit Verl Switzer so hard his helmet flew one way, the ball another. He knocked him right out of his shoes. It must have been ten minutes before they could get Switzer off the field. It was, without question, the greatest hit I ever saw.

The footnote to the story is what Vanisi told me later about what happened in the Packer locker room after the game. According to Vanisi, Switzer got up on one of the benches and asked for the team's attention. He said, "I'm telling you guys, if you ever open up the wedge and I get hit like that again, when I come to, I'll leave my shoes on the field and wave to the north, east, south and west. I'll drop my headgear next to my shoes and walk off the field. That's the last time I'll ever play a football game."

Football fans today have become accustomed to big hits as they watch the games on TV. When there is a tremendous collision of players, notably the one-on-one kind, we seem to see it over and over again on instant replay and watching Classic Sports on ESPN. Some of the hits we see are of the head-to-head variety which are vicious, dirty plays and have no place in football, college or pro. These hits, where the one player, usually on defense, flies through the air and hits helmet to head of the opposing player are done with the intent to physically hurt a player and put him out of action. George's hit, though devastating, had no malicious intent.

In George's day there was no instant replay. If you weren't at the game or didn't watch the telecast of the game, chances are you missed it forever. This is true especially of any hits that happened during a Bear game of that era. The reason for this is the Bear office had a fire many years ago which destroyed their film library and most of their records. Therefore, the only visual record of one of the most memorable hits in pro ball is an old Green Bay film which is of very poor quality. However, old-time Bear fans who were at the game still talk about George's hit on Veryl Switzer. It was a classic tackle that will be forever rated as one of the hardest "hits" in the history of pro football.

As an avid follower of pro football, I have watched all the big hits through the years as shown on television shows. I can say with conviction that George's hit on Veryl Switzer was the most devastating one I have ever seen. If there was the camera work then that there is now, and the film was preserved so George's play could be shown today, I am confident every sports fan who viewed it would agree; it was the classic hit of all time. For those of us who were at that game, there isn't even a doubt.

In addition to the George Shaw hit in the Baltimore game and the Veryl Switzer hit, George had a few other memorable individual hits. There was one in particular against the Rams, when he put one of the ends out of commission early in the game. George saw from the films and knew from experience that this particular player was killing the other teams with his quick slants over the middle. George described what happened:

This guy was killing the other teams with his slants to the middle and the yardage he gained after catching a pass. With his speed, I knew I couldn't cover him so I decided I had to slow him down. Early in the game, I saw him spread wide to the left, his favorite spot for running his slant pattern. I dropped back from my middle linebacker position and just as he cut across the middle, I hit him hard. He went down in a heap. He didn't play the rest of the game.

The Bears had won four straight games and were not only winning but doing so in an impressive way. In their eighth game of the season the Bears routed the league-leading Rams 24-3 in Wrigley Field for their fifth consecutive win and a tie for first place. George again was the dominant player on the field as he made tackles in the Ram's backfield, in the middle and near the sidelines. He seemed to be everywhere. As reported by Dave Condon of the *Chicago Tribune*,

The Bears' defense was outstanding; so outstanding that some of Chicago's offensive unit wanted to carry the defenders off the field when the conquest of Los Angeles was made official by the final gun . . . It was so outstanding that Co-captain Connor, eight seasons a Bear and second to the last to trudge into the dressing room, was awarded a game ball by teammates who let Co-captain Sprinkle do their talking . . . Sprinkle, 12 years a Bear, said simply: 'George Connor anchors our great defensive team.' Then Sprinkle slapped the football into the midriff of Connor.

After a second handshake by a jubilant Halas, George was congratulated by his former teammate, John Lujack. George expressed his feelings to Lujack:

John, this is the greatest group of spirited per-
sonalities I ever played with and that includes Notre
Dame. There's never been a squad like this one
before. It excels because that's the way the guys play
it. Somebody gets knocked down and, as he's falling,
somebody is up and ready to give him a rest. Nobody
is jealous of anybody else. The spirit is so outstanding. I've learned a brand new meaning of fellow-
ship. Sure they play for money. They also play for
pride. They battle to get the job done.

Near George and Lujack was Bobby Watkins, one of the young
backs on the Bear team. He said, "I've never heard a better description
of anything in all my life. I didn't realize it before, but now I know
what makes the Bears great."

The Bears won their sixth game in a row as they beat the Lions,
24-14. With three games remaining, the Bears were riding high,
perhaps too high as they played that awful disjointed game that all
teams dread. The degree of euphoria in the Bears locker room after
the Ram victory was in inverse proportion to the despair of the locker
room two weeks later, when the Cardinals soundly defeated the Bears,
53-14, to smash the Bears' dream of a championship. It was a humili-
ating and devastating loss. It was one of those games where the Bears
could do nothing right and the Cardinals nothing wrong. Even
though the Bears had twice defeated the Rams, it wasn't good enough.
The Rams had lost only one other game. The Rams were now in first
place and remained there for a division championship.

In a defensive battle, the Bears squeaked by the Detroit Lions, 21-
20, for their seventh victory of the season. George scored his only
touchdown as a pro when he scooped up a Lion fumble and raced for
48 yards to the end zone. The goat of the game was the All-Pro, Doak
Walker, who missed an extra point.

At that time, I was a special agent of the FBI assigned to the Miami,
Florida office. I was thrilled to learn that the Bear game against Detroit

would be televised in the Miami area. Part way through the game, my FBI roommates and I were interrupted by a call from the FBI office instructing the three of us to proceed immediately to the Miami airport to check out an arriving passenger who was possibly a wanted fugitive. We hightailed it to the airport, parked our car and entered the terminal. We checked the arrival board and saw that the flight we wanted was at a gate about 50 yards away and had just arrived. We also noticed that the game was on the television sets on the wall, spaced about ten yards apart. As we ran to the appropriate gate, slowed by making sure our revolvers did not come out of their holsters inside our coats, I kept glancing up at the TV sets. I saw George scoop up the fumble and race toward the goal line. I didn't see the rest of the play as I had reached my destination. I learned the next day that George did indeed score his only touchdown as a pro.

I didn't learn until years later that George's wife, Sue, has a story about his interception. George and Sue were dating at the time and Sue was at the game. It seems when George intercepted the pass, he kept looking back for a would-be tackler. Spotting a player, George kept zigzagging to avoid the player (it turned out to be one of the Bear players) which caused his 48-yard run to seem much longer. Sue kids George that she went out for a hot dog and coke and when she came back, he was still running.

In the final game of the season the Bears beat the Eagles, 17-10, for an 8-4 season and another second-place finish. In the championship game for the NFL title, the Cleveland Browns defeated the Los Angeles Rams, 38-14.

After the season when the All-Pro team was selected, George was named for the fifth time in his career, this time as a linebacker on the defensive team.

George had completed his eighth season as a Bear and in many ways it was one of his best. He had courageously come back to top form after a serious knee injury that might well have ended his career had it not been for that fierce determination of his. Because of his knee surgery, he wasn't satisfied with his level of play in the first two games. Then he had a breakthrough game in the third game against the 49ers. Once he knew he could again play with his usual reckless abandon, he seemed to push himself to an even higher level of play: this resulted in his having career-type performances against both Green Bay and the Rams and outstanding performances in the other games. Part of the explanation for this might be the fact that, for the first time in his entire career, he was playing mostly on defense. This no doubt gave him more stamina, but mainly, it was his strong desire to overcome adversity that was responsible for the return to stardom.

CHAPTER NINE

Turning Points

As George packed his bags in preparation for his annual trip to St. Joseph's College in Rensselaer, Indiana for summer camp, he had every intention of playing his ninth season with the Bears. He had just signed a new, two-year contract with George Halas and had told his coach, "I think the Bears are going to win the championship this fall and I don't want to miss out on it."

Upon arrival at camp he had a chat with Halas. The coach told George that he planned to use him as his "swing-man" linebacker during the coming season. He explained that George had played all three linebacking positions, both sides and in the middle and therefore could play wherever he was needed. He also advised George that, as one of the veterans of the team, he should ease into the practice routine and should not participate in the many contact drills and scrimmages until he felt he was ready. George, who had followed his usual off-season regimen of playing a lot of handball and watching his weight, knew he was in good condition. But he also realized it was only the previous year that he had had major knee surgery and had experienced a long, difficult rehabilitation. With that in mind, he welcomed the opportunity to ease into the grueling routine of summer practice.

George did his usual amount of running to strengthen his legs and helped some of the younger players with their techniques in the blocking and tackling drills. Within a week of the opening of camp, Halas held a scrimmage. George, who watched from the sidelines, recalled what happened:

After a few days in camp I was watching a scrimmage from the sidelines when I had the strangest feeling – sort of a detached feeling – as I watched my teammates scrimmage. Usually when I watched a scrimmage, I had a strong urge to be out on the field and be a part of it. This time I had no such feeling. Not only did I have no desire to play, but for the first time in my career, I couldn't even picture myself playing.

That evening I went to Halas and told him of my feelings and that I thought it was time to call it quits. He was very understanding. He said that sometimes that happened to a player who has played a number of years and that with some time to think about such a big decision, the player often changed his mind. He suggested I go home for a week and think about it; then return and give him my decision.

George drove back to Chicago to spend some time reflecting on his decision to quit playing football. He sought out his good friend, Gene McNeil, who had been his mentor and had always given him sound advice. In the true spirit of friendship, McNeil expounded on the pros and cons of such a life-changing decision. Then McNeil, in his direct way, told George he had just completed one of his best years and asked, "Are you going to get better? Do you have anything else to prove? Why don't you quit while you're on top?"

For several days George thought about McNeil's words. He then made a decision that he knew in his heart was the correct one. After playing 16 years of competitive football, eight of them with the Bears, he made the decision to retire. He was 31 years old.

He drove back to the Bears' camp and met with Halas. George explained to Halas that if he couldn't be the best at his position, then it was time to retire. Halas asked George if he was comfortable with that decision. George told him he was. George remembered the discussion:

Halas was very understanding. He said, 'Kid, the toughest thing a player has to do is realize when it's time to quit. You've thought it out and I respect your decision. Now, I have an offer for you.'

Halas asked George to become a part time defensive coach. They worked out the details: George would coach Monday, Tuesday and Thursday mornings and full time on the weekends. The pay would be half of what a full time coach would receive. George gladly signed his new contract and Halas tore up his player's contract. This arrangement was ideal for George. It allowed him to carry on with his box business, as he did when he was a player.

On August 6, 1956 the Bears held a press conference and announced that George had retired as a player and would be added to the Bears' coaching staff. George said, "I quit because if I can't be the tops, I don't want to play." Halas said, "George parlayed leadership and intelligence into one of the great careers of our time. We set high standards for him as a player; he exceeded them. We have set equally high standards for him as a coach; he will exceed them, too."

Jack Rosenburg wrote in the *Chicago Tribune*:

> Unlike another captain, the fictional Ahab of *Moby Dick*, Co-captain Connor quit when he was ahead. Professionally, Connor's greatest moments came as a linebacker rather than as a tackle. He first inherited his linebacking station in 1949 in a move designed by the Bears to combat the running of the Philadelphia's Eagles, Steve Van Buren. Thereafter, Connor became the scourge at backing up the line, an impenetrable force whose hulking form suggested that enemy ball carriers travel in other directions or face the consequences.

From Player to Coach

"I always thought coaching was fairly easy," recalled George "until I actually became a coach." He went on to explain that he did so many things on instinct while playing that he had to re-think how he did things and why. He enjoyed coaching until a defensive team meeting the Monday after the opening game of the season against Detroit. George remembered:

> I was conducting a meeting of the defensive team after one of our exhibition games – we had been beaten badly, by over 35 points. We were watching the game film and I was pointing out the many mistakes the defense had made. The players, many of whom I had played with the year before, were not having any part of my criticism. I heard remarks coming from the back of the room such as, "What do you know about it? I suppose you could do better? Didn't you ever make a mistake?" Now I was mad. I stopped the film, flipped on the lights and said, "I don't need this job. I make more money selling boxes. They don't pay enough to take the kind of guff you guys are giving me. Sure I made a lot of mistakes but I'm trying to coach you. If you'll let me point out your mistakes, I think we can improve. I'll tell you what; I'll take any one of you on. Or, I don't know how long I'll last, but I'll take all of you on one at a time if that's what you want. I'm going out the door and I'll be in the hall. You decide what you want to do." With that, I left the room.
>
> As I waited in the hall, I heard all kinds of noise. Then I heard the door open and waited with clenched fists to fight whoever came out. Who walked out but Doug Atkins, all 6-feet-8 of him. I thought, 'Oh my

God, what have I done?' I glared at him with my fists clenched and he stared back at me with his fists clenched. As he approached, he opened his fists and stuck out his big right hand and said, "Look Coach, we need you. Please come back in."

From that moment on, George was a coach – and a good one. He had an aptitude for analyzing offenses and designing defenses to stop the main thrust of the opposing team. As an All-Pro on both offense and defense, he knew the techniques of every position and was able to impart his knowledge to the players.

Thanks to George, in the Bear-Cardinal game during the season, the fans were treated to one of the best fights ever seen in Wrigley Field. Key players, Jerry Groom of the Cardinals and Bill Wightkin of the Bears, had played on the Notre Dame team with George. He knew their style of play. Wightkin, he knew, was a steady player but played at a more intense level when riled up. Seeing that both Groom and Wightkin had casts on their hand's and arm's from previous injuries, George devised a strategy for the game.

That day both benches were on the same side of the field and very close to each other. George roamed the sideline between the two benches.

Before the game, he warned Wightkin that Groom was going to hit him with his cast. Wightkin, an easy-going guy, told George that Groom would never do that because they were good friends. George said, "I'm warning you, Bill. He'll do it." George knew that when a player wore a cast it was virtually impossible not to hit someone in the heat of the game.

Sure enough, after the game had been underway for several minutes, Wightkin came to the sideline and told George that Groom had hit him with the cast. George asked him if he had talked with the officials about it. Wightkin told George he had talked to the officials and they did nothing. George said, "Bill, you have no choice. You have to hit him back."

153

After the next series of plays, Groom came to the sideline, spotted George and said, "Do you know what Wightkin did? He hit me with his cast." George responded, "If the officials won't do anything about it, I'm afraid you're going to have to hit him back to protect yourself."

Later Groom, now back in the game, hit Wightkin with his cast. By now George had acquired a bull horn. Depending on who hit whom last, George would bellow with the bull horn, "He's hitting you with his cast. Hit him back!" Before long there was plaster from the casts flying all over. It looked like it was snowing in Wrigley Field. Bill Downs, the official, warned Wightkin and Groom several times to stop their fighting but never called a penalty. After the game, Downs told George, "I wasn't about to stop it. It was the best damn fight I ever saw."

After the game, Wightkin and Groom made their peace and went to dinner together with their wives. George came in the restaurant where the Wightkins and Grooms were dining. It was then the true story of George, instigating and promoting the fight, was uncovered. Through the years Jerry Groom and George have had many laughs about the famous fight when it snowed plaster of Paris in Wrigley Field.

The 1956 Ram game was a big game for the Bears. According to George,

> The Ram game was a key one for us. Bill George and I were talking about the upcoming game and we agreed that we needed a good game from Ed Brown, our quarterback and Rick Casares, our big fullback. The problem was both were known to slip out after curfew, have a few drinks and maybe enjoy some female companionship. Bill and I decided we would take Brown and Casares to dinner and even have a few beers to keep them loose and then tuck them in bed.
>
> The next morning at breakfast, Brown appeared as rested as I had ever seen him before a game. Casares was a different story. He looked as though he

was out all night, which was probably the case. In the locker room before the game, I grabbed Casares and shoved him against a locker and said, "I know you were out last night. We need this game and we need you. I want at least 100 yards from you today or I'm coming after you."

Casares played the game of his life, killing the Rams with his hard running. In the third quarter, he hurt his leg but wouldn't come out of the game. I think he got 130 yards rushing that game which was a big factor in defeating the Rams.

During the season, George watched movies of the opponents on a daily basis, either at the Bear office or at home. He became quite proficient at charting how the opposition played in various down and yardage situations. This helped him design the defenses the Bears would use from week to week. The one hitch in the defensive game plan was the implementation of it on game day. On game day, George wanted to be on the field so he could have direct contact with his players in order to get their first-hand feedback. This would allow him to make on-the-spot adjustments. Instead of being on the field, Clark Shaughnessy, who was the overall coach of the defense and as such was George's immediate boss, assigned George to the coaches' booth high up in the stadium. This frustrated George and the players. None of the players had any rapport with Shaughnessy and George's instructions by phone to the bench were ignored by Shaughnessy.

Three veteran defensive players, Doug Atkins, Bill George, and Freddie Williams met with George hoping to solve the problem. They talked it over and decided a direct request to Shaughnessy for a change would never work, so they devised a scheme. The three players went to Shaughnessy and told him that having George on the phones from the booth was a waste because he (George) didn't know what he was doing. They told Shaughnessy they needed his input from the booth. Shaughnessy bought the scam and assigned himself to the booth for the remaining games. From then on, with George on the sidelines, the defense was superb making timely adjustments as needed. Shaughnessy never knew the instructions he called down to the bench from the booth were completely ignored.

The Bears enjoyed a very good season in 1956. They ended the regular season with a 9-2-1 record which earned them the Western Division Championship. The NFL championship game against the Eastern champs, the New York Giants, was scheduled to be played in Yankee Stadium two weeks after the regular season ended. George recalled:

> Since we had two weeks to prepare, I watched game films of the Giants against six different opponents. I charted all the Giants' tendencies and felt we were ready to stop anything they would do. The one contingency we were not prepared for was the weather. There was snow, sleet and generally very foul weather in New York. By game time, the field was a quagmire. The Bears had brought with them what they thought were bad weather shoes. But in reality, they were the same type of old shoe Bronko Nagurski wore in bad weather when he played for the Bears. Each shoe had a number "3" (Nagurski's playing number) on them to indicate they were the foul weather shoes. They had hard rubber cleats and were completely useless. The Giants, on the other hand, solved the shoe problem. Andy Robustelli, their great end, owned a sporting goods store. The Giants arranged to have sneakers from Robustelli's store delivered to the stadium prior to game time. As the Bears slipped and were unable to get sure footing, the Giants, with their sneakers, completely dominated the game, winning 47-7.

After the game, George went to Toots Shor's restaurant where many of the Giant players were celebrating. His good friend, dating back to the college all-star days, Charlie Conerly, now a Giant quarterback, took great delight in needling George with such taunts as, "Giants 47, Bears 7" and kept repeating the score. George could do nothing but take the abuse. However, years later, George did get his revenge! As George recalled:

> In the 1963 season, the Bears again played the Giants for the NFL championship. The Bears won, 14-7. Later in the evening, I thought of Conerly and how he had given it to me after the Giants won in 1956. I waited until about 1:30 in the morning and placed a person-to-person collect call to Conerly in Clarksdale, Mississippi. When he accepted the call, I immediately said, "Bears 14, Giants 7." Conerly said, "George, you finally got me."

George enjoyed his work as a coach, particularly developing young players and seeing them progress to good pro players. After a few years as an assistant coach however, George decided to leave the coaching ranks. Several factors entered into his decision. First, he never planned to stay in coaching as an on-going occupation. Second, he had an opportunity to stay connected with football by working as a broadcaster and third; he was finding it progressively more difficult to work with Clark Shaughnessy who was in charge of the defense for the Bears. George says that Shaughnessy was very secretive and did things to alienate his fellow coaches. As George says, "He never took the blame when he made a mistake and took credit for good things on the defense even when he had nothing to do with it. He was very difficult to work with and I didn't like being around him."

Despite his periodic clashes with Shaughnessy, George enjoyed his two years as a coach. George saw his protege Bill George earn All-Pro honors as one of the best middle linebackers in pro football. The following year the team did not fare as well, but the defense played well with Bill George again named to the All-Pro team, as well as Doug Atkins at end. It was a good run for George but he was ready to move on to the broadcasting booth.

George and Sue

While he was still with the Bears, George met Suzanne Dungan, an attractive, red-haired girl from Winnetka, Illinois. Sue is the daughter of Albert W. and Gladys Dungan of Winnetka where she was raised along with her siblings. Sue was not a football fan when she first started dating George during his last year as a player for the Bears. As a matter of fact, initially she wasn't aware George played professional football. After they dated a few times, George asked her if she wanted to attend a football game that Sunday at Wrigley Field. After she agreed, George asked her how she would get to the Field. Sue, wondering what kind of man would ask for a date and not pick her up, asked, "Where will you be?" George told her he had to leave early to get his ankles taped before the game. Now Sue wondered what was going on until George finally explained that he played for the Chicago Bears and it was a Bear game he wanted her to attend.

The two were married on December 27, 1962. George and Sue have two children, George, Jr. and Albert. Given George's background, it seems fitting that young George attended Notre Dame and Al went to Holy Cross. The boys were George's pride and joy which was always evident when he talked about them. George and Sue, as well as their boys, have always lived in Chicago.

When George was selected for induction to the Pro Hall of Fame, his boys learned for the first time what a famous father they had. As young George said, "My Dad and I were driving down Lake Shore Drive (in Chicago) and had a sports program on the radio. The announcement came on the air that George Connor was selected to be inducted in the Hall of Fame in Canton, Ohio. I asked, 'Is that you?'

All my Dad said was, 'Yeah."

Al, at home at the time, answered the phone and as he says,

> This man with a strong voice asked if my dad was home. I told him he wasn't. The man said, 'This is Hank Stram. Tell your father I called and want to congratulate him on his selection to the Hall of Fame.' I was old enough to know that Hank Stram was the coach of the Kansas City Chiefs. I was a big Chief's fan and was really impressed that this famous man would call to congratulate my father."

As the boys say,

> Even at this point, we didn't realize the magnitude of our Dad's accomplishments. We just never knew how good a player he was or that he even played football. In the apartment where we lived, there weren't any trophies or anything to indicate he was a player, let alone a great one. The only clue we had was one time when he took us to a White Sox game. We were not yet ten years old. The popcorn boxes had a place for autographs. About the second or third inning, little kids came up to our row with pens and popcorn boxes to get Dad's autograph. We wondered what all that was about. That's how humble our Dad was. He just never talked about his football career.

CHAPTER TEN

Life After Football

After his retirement from coaching with the Bears, it wasn't the shock for George, as it was for many former pro players, to face the challenges of life after football. He was accustomed to supporting himself from income earned as a salesman. Sure, he missed the routine of a pro athlete and the camaraderie of his Bear teammates but it was a smooth transition for him.

George had been a corrugated box salesman since his second year in pro ball and he was familiar with the business world. He knew his craft well and had progressed from a salesman covering local accounts to one responsible for covering national ones. Soon he was one of the leading producers in the corrugated box business. George knew that his name and association with the Chicago Bears and Notre Dame gave him an entree to see purchasing agents that most other salesmen didn't have. But he also knew that once in the door, he had to know the box business as well or better than his competitors. To that end, George kept current with the various designs of boxes and made it a point to visit Hoerner's box plants in Biloxi, Mississippi, Fargo, North Dakota and ones in between to know the production problems that the plant managers encountered. In this way, George felt he could service an account and merit their business.

He was known for his service once he landed an account. Not only did he follow an account closely and solve any problems that cropped up but made friends with the purchasing agents. Many of these friendships lasted for decades.

Broadcasting

George entered the broadcasting field serendipitously. He attended a cocktail party in the late 1950s hosted by Marty Hogan, Sr., the general manager of the radio station WCFL in Chicago. Hogan suggested to George that he might like to try his hand at broadcasting. After talking it over, he offered George the job of doing the color commentary for the home Notre Dame basketball games as a way of getting started in his new profession.

To say that George's first time on the air was a low budget affair is a gross understatement. In one of the most bizarre broadcasting arrangements one might imagine, George did the color of the games from the WCFL studios in Chicago while Frank Krousher, who usually broadcast for WHOT in South Bend, did the play-by play from the Notre Dame Fieldhouse. In other words, George did his analysis without the benefit of seeing the game either in person or on television. Perhaps the oddest part of the whole arrangement was Krousher was not aware anyone was doing the color commentary. George listened to the game in the studio in Chicago. When he wanted to comment, he would press a button which made his mike the live one. Thus Krousher, at Notre Dame, kept talking not knowing that during part of his broadcast, his mike was dead. How primitive that arrangement was, in contrast to today's highly technical broadcasts. A year after that season, George ran into Krousher at some function and commented that he enjoyed doing the color commentary of his broadcasts of the Notre Dame basketball games. Krousher said he didn't remember ever doing a broadcast with him. George then explained to him they weren't together and how the broadcast was set up with the live mike switching back and forth between the fieldhouse and the studio in Chicago. They both had a few laughs about the weird arrangement

Bill McPhail, the head of CBS sports, called George and asked him if he wanted to do the color commentary on television for the Green Bay games the following season. It should be noted that in those days each team had its own set of announcers unlike today when the network assigns one set of announcers for each game. McPhail explained that John Lujack, who had been doing the games with Ray Scott, the Green Bay announcer, was going to do the NY Giants games with Chris Schenkel. George immediately accepted the offer but it turned out there was a snag. When the president of the Packers heard that George was to be one of the announcers of their games, he objected. He felt that George was so identified with the Chicago Bears that he couldn't do an objective broadcast and might even be a spy of sorts for Halas and the Bears. At Scott's suggestion, George and Ray visited the Green Bay offices to discuss the matter. George described the meeting this way:

> The president of the Packers and I hit it off right from the start. He got right to the point and openly expressed his feelings about my identification with the Bears. I told him I could understand his reservations about having me on the Packer network, given my history with the Bears and the well-known animosity between the two teams. I said to him, "I'll make a promise to you. I'll be objective as I can be. I'll also make a deal with you. If you don't ask me for any information about the Bears, I promise you I won't divulge any information I learn about the Packers." He seemed to like that as he consented to having me on the announcing team.

About working with Ray Scott, George said:

> I loved working with Ray Scott. He was the epitome of class. He was the consummate professional yet he was very low key and a fun guy to be around. I remember my second game vividly. I was looking forward to leaving the booth at halftime to have a soft

drink and relax for ten minutes or so before returning for the second half. As halftime approached, I heard Scott say, "Now for your half-time commentary, I turn you over to my partner, George Connor," and with that, he left the booth. I think my jaw dropped a foot. I grabbed a program and quickly looked up the name of the band performing on the field. I didn't know what to say other than briefly re-cap the game and then talk about the band, even describing their uniforms. I looked at the glass window and there was Scott outside laughing and waving to me. At the time I could have killed him, but upon reflection, I knew he left me alone without warning to get me used to ad-libbing. Ray liked to kid me about my description of the color of the band uniforms.

After two years working with Scott, George accepted CBS's offer to do the Bear games with Red Grange, the famous "Galloping Ghost" of the University of Illinois and later a star with the Chicago Bears. George recalled the experience:

Red Grange was one of the finest men I ever knew. It was a wonderful experience getting to know him and working with him on the games. He knew his football but would occasionally make some mistakes in his play-by-play call. One time I received a call from someone at CBS in New York telling me I should correct Red's mistakes on the air. I said, "Who am I to correct one of football's legends? Don't worry about it. The fans and everyone listening love Red Grange."

One Sunday morning in Green Bay before the Bear-Packer game, I ran into Halas in the lobby of the hotel after he had returned from attending mass at the nearby Catholic church. I was about to leave for the next mass. Halas told me he thought it would be a good omen if Red Grange attended mass. He asked me to get ahold of Grange and bring him with me. I did, and the Bears won that day. Halas insisted I take Red to mass every Sunday. The Bears won five in a row, prompting Bill Gleason, the noted Chicago sportswriter, to say, "If Red Grange keeps attending mass, he will soon be known as the 'Galloping Holy Ghost.'"

After one of the seasons working with Grange, George was summoned to New York to talk to the CBS brass. At a meeting held in the evening, they informed George that one of the sponsors of the Bear games wanted someone they knew to replace George as the color analyst:

I knew that Halas had a lot of influence with CBS and, as the owner of the Bears, he also had a say as to who the announcers would be. With that in mind, I suggested we call Halas to get his viewpoint. One of them said, 'We can't call at this hour. Halas will be at home.' I told them it wasn't a problem that I had his number. They were impressed. What they didn't know was that his number was listed in the phone book.

Halas answered the phone. I told him what the CBS people had in mind about replacing me as the color analyst for the Bear games. He said, 'Put them on the phone.' Halas told the CBS executive in no uncertain terms that if I wasn't on the program he wouldn't allow CBS to broadcast the Bear games. That ended the matter.

After working with Grange, CBS assigned George to work with Lindsey Nelson, who had replaced Grange as the play-by-play announcer for the Bear games. Nelson, like Ray Scott, was a recognized top announcer. George recalled:

> Lindsey was a joy to work with. He was a real pro when it came to calling a game. He not only prepared studiously for each game and knew football as well as anyone but seemed to have a clock in his head. If the director told him he had 45 seconds to make his comments before a scheduled break, Lindsey would end his comments exactly on time. He was always loose and relaxed which put me at ease. Right from the start of our association, we had a chemistry that helped make a good broadcast. He had a great sense of humor and wanted his broadcasts to be an enjoyable experience. They were.

At this time, I was living in Chicago working for an investment-banking firm. There was an opening for a "spotter" (one who helps the announcers with identification of the players) to work with Nelson and George. My brother asked me if I would like the job. I jumped at the opportunity. In the ensuing four years I was the spotter for all the Bear games, home and away. Like George, I found Lindsey Nelson to be a class guy who was as nice a person as he was a complete pro as an announcer.

One example comes to mind. For a game at Kezar Stadium in San Francisco, we were in the visiting club's booth – an old wooden structure where we sat on card-table chairs with a long, old table to put our paraphernalia on. The booth was open facing the field which allowed the technicians to install a small TV monitor on the ledge of the booth. The announcers wore headsets with a microphone attached. Any information I wanted to pass on had to be done by pointing to the appropriate name on the spotting board, scribbling a short note on an index card, or by hand signals. During the game, with the three of us resting our elbows on the old, wooden table, it collapsed. This caused the TV monitor to fall and Nelson to be pinned by the table in such a way that prevented him from seeing the field. George and I were standing and had escaped the falling table. Without missing a beat, and without mentioning the incident and the fact that he couldn't see the field, Nelson kept right on with the broadcast. From my position in the booth, I could see the field and what was going on. Through a series of hand gestures from George and me, and with the use of the spotting board, George and I let Nelson know what was happening. He announced it as if he could see the action unfolding before his eyes. Neither the New York brass of CBS, nor anyone else for that matter, ever knew he did the broadcast for about ten minutes without the benefit of being able to see the game.

Nelson and George worked very smoothly together presenting the game to the viewing audience. They took a lot of pride in making their telecasts the best possible and I tried to do my part. I learned there is more to a good broadcast than a play-by-play man with a smooth delivery and an analyst who makes insightful comments. It also includes many little things the public is not aware of. For example, I recall a Bear-Colt game in Wrigley Field when Bert Rechichar of the Colts lined up to kick a field goal. I immediately noticed it would be a 58-yard attempt (the record at the time was 56 yards) and began writing a note to Nelson saying it would be an all-time record. Nelson called the yard line and without hesitation read my note and with proper excitement in his voice announced that Rechichar's attempt could set a NFL record if it was good. As soon as he said it, George passed him the NFL record book which gave the particulars of the record. Nelson told the audience about the old record without missing a beat. To a viewer, it sounded as though all this information was in Nelson's head. The kick was missed but the way it was presented was smooth and professional. We broke for a commercial after the kick. Nelson, unable to speak because of the headset, looked at George and me with a big smile and bowed his head as his way of saying "Thanks for making me look good."

From time to time George provided the color commentary for games other than a Bear game. During the course of his broadcasting career he was teamed with announcers such as Jack Drees, Brent Musburger, Jack Buck and Harry Kalas. One year he was assigned to do the color commentary on radio for the East-West Shrine Game in San Francisco. George had a good radio voice. It was strong with a well-modulated tone. Because of his years speaking on the banquet circuit, he seemed to be at ease at the microphone. However, like all broadcasters and despite years of experience, George occasionally encountered a word or phrase that for some reason or another he couldn't pronounce correctly. This happened to George at the Shrine Game. The Shriners were known for the great work they do with crippled children in their Shriners' hospitals. George had a problem with the word crippled. When he was describing the work of the Shriners, he came to the word, crippled, and said, "cippled crildren," said it again and finally said, "maimed children."

George sometimes had to use his ingenuity to arrange interviews. For the Bear versus Green Bay Packer game in Green Bay, he was instructed by CBS to get both Vince Lombardi, the great coach of the Packers, and George Halas, the Bear coach, for pre-game interviews. Both coaches had a well-known aversion to interviews, especially interviews before a game. George saw Halas coming out of church and approached him about the interview request. George said, "Coach, CBS asked me to ask you if you would do a live interview on the field before the game. It's a big game for them. For the first time the broadcast will go to Hawaii." Halas shot back, "To hell with CBS and the hell with Hawaii. I'm not doing an interview." "I understand coach," George replied, "I just thought I'd ask. By the way, Lombardi has agreed to be interviewed." "He has?" Halas asked, "Alright, I'll do the interview."

George then went to Tony Canadeo (the great Green Bay back) who did the color commentary for the Packer CBS network and told him he got Halas to agree to the interview and how he did it. Canadeo went to Lombardi and got him to also agree to the interview, once he heard Halas had consented.

The behavior of Halas and Lombardi regarding the interview was typical of the two. In any competitive setting the two would do everything they could to best the other. Yet, when it came down to true feelings, they each had the deepest respect and maybe even love for the other. In 1963, when the Bears won the NFL championship, Lombardi hosted a party for Halas in Green Bay. George, who emceed the affair, said the two acted entirely differently when not competing against each other. George remembered,

> Halas and Lombardi loved each other. There is nothing one wouldn't do for the other, except of course, when their teams played each other. Then it was all-out war. These two great men epitomized all that is good about pro football. When they competed, they gave everything they had and when the game was over there was great friendship and respect.

George was instrumental in one of the Bears' most memorable victories in 1961, six years after his playing days were over. That year, Red Hickey, the coach of the San Francisco 49ers, introduced the "shotgun" offense into the NFL which caused many of their opponents to go down in defeat. Some of losses were downright embarrassing, such as the drubbing of their arch-rival, the LA Rams, 35-0, and the win over a powerful Detroit team by a score of 49-0. Teams were obviously having a difficult time defending against this potent offense.

When the Bears played the 49ers, George was a CBS analyst assigned to do the game. On the field before the game, George visited with his good friend of many years, Gordie Soltau who, like George, was retired as a player and was also a CBS analyst on the 49er network. Naturally, the discussion got around to the phenomenal success the 49ers were having with the shotgun formation. During the course of the discussion, Soltau let slip that the 49er center always hated to play against Bill George. George then visited with the Bears' captain, his former teammate and good friend, Bill George. George asked Bill what defense the Bears were going to use against the near unstoppable 49er offense. Bill told him that Clark Shaughnessy, the Bear defensive coach, designed a three-man line and four-linebacker defense to attempt to stop the 49ers. George said, "Bill, it'll never work. Kilmer (the 49er quarterback) will have all day to pick the defense apart with his passes. When he's not doing that, their big fullback will chew you up running up the middle." Bill asked, "What should we do?"

Bill always thought of George as his mentor. To ask George for advice, even so close to game time, came naturally to Bill. My brother replied, "I know for a fact that their center is scared to death of playing against you if you played on his head. (Bill George for years played nose guard on defense.) I would go into a five-man line with you playing on the head of the center instead of your usual middle linebacker position. You'll have a field day against him and be able to put pressure on Kilmer. You'll also clog up the middle against the run."

When the game got underway, George observed that the Bears were in the three-man line formation on defense. The first four plays went as George had predicted with the 49ers taking the Bears apart. Then Bill George called a time out. When play resumed, Bill George was on the head of the center. Again as George had predicted, Bill George had a career day and mainly because of his play, the Bears stopped the shotgun and defeated the 49ers, 31-0. Shaughnessy took credit after the game for the brilliant Bear defense, but there were two people who unquestionably knew who was responsible for the brilliant defense, Bill George and George Connor.

Halls of Fame

In 1963, George was notified by the National Football and Hall of

Fame Foundation that he had been selected for induction into the College Hall of Fame during the annual ceremony held at the Waldorf Astoria Hotel in New York in early December. He became the ninth Notre Dame player or coach to be so honored. He followed such luminaries as Jack Cannon, Frank Carideo, Jim Crowley, George Gipp, Elmer Layden, John Lujack, Knute Rockne and Harry Stuhldreher. It was customary at the induction ceremony that a large school banner of each inductee be prominently displayed. George, out of his love and respect for Holy Cross College, asked the committee if they could display both a Holy Cross and Notre Dame banner when he was inducted. They granted his request.

Our Dad and I traveled to New York to attend the ceremonies. The evening before the party at the Waldorf, George asked Dad if there was any place in New York he would like to see. Dad had one request. He wanted to meet the famous Toots Shor who he had heard so much about. When George, Dad and I arrived at Shor's restaurant, there was a line out to the street waiting to get in. Led by George, the three of us edged through the crowd until George spotted Shor, caught his eye and motioned to Dad. Toots caught on immediately and went straight to Dad and said, "You've got to be Dr. Connor, welcome." With that, he led us to table number one, asked the occupants to move and seated us there. We were joined by Bob Considine, the great New York sportswriter and Toots. Dad immediately got into a discussion with Considine and Toots about various sports stories. George and I became spectators watching Dad, Considine and Shor in an animated discussion. The wonderful look on Dad's face alone made the trip to New York a memorable one.

During George's years as a broadcaster, he continued with his successful box business. To help his business, George put out a weekly newsletter during the football season called "Professionally

Speaking." George would meet on Monday after the pro games with his good friend, the noted Chicago sportswriter, Bill Gleason. George would review the past games and give his thoughts about the upcoming pro contests as Gleason took notes. Bill would then ghost write the newsletter that was sent to the many Hoerner-Waldorf box customers around the country. The newsletter was so popular that George enlisted the help of his good friend, golfer Bob Goalby, the former Masters champion, to collaborate with Gleason in continuing the newsletter during golf season.

In no small measure, the newsletter was responsible for additional box clients for George, as well as a demand for speaking engagements in various parts of the country. George recalls vividly one such engagement. He was in Fargo, North Dakota giving a talk for one of his customers when he was asked to go on the local radio station for an interview. After the radio interview, there was a call-in segment to the show. A woman called in to say her sister had met George many years before in Delavan, Wisconsin. She said her sister had George autograph his picture for this woman's young son. George asked her if she still had the picture. She replied she did and after she retrieved it, George asked her to read the inscription. It read: "To Roger Maris, I hope you grow up to be a great football player someday, with best wishes, George Connor."

George chuckled as he said, "I sure can pick them, can't I?" The young Roger Maris was, of course, the famous Roger Maris of New York Yankee fame who broke Babe Ruth's single season home-run record by hitting 61 homers.

George's long-standing affiliation with Hoerner-Waldorf ended when Champion Paper purchased the Iowa-based firm. George continued on as a salesman for Champion but, as with so many companies that absorbed a smaller company, the working atmosphere was never the same. Champion, it seemed, never understood the value of a salesman's relationship with his client. The management re-assigned many of George's national accounts to another salesman thus shrinking George's commissions. The fact that Champion lost these accounts to competitors without George covering the account, didn't change the way they operated. In evaluating his status, George opted to leave Champion and formed his own company, Connor Sales.

As part of his broadcasting duties George had to do many interviews. By far, the interviews with Dan Devine, Notre Dame's head football coach, were the oddest. George would notify Devine in advance that he wanted to do an interview and even suggest the topics he wanted to cover. Devine would stall his response and then finally set a time when the interview would be held.

The problem George encountered was that Devine had his own agenda for the interview. The agenda all centered around Devine trying to prove he was a better coach than his predecessor, Ara Parseghian. It seemed no matter what question George asked, Devine would quote some statistic or give some evidence why he was a better coach than Parseghian. If George was patient enough he would eventually get Devine to answer his questions. What should have been a 10 to 15-minute interview usually took well over an hour.

George still chuckles about the time Devine, to show his football genius, pulled out of his drawer a play he had diagramed. Devine said he would use the play in the game the following day and that, in his opinion, it was unstoppable. Later, when George had left Devine's office, he examined Devine's play. George had to agree with Devine. The play, if executed properly, might well be unstoppable but not for the reason Devine thought. The reason the play seemed so good is that Devine had put 12 men on the offensive team.

George's last stint as a broadcaster was doing the Notre Dame games with the veteran announcer, Harry Kalas. The television broadcast was taped and was shown the following day so that Notre Dame fans who missed the game when it was broadcast live would have the opportunity to watch the game. These broadcasts which lasted about five years had a particularly large audience in the Chicago area.

◆

◆

◆

In 1975, George was notified that he had been selected for induction to the Pro Hall of Fame. He was the 15th Chicago Bear named to the Hall. Upon hearing the news, George said, "I'm thrilled beyond words. It's like a dream come true. It's great to join my teammates in the Hall – Bulldog Turner, Sid Luckman, George McAfee and Bill George."

George credited his success to his line coach, Hunk Anderson, who made him a linebacker before the 1949 Philadelphia Eagle game. "The Eagles had an end run nobody could stop led by Steve Van Buren and Joe Muha," recalled George. "Hunk told me I was to line up across from Pete Pihos and my job was to turn in the play and knock down the interference. We won the game 38-21, the only team to beat the Eagles before they won the league championship. From then on I was a line-backer, left, right and in the middle, but I still played offensive tackle."

When the news of George's selection was announced, George Halas said, "If ever a man deserved to be in the Hall, it's George Connor. He was one of the best players to ever play pro football. He consistently made more tackles than any player who played the game and was always an inspiration to his teammates."

As was written about George in a press release by the Hall of Fame:

> George Connor is one of the men who bridged the gap between the old and the new. He was one of the last two-way players, playing offensive tackle and line-backer while making All-Pro five times. He was also the first of the big linebackers, and his success in that position made it almost mandatory that linebackers who followed him be as he was – big, fast and mobile. George was always one of the smartest men on the field wherever he played. He seemingly instinctively knew about keys – the tips that movements of certain offen-sive players will provide to the alert defender as to which way the play is going – long before keys became the vogue.

The official record at the Pro Hall of Fame in Canton shows the following about George:

All League Teams:
>   1950 (Tackle, AP, UP)
>   1951 (Offensive Tackle, AP; Defensive Tackle, UP)
>   1952 (Offensive Tackle, AP; Linebacker UP)
>   1953 (Offensive Tackle, AP; Linebacker UP)
>   1955 (Linebacker UP)
>   (Five different years at three different positions)

Receiving: No.: 5, Yards: 89, Average: 17.8

Interceptions: No.: 7, Yards: 66, Average: 9.4

Fumbles Recovered: No.: 8, Yards: 73, Average: 9.1,
>   Touchdowns: 1

It should be noted that in George's day, there were no league statistics for sacks, hurries and solo tackles as there are today.

It was one of the hottest days anyone could remember that mid-August day in 1975. Canton, Ohio was jammed with people attending the induction of four of the National Football League's greatest players into the Pro Hall of Fame: Dante Lavelli of the Cleveland Browns, Roosevelt Brown of the New York Giants, Lenny Moore of the Baltimore Colts and George Connor of the Chicago Bears.

George had been invited by the Hall of Fame to come to Canton the Tuesday before the Saturday induction ceremony. En route to Canton, George had no idea what was in store for him that week. He knew the schedule of course, but no one prepared him for the emotion-packed week he was about to experience.

Before the induction ceremony, the days were filled with a series of luncheons and golf outings. One surprise for George was that at each luncheon and dinner the speakers would recount the careers of the inductees but the inductees were not allowed to respond. This strategy made the inductees realize the importance of Saturday's ceremony and no doubt partially explains why so many of the inductees are overcome by emotion during their acceptance speeches.

George's wife, Sue, and sons, George Jr. and Al, made the trip from Chicago as did Mother, our sister, Mary Ellen, myself, my wife, Alice, our kids and numerous other relatives and friends. In addition, George's Notre Dame teammate and close friend Ziggie Czarobski led a large contingent from Chicago to Canton in order to celebrate with George. Statistics kept at the Hall of Fame indicate that as of several years ago more people traveled to Canton to support George than all other players except Roger Staubach of the Dallas Cowboys.

During the course of the many activities, I spotted Paul Stenn who had been George's teammate on the Chicago Bears. I was surprised to see Stenn there because I was aware that he and George had not been good friends when they played together on the Bears. I approached Stenn, introduced myself and inquired why he was there. To Stenn's great credit and my brother's, he replied, "George and I didn't always get along when we played together on the Bears but he was a great player – one of the best. I just wanted to be here and show my respect for him and support him."

On Saturday just before the induction ceremony began, George appeared more nervous than his family had ever seen him. He told them he was worried about breaking down in his talk when he mentioned his brother Chuck, who had died the previous February and his father, who had died in 1971. After talking it over with family members, George decided to leave that part until the very end of his talk.

George Halas, the legendary owner and coach of the Chicago

Bears, was George's presenter. The story of how that came about is worth recounting. Soon after George received notification from the Hall of Fame that he had been selected to be inducted, he made an appointment to see his former coach. Halas had long since retired from active coaching but as the owner of the Chicago Bears he was still very active in the team's affairs.

Prior to the appointment with Halas, George planned his strategy for the meeting. He was aware of the fact that Halas did not like to be a presenter and had spurned previous requests from other Bears players to present them at the Hall of Fame ceremonies. Still, George was convinced Halas was the right one to present him in Canton. So, with his trademark dogged determination, he developed a plan to convince Halas he was right.

In Halas's office, George got right to the point of his visit and asked Papa Bear (the press' nickname for Halas) if he would be his presenter at the induction ceremony. Halas told George he was flattered to be asked but said that the presenter's role was one he had been asked to do by several former Chicago Bear players when they were up for induction and that he had refused each request. He told George he was declining this request as he did with all the ones in the past and suggested George get someone else. George had anticipated this response. The dialogue that followed would no doubt amaze anyone who did not know my brother well.

George responded, "Coach, I know you are a very busy man. I also know that you have extra room in your apartment since Min (Halas' wife) died. So I'm going to go home, pack some pajamas and other things, then I'll move in with you."

Halas looked at George with a perplexed look on his face and asked, "George, are you kidding me?" "No, I'm not," George replied. "You always told us players that if we wanted something badly enough we should go after it with all our heart and never quit. Well, I want you and only you. I'm not going to take no for an answer even if I have to move in with you and keep asking you until you say you'll do it."

Halas had seen that determined look on George's face many

times over the years. He also knew George would never let up until he agreed to George's request. After one of those moments that seem to last an eternity, Halas got out of his chair. He came around the desk, shook George's hand and said, "Okay kid, you win. I'll do it."

During his opening comments, Halas described how George looked when he first saw him by using the words once used by Grantland Rice, the noted sportswriter. "George Connor had a physique that was the nearest thing to a Greek God since Apollo." Halas then went on to say some glowing words about George's career. When it was George's turn to speak, he gave a short, but eloquent talk ending as planned with the words, "I only wish my brother Chuck and my Dad could be here today to see this."

CHAPTER ELEVEN

Paying The Price

To say that George paid a price for his many years of playing football is a terrible understatement. One only has to count the number of surgeries he had to draw this conclusion. In total, he had 32 surgeries. A few had nothing to do with football, but most were directly related to playing football.

A quick review of the football-related surgeries shows that his entire body was damaged from top to bottom to one degree or another. He had five shoulder surgeries, one for elbow, four knee surgeries, three hip surgeries, two foot surgeries and five major back surgeries. The doctor who operated on George's back says that George had the worst back he has ever seen. In addition, George had many artificial parts: a knee, a hip and both big joints on both feet. He had an artificial shoulder joint put in but it never functioned correctly and after several infections it was removed permanently. Since 1990, George was without a joint in his right shoulder.

It's one thing to list these surgeries as if they are merely notations on a medical chart; it is quite another matter to contemplate all the suffering that George has endured as a result of the injuries which necessitated these surgeries. In that light, one has to think about the countless hours of painful rehabilitation connected with these procedures. As his brother and one who has closely observed him, I can say without hesitation that I have never known anyone who has been in constant pain over as long a period of time as George. Through all this, he showed remarkable fortitude. He was always upbeat and optimistic with an attitude that believes tomorrow will be a better day. He attacked his physical problems with the same gritty determination to overcome his ailments that he showed while he played football or undertook any meaningful task throughout his life.

Like so many of his fellow pro football brethren who have suffered similar injuries and surgeries, George says he would do it again – follow the same path and be a football player. For those who never played competitive football this is no doubt incomprehensible. For those who did compete, it might be remotely understandable. In my opinion, it is only the true warriors, men such as Chuck Bednarik, Doug Atkins, Jerry Groom and Jim Otto who completely understand George's feelings about doing it again.

Unlike some other professional athletes who blame their team or their team doctors for their problems, George did not blame anyone – the Bear organization or the team doctors for his football-related injuries. On the contrary, he always had a close relationship with the owners of the Bears, the McCaskey family. When George Halas was alive, George had a marvelous relationship with his former coach. The team doctor while George played with the Bears was Dr. Theodore Fox, who George regarded as a dear friend. Their relationship continued long after George's career as an active player was over. Their relationship was such that George was one of the speakers at Dr. Fox's funeral services.

All his surgeries and medical problems brought George one piece of good luck. In 1980, George went to see his regular doctor, Warren W. Furey. Dr. Furey examined George and ordered some tests. The following Saturday, George received a call from Furey informing him he had cancer of the colon. On Furey's recommendation, George elected to have surgery. Dr. Furey's early detection of George's cancer proved to be life-saving as George had no later signs of cancer.

The one aspect of George's playing pro football that has been unfair is the treatment he and others like him have received from the NFL Players' Pension Fund. When George first entered the NFL, there was no pension fund or Players' Association. The idea of a Players' Association dates back to the early 1950s when there began to be talk among the players from various NFL teams of forming a players' union.

The reason for wanting to form an association was to get bargaining power against the owners of the NFL teams. At that time, the players in the NFL enjoyed no group benefits. Amazingly, there was no hospitalization program, no life insurance, no pension plan, no injury clause in the contract and only one or two NFL clubs paid the players for pre-season games. Three Cleveland Browns players, George Ratterman, Abe Gibron and Dante Lavelli, approached Creighton Miller, the former Notre Dame All-American and an outstanding attorney, and asked him to be their lawyer. Miller declined. Several years later, he was again approached by various players requesting that he assist them in setting up an association similar to the one which existed in major league baseball. This time Miller accepted the offer.

In late November, 1956, after groundwork by Miller and much talk among the players, the first official meeting of the newly formed Players' Association was held in New York . At the meeting, Creighton Miller was chosen attorney and Kyle Rote (Giants) and Norm Van Brocklin (Rams) were selected as Eastern and Western representatives. They met with Bert Bell, the Commissioner of the NFL, and presented their demands. Initially the league officials refused to recognize the Players' Association but after a favorable court ruling and a threatened anti- trust law suit, the NFL acquiesced and recognized the Association.

After Bert Bell died, the Players' Association representatives continued to meet often with Pete Rozelle, the new NFL commissioner, and much was accomplished. By 1960 they had achieved the following for the players: a minimum salary; an upgraded and uniform travel allowance; $50.00 for each exhibition game; the inclusion of an injury clause in the player contracts; the adoption of a hospitalization and life insurance program for all players; legal advice at no individual expense; a pension fund which had $153,792.81 deposited and over $600,000 committed for the next two years.

Before leaving as general council for the Players' Association because of the press of his other legal business, Creighton Miller made sure the stated objective of the pension fund was, "to grow as the league grows." This is exactly what happened. The NFL's growth since 1960 has been beyond anyone's wildest dreams. The league has expanded from twelve teams to 32 teams in as many cities. The revenue from television is staggering. By any definition, it is big business. As Creighton Miller had hoped, the Players' Association has indeed grown proportionally with the league. It has a pension fund of approximately a billion dollars.

As a player in the pre-1959 category, George was not included as an eligible participant from the very start of the pension. This is understandable in that the fund was not large enough at the inception to include all pro players. However, as the fund grew to a size no one could have imagined, it became an embarrassment not to have the pioneers of the game included. These men threatened a law suit and after many years of receiving nothing, the pre-'59 players were finally given $80 per month for each year in the league. In George's case, this amounted to $640 per month ($80 times 8). It was nice to receive something, but this sum did not cover his medicine and therapy bills, let alone the cost of his many football related surgeries. The medical bills were handled by George and his private insurance.

A few years ago, the pre-'59 players received an increase from $80 a month for each year played to $100 a month. In 2001, the players and owners reached an agreement to extend the current contract through 2007. Along with the extension, the deal, which took effect in 2002, included a new wage scale designed to make it less likely for veteran players to be cut in favor of younger, lower-salaried athletes. Included in the package is a 100 per cent increase for the older retirees. For George, this meant an increase from $100 a month for each year of service to $200 a month. This compares to other retirees who receive $425 a month for each year in the league, more than double the amount of the older players.

Putting this in perspective, no one can dispute the fact that the pre-'59 players, men such as George, Otto Graham, John Unitas, Doug Atkins, Sammy Baugh, Chuck Bednarik, Jim Otto and their fellow players, helped make the NFL what it is today. They paid a high price for doing so. It is safe to say that without these men, there would be no NFL as we know it today. Further, no one disputes the fact that the NFL Player Retirement Plan was drafted and amended in accordance with current laws. However, what is disputed is that from an ethical, moral and equity viewpoint, these men have been virtually ignored in relation to the amount of pension money they receive.

With all this, George never complained nor was bitter about perceived injustice to the old-timers. About a year ago, George was interviewed by phone for a radio talk show and this subject was discussed. It was one of the rare times George voiced an opinion on the matter. In response to a question, George said, "I am disappointed in the way the Players' Association has treated the pre-1959 players. With about a billion dollars in their pension fund, you would think they could well afford to give us some kind of lump payment and increase our monthly payments to equal that of the current players. When they can turn down a great player like Johnny Unitas for a disability claim, it doesn't look good." When asked if the old-timers would sue, George replied, "No, that's not our way."

Those words, "That's not our way," seem so appropriate for true warriors. They don't complain and they don't sue. There is no question George and the other pre-1959 players would love to receive some money from the Players' Association to help them in their later years. Being the type of men they are, they know what their contribution to football and the NFL was. In their hearts, they do not need additional compensation to authenticate their contribution.

CHAPTER TWELVE

Giving Back

George had a healthy enjoyment of his celebrity status. But rather than focus on himself, it gave him a strong desire to render service back to the community that had been so good to him. Soon after retirement from football, charitable organizations became his passion. Three in particular became especially dear to him: Maryville Academy (an orphanage located in Des Plaines, Illinois headed by his close friend, Father John Smyth, a Notre Dame alum), the Chicagoland Sports Hall of Fame, and the Leahy Lads.

Maryville Academy

This is the charity that George's great friend, Ziggie, devoted the latter years of his life to. Ziggie's involvement began in the late '60s when Maryville was in dire financial straits. He called Father John, who was well known to all the players from Notre Dame because he was not only a graduate but had been a star basketball player there in the mid-1950s. Ziggie told him, "I have to have a meeting with you and some of the guys. We're going to make a lot of money for you."

At the meeting Ziggie said, "We're going to have a picnic," and repeated, "we're going to make a lot of money for you." In recalling the meeting Father John said, "I'll never forget my words. I said, 'Ziggie, how are you going make any money on a picnic? This is the dumbest idea I ever heard.' Ziggie never took no for an answer, so he kept right on going. 'We're going to have a picnic. It will be on the last Sunday in June. We'll call it the Chuckwagon Day.' I asked, 'What's a

Chuckwagon?'"

Father John continued, "Ziggie said, 'That's where you eat off the wagon.' I said, 'Fine, let's have a picnic.' That's how the first Chuckwagon was born."

Ziggie enlisted the help of his pal George and a host of Chicago sport's celebrities. Much to Father John's surprise and delight, the first Chuckwagon Day made $24,000. Through the years the fundraiser has grown to be, and has been reported for a number of years, as the largest such event in the United States.

It seems fitting that because of his close relationship with Ziggie, George continued to work every single year for Father John and Maryville in their annual fund-raising event. As we will see, Maryville also became the home of the Chicagoland Sports Hall of Fame.

Chicagoland Sports Hall of Fame

George always had a deep appreciation for the players and coaches of the Chicago area where he learned to play sports. One evening, when George and I roomed together in an apartment on Chicago's south side while I attended law school and he had just completed his third season with the Bears, George informed me he would be out late. He was the speaker at the Fenwick High School football dinner. A few nights later, he was off to the Leo High School football banquet to be their speaker. Then a few days after that, he was the speaker at some other high school football banquet. After yet another banquet, I finally said, "George, you have been out so much at these banquets; you stay up late and get up early for work. Why don't you turn down some of the requests before you kill yourself?"

I'll never forget his answer. "Jack, where would I be if not for the great high school coaches who sacrificed so much so that young players like me could learn how to play football? I owe so much to De La Salle, the Catholic League and all my coaches that I can never repay them. That's why I go to these banquets and I'll continue to go

186

as long as they ask me," he said.

Years later, when George was inducted into the Chicago Sports Hall of Fame (now the Chicagoland Sports Hall of Fame), he requested that his presenter mention just two people – his high school coach, Joe Gleason, and his high school captain, Alfie Fleming. After George was inducted into the Hall of Fame and became familiar with its purpose, he devoted much of his life to making that Hall one of the best. When he became Chairman, he reorganized the selection committee and the induction ceremony to allow as many great athletes with a Chicago connection as possible to be recognized for their accomplishments in their particular sport.

For years the museum for the Hall of Fame was housed at Ditka's restaurant in downtown Chicago. When the restaurant closed several years ago, the Hall of Fame was in crisis. All the memorabilia had to be stored until a new home could be found. George, with immeasurable help from his nephew (my son) Kevin Connor, made arrangements for storage at the Chicago Park District with the help of one of its officials, Gene Sullivan. George spent months tirelessly looking for a new home for the hall. Through a fortuitous circumstance, George and Father Smyth met for lunch. On impulse, he asked Father John if he would consider having the Hall of Fame at Maryville. As George says, "It took all of about five seconds for Father John to think about it and reply, 'Let's do it.'"

Since Maryville is in Des Plaines, Illinois and because of the Chicago area feature of the Hall, it was re-named the Chicagoland Sports Hall of Fame. Father John became its Chairman and George continued as President. Father John had the old Monticello building on Maryville's campus renovated to serve as the new home of the Hall of Fame. With the help from devoted friends and sports enthusiasts, George and Father John transformed the Hall into one of the premier sports halls in the country. The annual induction ceremony grew from several hundred attendees to 1,000.

George enjoyed his work with the Hall and took pleasure in seeing that deserving men and women from various sports were honored with induction. During his time as president, there were more inductees than in any other time in the Hall's history. One of George's satisfactions in his work was reconciling inductees with those who until that time, held some sort of grudge against either him or another inductee. Lou Rymkus is a good case in point.

Rymkus was a star Notre Dame lineman for Frank Leahy in 1941 and '42 and with the Cleveland Browns under Paul Brown after the war. After his playing days were over, Rymkus was head coach of the Houston Oilers. While he was playing for the Browns in the late 1940s, he and George, who was then with the Chicago Bears, played against each other. In the heat of battle, George hit Rymkus and cost him a few teeth. Ever since that day, Rymkus held a grudge against George. In addition, while he was the coach of the Oilers, Rymkus benched George Blanda (the starting quarterback). This caused a rift between him and Blanda.

George was well aware of Rymkus' feelings towards him. He was also aware of how Rymkus and Blanda felt about each other. Despite this, George thought they both deserved to be honored and pushed hard for both to be inducted into the Hall of Fame. George never told the committee about any potential problem with getting Rymkus to attend given his feelings about George. Nor did he tell the committee that both Blanda and Rymkus might pass on the induction ceremony if either knew the other would be part of the program. George was confident he could handle the situation.

The first call George made was easy; it was to his former Bear teammate and good friend George Blanda, who was delighted with the news of his selection to the Hall of Fame. He promised to be at the dinner the evening before the induction ceremony. George did not tell Blanda that Rymkus would also be at the same dinner.

George's call to Rymkus wasn't as easy. It required more salesmanship, as George had anticipated. When George got Rymkus on the line, he explained that he was calling in his capacity as president of the Chicagoland Sports Hall of Fame to inform him he had been selected for induction at the upcoming ceremony. He invited Rymkus to come to Chicago on an all expenses paid visit. Before Rymkus could turn him down, George continued, "Lou, I know you have been mad at me because you lost a few teeth when we played against each other. I want to tell you it wasn't deliberate and I'm sorry it ever happened. What you don't know, because I never had the opportunity to tell you, is I have admired you as a football player going back to your days at Tilden Tech." George went on to say how he watched Rymkus play high school football in one of the rare indoor football games played in Chicago at the old Chicago Amphitheater and saw him put the ball through the goal posts on the kickoff. "You remember that?" asked Rymkus. "I remember a lot about you," George went on. "Frank Leahy used to say you were one of the best pass blockers in all of football. Hee was right, as I learned when we played against you when you were with the Browns."

Everything George told Rymkus was true. George's sincerity in talking to Rymkus must have come through because by the time the two were finished with their conversation, they were at peace with each other. Rymkus accepted the invitation to come to Chicago and promised to be at the dinner the night before the induction ceremonies. George's problem was now how to bring Blanda and Rymkus together.

George had asked Rymkus to arrive at the dinner early so they could talk. At that time, George told Rymkus that George Blanda was also being inducted on the same program with him. Before Rymkus could protest, George went on to tell Rymkus that he and Blanda were good friends and that Blanda had often told him what a great coach Rymkus was and how much he had helped him with his career. George went on, "Lou, I know you have some reservations about Blanda but he is one of your biggest supporters so I hope you take that into account when you speak and maybe say some nice things about him."

At the dinner, George intentionally called on Rymkus first to speak. As hoped, Rymkus praised Blanda as a great player and told how proud he was to be inducted with him. When it was Blanda's turn to speak, Blanda was gracious in his comments about Rymkus. At dinner's end, Rymkus and Blanda hugged each other as a smiling George looked on.

After many years of working diligently for the Hall of Fame, George felt it was time to turn the reins over to some younger person who would love the Hall as he did and would devote considerable time and effort to see that it flourished. He knew he had his man in his life-long friend, Charlie Carey. George and Charlie's father were the best of friends, so George had the benefit of watching Charlie mature into a dynamic doer on Chicago's Board of Trade. George then became President Emeritus of the Hall of Fame.

The Leahy Lads

George, Ziggie and many of the players who played for Frank Leahy in the 1940s stayed in close touch with each other after they left Notre Dame. Ziggie, who kept the team loose during his playing days, was the catalyst for bringing the group together in the years that followed. He organized a yearly reunion and together with George arranged for the group to meet often in Chicago, South Bend and in other parts of the country. As often as they could, George and Ziggie made sure Coach Leahy, Moose Krause and some of the other coaches joined us at our gatherings. If at all possible the teammates, as Ziggie called us, tried to make as many of the gatherings as possible. You could always count on a good time, many laughs and a lot of story telling. It was during this time we started to hear the often repeated refrain, "Somebody has to write a book about all this." All of us who gathered realized that we were privileged to play at Notre Dame on arguably the greatest college teams that ever played college football. But more than that, we also knew that our bond with each other was unique and the stories that were told were priceless gems that somehow had to be preserved.

After Ziggie died in 1984, the idea of someone writing a book about our group began to gain momentum. At George's suggestion, I began to tape our story-telling sessions with the idea some writer, yet unidentified, could use them for the book we all knew had to be written. Little did I, or anyone else for that matter, realize at the time that I would be the one to write it.

At our annual reunion in 1989 now affectionately called the "Ziggie Reunion" in honor of our beloved Ziggie, there were more stories told than ever. It seemed everyone had a favorite Ziggie story. We heard the now familiar words often, "Somebody has to write the book." As I drove alone back to Chicago, I reflected on my blessings to be a part of such a great group of people, and recalled the laughs and tears we shared at the reunion. I actually laughed out loud as I thought of some of the stories and heard myself say, "Somebody has to write the book."

As it turns out, I wrote "Leahy's Lads" which was published in 1994. Shortly afterward, my good friend Bud Maloney, who was an enormous help to me in editing and consulting on the book, told me that whether I knew it or not, I had coined a name – "Leahy's Lads." He said as time went on, our group, the players who played under Frank Leahy at Notre Dame, would be known as the Leahy's Lads. Bud's prophecy turned out to be correct. The players who played under Leahy are now universally known as the Leahy Lads.

What no one realized at the time was that the book would be the springboard for other undertakings by the Lads. The Lads had always talked about doing something concrete to honor Frank Leahy. They felt that he was one of the greatest coaches of all time and that there wasn't sufficient evidence at the University of Notre Dame to show his proper place in football history. At the 1994 Leahy Lads' reunion (formerly the Ziggie Reunion), there was more talk about doing something to honor Leahy. George and Angelo Bertelli were particularly vocal in saying it was about time we got going in doing something. When George and Bertelli talked, everyone listened.

The following week, George called a meeting in Chicago to decide what should be done. The committee included George, Jerry Groom, Tom Carey, Jack Leahy (the Coach's nephew), Patrick O'Malley (Chairman Emeritus of Canteen Corp) and me. It was clearly the wishes of the committee to have something visible, some kind of monument on the Notre Dame campus grounds for students, alumni and fans to see. Secondly, the committee wanted the tribute to be a lasting one and truly representative of how the Coach emphasized academics and was an educator in the best sense of the word. The idea of the Frank Leahy Scholarship Fund to educate young deserving students at the University of Notre Dame was conceived and became the second part of our tribute.

The plans of the committee were presented to the University in the form of a written proposal. Eventually, there was a face-to-face meeting with Father Beauchamp, the executive vice president of the University, who asked some tough questions. When he was satisfied the Leahy project would be handled properly, he accepted the proposal with enthusiasm. The Lads began a fund-raising campaign (which is still on-going) to raise the necessary funds to pay for the sculpture and to endow the scholarship fund.

Jerry McKenna, a 1962 Notre Dame graduate, was selected as the sculptor. After months of painstaking work crafting a one-and-a-half life-sized, bronze sculpture of Frank Leahy, McKenna's work was ready for viewing. When the sculpture was first seen by a small group at McKenna's ranch in Boerne, Texas, he received the ultimate compliment when the coach's son, Jim, exclaimed upon seeing it, "It's Dad!"

As is McKenna's custom, he personally delivered the sculpture. He loaded "Leahy" on a flat-bed truck and drove it to Notre Dame Stadium. Since it was on his way, plans were made for McKenna to stop at our house in Chicago so that George, my family and some neighbors could view it before it arrived at the stadium. My wife, Alice, and I had a small crowd at our house waiting for McKenna to arrive with the sculpture. George sat in a chair at curbside. McKenna, with "Leahy" strapped in place on the truck, was about 15 minutes late in arriving. When he parked the truck in front of the house it came to rest directly in front of George. George looked up at Leahy and said, "Coach, you're late. Take ten laps around the block."

192

In the fall of 1996, the Frank Leahy Scholarship Fund was activated when three young women became the first recipients. Since then, four students each year are awarded scholarships (non-athletic) based on financial need as determined by Joe Russo and his staff in the financial aid office of the University.

On September 19, 1997 the McKenna sculpture was dedicated outside the east side of Notre Dame Stadium where it now stands. It is viewed by thousands of people annually and is among the most photographed landmarks on campus. George took great pride for his part in seeing that the name Frank Leahy is never forgotten and, as with Leahy's Lads who are active in the fundraising, enormous satisfaction in knowing that young men and women who otherwise might not be able to afford it, are being educated at that special place that Frank Leahy loved so much.

A major segment of the fundraising enterprise that George and all the Leahy Lads love is what we call our "Roadshows." These events include golf outings, dinners and lunches held throughout the country. Jerry "Boomer" Groom (one of Leahy's greatest All-American players, captain of the 1950 team and Hall of Famer) and I plan and run these events. George loved these events and attended as many of them as his health permitted.

In May, 2001, at an event in South Bend sponsored by the Heisman Foundation and the College Hall of Fame to honor the Leahy Lads, George stole the show with his remarks. He asked all the Heisman winners to stand. Four men stood – Leon Hart, Johnny Lattner, Paul Hornung and John Lujack. George then asked all those who were Outland Trophy winners to raise their hand. George was the only one who's hand was in the air. "See," said George, "it's what I've always said, 'Heisman winners are a dime a dozen.' Now the Outland Trophy, that's really something." Rudy Riska, the President of the Heisman Foundation, was in the audience. He thought George's poking fun of the Heisman was spectacular. He could hardly stop laughing.

Honorary Teammates

One year while planning for our annual Leahy Lads' reunion, someone suggested we honor one of the great players who played against Notre Dame. George suggested Alex Agase, the Hall of Fame guard from the University of Illinois. The committee unanimously agreed that Agase would be the ideal person to honor first. He had played for the Illini in Notre Dame's opening game in 1946 and was selected as an All-American and was inducted into the College Hall of Fame in 1963. Agase was well-known to many of the Lads as many of them played with or against him in pro ball. It turned out to be the perfect choice. Agase attends many of our functions and takes pride in being the first of the Leahy Lads' honorary teammates.

Other honorary teammates quickly followed as Otto Graham and Dante Lavelli of Cleveland Browns' fame were honored at our next Roadshow. This practice started with nothing more in mind than a way to tell the great players from other schools how much we admired them as individuals and how much we appreciate their accomplishments and devotion to the game of football. We can think of no better tribute than to say we would like to be your teammate.

Through no great plan or design, the Lads have produced a new brotherhood of former football players. Our group of Honorary Teammates is distinctly different from other groups such as the Heisman winners or Hall of Fame members because there are no rigid standards to become eligible. Rather our selection is based upon admiration, respect and love. It is because of this that the Honorary Teammate program means so much to both the Leahy Lads and the recipients. A partial list of honorary teammates includes:

Alex Agase-Illinois (Hall of Fame)
Barry Alvarez-Wisconsin
Reds Bagnell -Penn (Hall of Fame)
Joe Bellino-Navy (Heisman Winner)
Bobby Bowden-Florida State

Mike Ditka-Pittsburgh-Chicago Bears (Hall of Fame)
Bump Elliott -Michigan (Hall of Fame)
Pete Elliott -Michigan (Hall of Fame)
Otto Graham-Northwestern-Cleveland Browns (Hall of Fame)
Larry Kelley–Yale (Heisman Winner)
Frank Kush–Michigan State (Hall of Fame)
Buddy Leake-Oklahoma
Bernie Lemonick-Pennsylvania
Dante Lavelli-Ohio State-Cleveland Browns (Hall of Fame)
Ray Lumpp-NYU
Jim Manley-Pennsylvania
Joe Manzo-Boston College
Don McAuliffe-Michigan State (Maxwell Award)
Frank Nastro-South Carolina-Camp Lejuene Marines
Steve Owen-Oklahoma (Heisman Winner)
Jim Plunkett-Stanford-Oakland Raiders (Heisman Winner)
Kyle Rote-Southern Methodist -NY Giants (Hall of Fame)
Roger Stauback-Navy(Heisman Winner)
Fuzzy Thurston-Valparaiso-Green Bay Packers
Billy Vessells-Oklahoma (Heisman Winner)

The custom of making an Honorary Teammate of players from other schools naturally evolved into making Honorary Teammates of Notre Dame players from other eras.

Taking a page from our beloved Ziggie Czarobski, who used to call a friend whom he admired "Teammate," the Leahy Lads have borrowed this practice by adding non-players who have helped the Frank Leahy Scholarship Fund in a significant way to our list of Honorary Teammates.

Several years ago at the annual Leahy Lads/Heisman luncheon in New York, Bobbie Bowden of Florida State was honored as a Legends Coach. Since then the following coaches have been so honored: Barry Alvarez (Wisconsin), Mike Ditka (Chicago Bears), Frank Kush (Arizona State), Ara Parseghian (Notre Dame), John Ray

(Notre Dame/Kentucky), Steve Spurrier (Florida) and Marv Levy (Buffalo Bills).

When the Leahy Lads honored Marv Levy for his many contributions to football, he, in turn, honored us with a poem he had written for the occasion. Later that night my daughter, Terri, remarked that it was a testament to the uniqueness of the Lads that someone of Marv's remarkable reputation would feel comfortable delivering a poem to a room full of men.

ODE TO LEAHY'S LADS
by
Marv "O'Levy"

They were young and bold, swift and proud
When they first put on their pads.
And their collisions on Cartier Field were loud;
And they were known as Leahy's Lads.

They took the field with spirit and flair;
They were sons of Notre Dame;
Cheers and excitement filled the air
Whenever they played the game.

Tales of their exploits echo still;
They're part of that Notre Dame lore;
Those Golden Domers! Oh what a thrill,
To recall those warriors of yore.

The years have passed; they no longer play;
They no longer don those pads;
But their legend lives on to this very day.
They're still known as Leahy's Lads.

Ridge Country Club 7/29/02

George, as well as all the Leahy Lads, are thrilled to be able to honor these outstanding players and coaches. Each one of them has made his mark in football and has been a credit to their respective schools and organizations. Some wonderful friendships have been made as a result of the Lads getting to know these outstanding men.

CHAPTER THIRTEEN

Leahy's Lads Stories

Whenever the Lads gather, stories abound. They never seem to tire of hearing their favorite reminiscences about Ziggie, Coach Leahy and their days at Notre Dame. George's favorite stories never fail to entertain.

McAllister and Lattner

Mac MacAllister, the long time equipment manager at Notre Dame, had died. He had been the equipment manager since the Rockne days and was a favorite of all the players. Among the pallbearers at Mac's funeral were Frank Leahy, George, Ziggie Czarobski and Johnny Lattner, the former Heisman winner. Leahy was not feeling well at the time so his fellow pallbearers told him not to lift the casket, but Leahy insisted on doing his part. At the conclusion of the burial services at the grave site, the pallbearers went back to the limousine for the ride back to the funeral home. As they were driving along they began to tell MacAllister stories, particularly ones of how he liked to harass incoming freshmen football players. Lattner told of his first reporting as a freshman to draw his football equipment from the legendary MacAllister. As Lattner told it, Mac would not issue any equipment to him for almost a week. Leahy piped up, "Oh John, if I had known that, MacAllister would have been under the ground twenty years ago."

Frank Leahy Pallbearers

Frank Leahy was buried in Portland, Oregon. His eight pallbearers were Moose Krause, Joe McArdle, Ed McKeever, Bob McBride, Bill Sullivan, Tom Sullivan, Johnny Lattner and George. At the cemetery, the undertaker asked the pallbearers if they wanted to carry the casket some three hundred yards to the grave site or did they want the casket wheeled. Before anyone else could speak up McBride said, "We'll carry it."

According to George:

> Krause, McArdle, McKeever and McBride all had some heart problems so they weren't much help. The two Sullivans together couldn't lift a wet towel, so that left Lattner and me to do all the work. After about two hundred yards it was becoming a strain to carry the casket, and we almost dropped it. Fortunately the undertaker rescued us by putting the wheels under the casket.

After the services, Lattner said, "George, remember Leahy always told us the last ten yards were the hardest. Well, he just gave us his final lesson."

Leahy and Clashmore Mike

Prior to the leprechaun, the Notre Dame team mascot was an Irish terrier named Clashmore Mike. One Friday before a Saturday game, Leahy had the team practice in the stadium. This in itself was unusual, but the players were used to Leahy's idiosyncrasies and thought nothing of it. The first team was running plays against a defensive unit when all of a sudden Clashmore Mike, the team mascot, ran on the field. He started snipping at the football, completely stopping practice.

The players tried unsuccessfully to shoo Mike away from the football. Leahy was always intolerant of anything or anybody who caused a practice session to be delayed in any way. The players were amazed to see Leahy calmly watching the dog run around the field disrupting their practice. It would have been more in keeping with Leahy's usual behavior to order the dog captured, or maybe even shot, yet here he was as calm as the players had ever seen him on a practice field

The reason for Leahy's strange attitude towards Clashmore Mike that day was discovered years later by the players. It seems that Leahy wanted a way to delay a game if he was out of time outs. He instructed Mike's trainer to teach the dog to run on the field and disrupt the game. Leahy would nod to the trainer, who would give the appropriate command to Mike to do his thing. What the players saw that day was Leahy having the dog practice his act.

Ziggie, The Student

In Ziggie's time, final semester exams were held after the Christmas holiday season during the first week in January. Since Ziggie would be a participant in the 1948 East-West Shrine Game played in San Francisco, he would miss semester exams. With his usual cunning, Ziggie made plans for the make-up exam he would have to take upon his return to the Notre Dame campus.

Ziggie's big exam was a comprehensive in his major subject. He asked the smartest student in his class to come to his room for a special meeting. Ziggie was so popular with his fellow students that his guest was thrilled to meet with him. Ziggie explained to his guest that he would be away for the semester exam and requested that the man remember the exam questions and write them down for Ziggie to see upon his return to the campus with, of course, the answers.

A few days after his return to the Notre Dame campus, Ziggie, armed with the list of questions and answers which he had practically memorized, took the make-up exam. As Ziggie had counted on, the professor didn't bother to change the exam. Several days after the exam, Ziggie and the professor met. "Congratulations on your test result. You ranked third in the class," exclaimed the professor. "You must have studied very hard while on your trip." "Actually," replied Ziggie (with a straight face), "the books were never far from my side. I studied both ways on the train and stayed in at night to study while the others were out having fun. But I don't regret it – my studies are that important to me."

The professor told Ziggie that his placing third in the class presented a problem. He went on to explain that since Ziggie took the exam at a later date than the rest of the class, it might appear that Ziggie had an advantage because of more time to study. Ziggie took a little time to think about this and said, "I can see your point. Why don't you rank me 13th in the class. I think that would be fair." A relieved and smiling professor shook Ziggie's hand and said, "That's very gracious of you and yes, it's very fair."

A smiling Ziggie left the meeting knowing he had once again beaten the system.

More Ziggie

Several years before Ziggie was inducted into the College Hall of Fame, George and I took Ziggie as our guest to New York for the annual Hall of Fame induction ceremonies. The three of us met at O'Hare Airport in Chicago on the morning of departure. As we checked our luggage, George noticed that Ziggie was carrying a large, brown paper bag. "76, what's in the bag?" George inquired.

"Some Fannie May candy for the stewardesses."

George knew Ziggie's routine with the candy, but George loved to needle Ziggie, so he said, "76, you're a passenger. You don't have to bring the stewardesses candy when you go on a plane ride."

Ziggie replied, "Moose, these girls work hard, so I just want to show them I appreciate what they do."

We were the first to board the plane. Ziggie immediately called the closest stewardess over to where he was seated, which was across the aisle from George and me. "My dear," Ziggie began as he kissed her hand, "my name is Ziggie (he ignored George and me). Here is a box of candy for you for the wonderful service I know you will provide during the trip. If you will call the other girls over, I would like to meet them and also give them a gift."

Within a few minutes, three other stewardesses came to Ziggie and he went through the routine with each of them. "Look at him," said George. "Here we are paying his way and he'll end up with all the service."

Sure enough, George and I were lucky if we got a drink, while Ziggie was waited on all through the flight.

Bill Wirtz, the owner of the Chicago Blackhawks hockey team, was also on the flight. Wirtz was a good friend of George's, but had never met Ziggie. After George introduced them, Ziggie entertained Wirtz for most of the flight with his many stories. You could tell Wirtz was really enjoying his time with Ziggie.

I had been warned by my New York office that there was a cab strike in the city. Accordingly, they had a limousine waiting at LaGuardia Airport for our transportation downtown. I told George and Ziggie about this.

As we were about to leave the plane, Ziggie asked Wirtz, "Bill, are you aware there is a cab strike in New York?"

Wirtz said, "No, I didn't know that. That means I'll probably be late for the league meeting."

"Don't worry, Bill," Ziggie said, "I knew about the strike, so I have my driver and limousine at the airport. I'll be glad to drop you off wherever you want to go."

George poked me and whispered, "Now it's his limo. We might as well have some fun with this." After we departed the plane and retrieved our luggage, George and I arrived at the limousine before Ziggie and Wirtz. George told the driver what he should say and he agreed to go along. As Ziggie and Wirtz approached the limousine, the driver went directly to Ziggie and said, "Good morning, boss. I hope you had a nice flight."

Without batting an eye, as if he did this every day, Ziggie said, "Good morning, Henry. (He did not have the slightest idea what the driver's name was). Yes, we had a delightful flight. I would like you to drive directly to Madison Square Garden to drop off my good friend, Mr. Wirtz, who has an important meeting there."

"Henry" drove directly to the garden. As we stopped at the curb, Ziggie got out first. Joey Giardello, the former middleweight champion, happened to be at the curb and when he saw Ziggie, rushed to him and gave him a big hug. "Ziggie, my old pal, so good to see you."

Later Wirtz talked to George and said, "Who is this guy Ziggie? What does he do? He seems to know everybody. I never met anyone like him." George could have answered, "And you never will."

Creighton Miller – Northwestern

Without a doubt, George's and the Lads' favorite story is the one Creighton Miller was requested to tell at all our gatherings. It has become known as "The Northwestern Story." I say, "was requested," because Miller died unexpectedly in late May, 2002. In honor of Creighton, the story is repeated below in his words but with a caveat – only Creighty could do justice to the story with his incomparable delivery, unique sense of timing and his self-effacing manner.

"In 1943, we played Northwestern at Dyche Stadium in Evanston. What happened is a little embarrassing. We had won seven consecutive games and Northwestern was in the top ten with some great players like Otto Graham. I had gotten some tickets for some friends from Winnetka. As we were warming up before the game, I spotted them sitting near the

50-yard line just a few rows from the field. Our coach, Frank Leahy, called out, 'On in, it's ten to two, game at 2:00.' I thought I had time to run up in the stands to say hello to my friends. I misjudged the time. When I looked back at the field I saw the last of the team at the five-yard line where you had to go up several rows before you went down the steps to the locker room."

"Not wanting to go on the field alone, I headed up the stairs till I found the stairs leading down. On the lower level, I found none of the doors had a name on them. I tried some doors but they were all locked. Now I'm starting to get panicky. I had passed a concession stand so I went back to ask one of the men who worked the concessions where the visiting locker was. I pushed my way through the line to the front of the line when the concessionaire said, 'Hey buddy, that uniform don't cut any mustard with me. Get to the back of the line.' As I started to the back of the line, I heard him say, 'These fans that come to a game dressed in a uniform crack me up. And this character is even wearing cleats.'"

"As I was standing in line, I saw Father John Cavanaugh, the Vice President of Athletics at Notre Dame approaching with a man I recognized as the President of Northwestern. Father Cavanaugh came up to me and said, 'Creighton, what are you doing in the hot dog line?' 'Father, it's not what it seems.'"

"Father Cavanaugh turned to the President of Northwestern and said, 'Remember our conversation at lunch yesterday when I predicted that Northwestern should do well against Notre Dame? Well, here we have one of our starting halfbacks in a hot dog line just five minutes to game time. See what I mean?'"

"Just then the team manager came along and rescued me and led the way to the visitor's locker room. As we entered, Coach Leahy rushed up to me and asked, 'Creighton Miller, where have you been? Where could you possibly go with that uniform on?' Leahy quickly added, 'No, don't tell me – don't say anything, I don't think I want to know. I just don't want to know.'"

Miller got over his pre-game embarrassment and during the game he was outstanding. He gained 151 yards rushing the ball and scored a touchdown as Notre Dame beat a very good Northwestern team 25-6.

CHAPTER FOURTEEN

Looking Back

When one looks back at George's career in competitive athletics, it is clear that he began playing at a time when the world was a simpler place. It was a time when the country was at peace, a time when a young man's dreams of the future were unencumbered by thoughts of war, drugs or big money. You played because you loved the game, loved the action and loved to compete. It was football that brought George fame but he also loved basketball and at one time in his life, thought that was his best sport.

Despite all his honors from football, George often talked about playing basketball. One of his fondest memories was winning the top amateur basketball tournament in Chicago in 1947 while he was a student at Notre Dame.

In those days, there was an annual tournament which featured the top amateur basketball players in March at St. Sabina School on Chicago's south side. George, having played a lot of basketball in Chicago, was very familiar with the event and always wanted to play in this tournament.

Politics

He organized a team that was called "The Senator Daley Hamburgs." (The sponsor, Senator Daley, would later become the well-known Mayor of Chicago, Richard J. Daley.) Included among the players George recruited were: John Foley, Leo Barnhorst, Jim O'Halloran and Frannie Curran; all from the Notre Dame basketball team. Former Leo High School players on the squad were Bob Baggott, Jerry Richards, Lou Knox, Jack Dunne and Jack Schaller. Added to the team was a high school phenomenon, the high-scoring Jake Fendley, who would later star at Northwestern.

Over a thirteen-day period, the Hamburgs won five games against some excellent teams to give them the championship. It was a very happy Senator Daley, sponsor of the winning team, who accepted the trophy. George was thrilled to play a key role. Perhaps, of greater importance than winning the tournament from an historical point of view was that this event brought him in close contact with Richard J. Daley. The two formed a friendship which would bring them together many times in the years to come. George and the Mayor had many things in common: both had a passionate love for Chicago, both were De La Salle graduates, both were members of the Lake Shore Club, and both were avid sports fans.

This friendship led to the Mayor asking George to serve on a committee to study and recommend a new sports stadium for the city. The Mayor also was responsible for the St. Patrick's Day committee selecting George to be the Grand Marshal for the parade in 1957. Since both the Mayor and George were members of the Lake Shore Club on Michigan Avenue, they saw each other often. Through Daley, George got to know many Chicago politicians. Among them were the Mayor's law partner Senator Bill Lynch and one of Chicago's well-known public servants, George Dunne, who was leader of the Democratic Party as well as Chairman of the Cook County Board.

When Daley had been Mayor of Chicago for a number of years, he decided he wanted to have a party to honor George. Within a week, George and the mayor's staff had agreed on a date, invitations were printed, the main ballroom at the Bismarck reserved, and the Mayor began a search for an appropriate gift. The Mayor told his driver to find the largest wristwatch he could find. During the next few days, the Mayor was shown several wristwatches but didn't like any of them. In his frustration, the Mayor said, "I don't want some dainty watch. Georgie is a big man so I want da watch to look good on him."

A crowd of approximately 300 people attended the Mayor's party for George. It was a cocktail party with no speaker's table. The Mayor acted as the emcee and was the only speaker other than George. That evening Mayor Daley was all smiles as he mingled with guests – he appeared to be having the time of his life. Friends who knew the Mayor well said they never saw him so loose and enjoying himself as he did that evening. When he spoke, he was eloquent. This might surprise some people, but those who knew him well knew that when he was among friends, he could be a smooth talker. He was that evening. He praised George for the life he had lead as an athlete, a Christian gentleman and a dedicated Chicagoan. He then presented George with a very large wristwatch suitably engraved. As the crowd was dwindling, the Mayor seemed not to want to leave. Those who were there were treated to an evening to remember – George and the Mayor sharing their friendship.

The only favor George ever asked from Daley was for someone else. George made an appointment to see the Mayor at his office. The two greeted each other warmly and Daley asked George what he could do for him. George got right to the point. "I'm here, Mr. Mayor, on behalf of Wally Fromhart. You might remember him as a Notre Dame football player who coached at Mt. Carmel High School for a number of years and won several city championships. He then coached at Loras College and the University of Detroit. He's now back in Chicago and out of a job. As a good coach and wonderful man, he devoted his life to teaching young men how to play football. It seems to me that this is the kind of man the city of Chicago should look after. Is there anything you can do for him?"

Without saying a word, the Mayor lifted the phone and called someone at the Chicago Park District and said, "A man named Wally Fromhart will be at your office at 9 a.m. Monday morning. He needs a job. Take care of him." He turned to George and asked, "Now, what can I do for you?" George replied, "You just did it. Thanks, Mr. Mayor." Fromhart went on to have a good career with the Park District until his retirement years later.

Through the Mayor, George got to know George Dunne and the two became good friends, a friendship that lasted a lifetime. Like Mayor Daley and George, Dunne was a member of the Lake Shore Club and he saw George there often. Dunne ran for county-wide re-election as County Board President every four years. And every four years for 20 years, George served as his campaign manager and master of ceremonies at each of the campaign fundraisers.

According to Dunne, these "road shows" were never the same twice but all were highly entertaining. "George would bring Ziggie and a few other former players. They just took over. They would kid me. They would kid each other. They would kid the audience and people liked it so much they forgot they were at a political fundraiser."

In recent years, George continued to be active politically in and around the Chicago area. Using his considerable contacts, George worked his nearly illegible personal phone book as only he could, to put together a host committee of former professional athletes, coaches and Heisman award winners known for the night as "The Legends" to honor Cook County State's Attorney, Dick Devine in June, 2001.

Despite recovering from yet another surgery and needing to use a cane, George attended with his close friend, Tony Golden and his wife Kaye. George's niece, my daughter Terri Connor Brankin, began the program from the podium microphone by passing along George's threat to "come out of retirement and personally remove" whoever talked longer than 2 minutes and 30 seconds. This, of course, got a laugh and a nod toward George who waved his cane and gave "the Look." Anyone who has faced George on the football field, knows "the Look." George wasn't kidding.

After Devine was introduced by a well-known Chicago sports figure, Gene Sullivan, the State's Attorney faced the crowd of athletic legends gathered in Hawthorne Race Course's beautiful Turf Room and talked about having Gene Sullivan as a coach. Devine talked about how important it was to have true mentors in life as in sports. He talked about the progress he had made in the State's Attorney's office since his upset election in 1996.

And then George's cane was up in the air and waving from all the way across the room. George started to get up from the table.

"OK! I see you George! Guess my time is up. Thanks for coming everyone." Devine left the podium and the "Look" left George's face. The room burst into applause.

Baseball

In addition to his football career and early days playing basketball, George had a very brief moment of glory as a baseball player. Since high school, George and Charlie Comiskey (of the family who owned the White Sox baseball team in Chicago), had been good friends. One day when George was still playing for the Bears, Comiskey invited George to attend a Sox practice, don a uniform and work out with the Sox team. George was delighted to take him up on his offer. Our father had been the personal physician to Charlie's father and also attended to many of the Sox players in the 1930s. George was a Sox fan to the core.

Charlie and George both put on Sox uniforms and went on the field at Comiskey Park to participate in the practice. After doing some running in the outfield and catching some fly balls, Charlie asked George if he would like to take a turn in the batting cage. George, who had played a lot of softball as a kid and also played briefly on the baseball team at Holy Cross, was thrilled with the opportunity to try his hand at hitting. After fouling a few balls, George connected and put one in the left field seats. A few pitches later, he hit another into the seats. By now, the Sox manager, Jack Onslow, was paying attention. After George hit a few more in the seats, Onslow had visions of a new power hitter for the Sox. He signaled the pitcher to throw some curves to see if George could handle them. George took some powerful cuts but never came close to hitting the curve ball. Onslow's dream of a new power hitter for the Sox evaporated quickly. Thus ended George's moment of baseball glory.

Clubs

The story of George's life would not be complete without mentioning his many years as a member of the Lake Shore Club on Lake Shore Drive, Bob O'Link Country Club in Highland Park, Illinois and the East Bank Club near downtown Chicago.

Shortly after George graduated from Notre Dame and joined the Chicago Bears, he became a member of the Lake Shore Club. He loved to play handball and the Lake Shore Club had excellent handball facilities. During the off season, George could be found in the handball courts almost every day. He and his fellow handball players belonged to a club within a club called the Hinder Club. His buddies, Elmer Angsman, Buddy O'Brien, Harvey Jackson and a host of others, if not in the handball courts could be found in the Grill Room having a few cool ones and swapping stories.

George used the dining room to entertain family members on various occasions. When our parents moved to Fort Snelling, Minnesota in 1953, George liked the club so much he got a permanent room and lived there for a couple of years. It was a sad day for George and most members when the club was sold many years ago.

Many members of the Lake Shore Club were also members of Bob O'Link Country Club. George joined the men-only club in the early 1960s when his mentor, Gene McNeil, said to him, "Kid, I think you're ready for Bob O'Link."

The story is told of a wife of one of the members who called and said, "I'd like to inquire if my husband is there." Before she finished the Bob O'Link employee said, "No, he isn't." The wife shot back, "How do you know? I haven't given his name." To which the employee responded "Lady, we don't have any husbands here, only golfers," and hung up. George's boys tell the story of riding to the club to pick up their Dad. When they arrived, they ran into the club to get him. Then an attendant told Sue she wasn't allowed in the club but he would be happy to serve her a drink while she waited in the car. Years later George and Sue joined the Saddle and Cycle Club and Sue turned the tables on George. As they arrived at the club for a dinner for new members, Sue said, "George, why don't you wait in the car while I find out where we should go?" As soon as she was inside, Sue talked to a waiter and had him bring a drink to George outside waiting in the car, just like at Bob O'Link.

In 1975, when it was announced by the Pro Hall of Fame that George was selected for induction, the members at Bob O'Link decided to hold a "George Connor Day" as a way of honoring him. It was one of those perfect summer days, as George enjoyed a round of golf with his good friend Bob Goalby, the former Master's champion, and Ken Venturi, the well-known Open champion and golf analyst. The dinner following the golf was attended by 200 fellow Bob O'Link members and guests. It was one of those memorable evenings of camaraderie for George.

In more recent years, George enjoyed his membership at the East Bank Club. Although his handball days were over, the facilities offered George a place to exercise in the pool and enjoy the company of good friends at the bar where he was known to hold court and tell Ziggie stories and others in his repertoire.

George's Bear Career

In looking back over his career with the Bears, George had this to say:

> It was a great experience to play eight years with the Bears. When I first joined the club in the late summer of 1948 at Rensselaer, Indiana many of the players from the great Bear teams of the early 1940s and the 1946 championship teams were on the team – players like Sid Luckman, George McAfee, Bulldog Turner, Fred Davis, Ray Bray, Ken Kavanaugh, Jim Keane, Ed Sprinkle plus many others. And, of course,

George Halas was the coach with Luke Johnsos and Hunk Anderson as his top assistants.

Being a lineman and later a linebacker, my immediate coach was Hunk Anderson. He was as tough as they come and the best defensive strategist in the game. As my fellow tackle Fred Davis said after we were through playing ball, 'Hunk never put us in a bad position.' And it was true. Hunk had a way of designing defenses that would allow each of us to play our best. I remember the Eagle game when I first played linebacker. Hunk told me to key on Pete Pihos, their end, and to follow him all over the field. On one play, I guessed they were going to run Van Buren. I didn't pay any attention to Pihos, who went downfield and caught a touchdown pass. When I came off the field, Hunk asked me what happened. I told him it was my fault, that I thought on my own and ignored Pihos and added, 'I won't do it again.' All Hunk said was, 'Thata boy.' I would have had a very different career had he not switched me to a linebacker, so I'm very grateful for what he did for me.

I loved Papa Bear George Halas and I loved being a Chicago Bear. I enjoyed playing for them. I liked to practice, I enjoyed the camaraderie of the locker room and loved playing in the games. It was a thrill for me to play with and against so many great players. The friendships I made with my teammates and some of my opponents have lasted a lifetime. I wouldn't have missed the experience for anything.

George Comments on his Bear Teammates

Sid Luckman

My first three years with the Bears overlapped with Sid Luckman's last three years. Sid's skills were diminishing by then but there were still times when he was brilliant. One thing he never lost was his great competitive spirit. I remember one game when we were losing by about three touchdowns late in the game and we went on offense on our 20-yard-line. In the huddle, Sid looked around and said, 'There's no way we can win this game but we're still the Chicago Bears. We're going to take the ball 80 yards to score and show them we are still the Bears.' Sid's talk fired the guys up and we did march down the field to score. To me that says a lot about the way Sid played the game. As a friend, Sid was the best. After my playing days, I didn't see Sid very often; but when I needed a favor in business, an introduction to a potential customer for example, Sid would respond immediately. He was a class gentleman and epitomized the spirit of the Chicago Bears.

Bulldog Turner

I played five seasons with Bulldog Turner. He was a great, two-way player as an offensive center and a linebacker on defense. He was one of the smartest football players I ever played with. He knew everyone's assignment for every play. They tell the story of a game before I joined the Bears where the Bears' halfbacks were all injured by the fourth quarter. Bulldog moved to halfback and on the first play he ran 65 yards for a touchdown. Not many centers could do that. He was a great player and a great teammate. He was inducted into the Hall of Fame in 1966.

Don Kindt

My best friend on the Bears through all the years I played was Don Kindt. As a star at Wisconsin, he was the Bears' number one draft choice the year before I joined the Bears. For the first few years Don played a lot of offense as a hard-running back and then settled in as one of the premier defensive backs in the league. Don had a great sense of humor and was a first-class storyteller. He was fun to be around. When he died several years ago, it was a real blow to me. I still miss him.

Ed Sprinkle

Ed Sprinkle was one of the toughest players in the league and a good friend. In one of my first games with the Bears, Ed hit the opponent's passer after he had thrown a pass and was assessed a 15-yard penalty. I asked him why he did it and reminded him it cost us 15 yards. Ed's reply was classic, 'Yes, George, but it's early in the game and the 15 yards isn't going to hurt us. Watch and see how he hurries his passes the rest of the game.' We played before the league kept records for sacking the quarterback. If they kept records then, Sprinkle would probably have sack records that would still stand as he was one of the best pass rushers in pro football. In my opinion, Ed should be in the Hall of Fame at Canton. Several years ago I was on the old-timers selection committee and proposed Ed's name along with Elmer Angsman's for induction. A couple of former players on the committee voted against Sprinkle because they thought he was a dirty player. There is no doubt Ed was tough, and played hard, but he played within the rules. I still think it is a shame he is not in the Hall of Fame.

Bill George

Bill joined the Bears in 1952 which was my fifth year with the Bears. You could tell from the start that he had the makings of an outstanding player. He was a complete player. He could play offense and defense, was tough and very agile. Initially he played offensive guard. He then switched to defense, first as a down lineman and to middle linebacker where he earned his fame. Bill had an outstanding career with the Bears and was inducted into the Pro Hall of Fame in 1973.

Bill and I hit it off immediately and became good friends. I like to think of him as a protege of mine. I helped when he began playing linebacker and was his coach for two years. It's a shame he died so young. He was a good friend and great ballplayer.

George Blanda

George joined the Bears in 1949, the beginning of my second year. He was very well built, surprisingly strong and tough, which no doubt played a part in Halas' decision to have him play linebacker for a while. We were together for seven years on the Bears and became good friends. George was a very talented competitor, who was always in shape. It was no surprise to me when he went on to an un-believable Hall of Fame career.

Ray Bray

Ray Bray was the strongest man I ever knew. He would do finger pushups with the right hand and then switch and do it with the left hand. He was a tough player.

Ken Kavanaugh

Ken was a superb pass receiver. He didn't talk very much but when he did his teammates listened. Occasionally in the huddle, Luckman would ask, 'Got anything, Ken?' Ken would usually say, 'No.' But when he said he had something and named the play that he thought would work, nine out of ten times it went for a touchdown on a Luckman to Kavanaugh pass play.

Doug Atkins

I played with Doug one year (1955) and coached the defense for two years when Doug was playing. Doug was not only big – 6 foot 8 and 270 pounds – but he was very agile and as tough as any player in the league. When he got mad, there wasn't any player we played against who could handle him. I loved playing with him and enjoy seeing him when our paths cross.

Rick Casares

Rick was one of the hardest running backs in pro football. He also was one of the toughest players in the league. They tell the story about when he was a 16-year-old amateur boxer in Tampa, Florida. Rocky Marciano, the heavyweight champion, went to the gym where Casares was working out. After Marciano watched Rick spar a few rounds with an experienced fighter, he turned to his manager sitting beside him and said, 'Don't ever let me go in the ring against that kid. He's the best I've ever seen.'

Rick displayed his toughness on the field. He ran hard, played when he was hurt and was a team player. If I was a coach and had 11 Rick Casares, we could beat any team.

Opponents

When asked who was the toughest player he ever played against, George didn't hesitate, "Arnie Weinmeister. Weinmeister was not only tough but also was the only lineman in the All-Star camp who could beat him in a race. Arnie played six years of pro ball, his first two years with the New York Yankees and the next four with the New York Giants. Arnie was the dominant defensive tackle of his time. He was All-AAFC in 1949 and All-NFL, 1950-1953, and was named to four Pro Bowls. He was enshrined in the Pro Football Hall of Fame in 1984. It was during the time spent at the Pro Bowls that George got to know Weinmeister on a personal basis. The two became better friends in their years after football.

George did some kind of favor for Arnie and as a way of acknowledging the favor, Weinmeister sent George a salmon. Unfortunately it arrived at George's Chicago office late on a Friday and remained there for the weekend. When George entered his office the following Monday, the place reeked with the odor of decaying fish. The dry ice that was packed with the salmon had melted. Not wishing to offend Weinmeister, George never told him about it.

George cited Hugh McElhenny of the San Francisco 49ers as one of the best backs he ever played against. After a game when McElhenny scored four touchdowns, a reporter asked George how it felt to tackle the elusive back. George replied, "I don't know. I never laid a hand on him the whole game."

When old-timers such as George talk about players they played with or against, the highest compliment they can pay to a player whether a lineman or back is to say, "Was he tough!" In that vein George named Steve Van Buren of the Philadelphia Eagles and Elmer Angsman of the Chicago Cardinals as the hardest running backs he ever faced and, in addition to Weinmeister, Pete Pihos of the Eagles as the toughest lineman.

As George looked back at his life there were so many memories, good times, tough times, so many teammates and friends who came to mind and most of all, so much to be thankful for. He has been asked many times whether, given his many surgeries as a result of football, would he do it again? As stated earlier, his answer is always the same. Yes, he would do it again. As he says, "My only regret about playing with the Bears is that we never won a championship." The Bears came in second in the division in five of the eight years George played, 1948, '49, '50, '54 and 1955. George recalls, "In each of those years, we were just a player or two from going all the way. Halas, either because of his reluctance to pay for a top player we needed, or in some cases loyalty to a veteran player, kept a few beyond their usefulness, costing the Bears a few championships."

Changes to the Game

George's football career from high school days until he retired from pro ball spanned 17 years, from 1938 to 1955 during which time many changes in the game of football took place. George was there for many of them and at the center of some. He also has a number of "firsts" to his credit.

During the late 1930s and early 1940s, offensive linemen had their tails down as if they were resting on their haunches. When George arrived at Holy Cross as a 17-year-old freshman in 1942, he was fortunate to have a line coach named Lud Wray. Wray was attuned to the more modern game. As a result, he taught his linemen to have their tails up, with weight on their down arms, ready to spring forward to block or to quickly pull out to trap an opponent or to lead the interference. George was in on the new change early in his career.

In his first summer practice at Notre Dame preceding the 1946 season, George broke his hand in a scrimmage. The hand was immediately put in a cast. In order to continue to practice, Hughie Burns, Notre Dame's outstanding trainer, devised a removable cast to go over the regular cast. This allowed George to continue to play without losing valuable practice time. A few days before the team's opening game against Illinois, the regular cast was removed but the hand was still tender. Prior to the game, Burns meticulously taped George's bad hand using foam rubber on the top to protect the hand from further injury. Burns and the coaches knew that Illinois would be aware of George's injured hand. To prevent the Illinois team from targeting George's bad hand, Burns taped the other hand exactly as he did the bad hand. Thus George became the first college or pro lineman to have his hands taped, much like a fighter's hands before he dons the boxing gloves.

Until that time, most linemen taped just their wrists. By mid-season that year, almost all Notre Dame linemen taped their hands like George without the foam rubber even in practice. By the next season, most linemen in the country adopted the new taped hands à la George.

In 1941, the college substitution rules changed which allowed platoon football possible. Even though, players continued to play both ways on offense and defense in both college and professional football. The age of the specialist began to emerge particularly as to a place-kicker and a defensive back or two when substitution rules changed. In 1948 the college rules were modified to allow unlimited substitution when the ball changed hands as opposed to unlimited only when time out was called. Whether this was the trigger for the offensive and defensive specialist that came into being in the 1949 college season or whether it was a natural evolution is not clearly discernable but whatever the case, platoon football (offensive and defensive players) became the order of the day. The pros followed suit and by the 1951 season most pro players played either on offense or defense. George was with the Bears when this change occurred and made history as one of only a few players who continued to play both ways. George was a bridge between the old, two-way players and the modern game of specialty players.

When George came in the league in 1948, there were many players who didn't wear face masks. Most of the interior linemen wore them, but the backs and ends for the most part did not. By the end of his career in 1955, almost all the players in the NFL, including quarterbacks, were wearing some type of face mask. George was one of the exceptions. He never wore a face mask during his entire football career.

One of the so-called trick plays in George's era was the tackle-eligible play. The end on the would-be tackle receiver side dropped a yard back and a flanker on the other side of the line lined up on the line of scrimmage thus making the tackle an eligible receiver. George, because of his speed, was a natural to use on the tackle-eligible play.

The Bears started to use the play often to take advantage of George's speed and ability to catch passes. George caught five such passes for an almost 18-yard average before the league outlawed the play. George's success with the play caused many of the NFL clubs to lobby for the rule change to outlaw the play. These clubs argued to the league that it was too hard to police. One has to wonder whether these clubs would have wanted such a rule change if they had on their squad a tackle who was as gifted athletically as George.

Some of the firsts for George include: the first-ever recipient of the Outland Trophy and likewise for the Lineman of the Year Award in 1946. Another first for George is the fact that he was the first of the big, mobile linebackers when he was switched from tackle to linebacker in the 1949 Bear-Eagle game. George perhaps wasn't the first but he was the first to be known for the art of "keys" or "reads" as a way of diagnosing plays.

Training

In George's day there were no mini camps, weight rooms and other team facilities where a player could workout and stay in shape in the off-season. Coaches did give their players an instruction sheet for what they should do in the off-season to maintain their physical fitness. It never mentioned weight training which was considered a no-no in those days. The main emphasis was on running to keep the legs in shape and watching one's weight, especially for the linemen. But in the end, if a player was not self-motivated, he probably showed up for summer camp somewhat overweight and out of shape.

George never had a diet problem. In fact, up until he was a teenager, he was almost a vegetarian. It wasn't until he started his big growth stage that he began to crave more of a meat and potatoes diet, and did so big time – but always with vegetables. His prodigious appetite stayed with him until he went in the Navy. From then on he still had a good appetite but no more so than anyone his size.

Since working out with weights was not in vogue when George was in high school, he had to find other ways to add muscle and strength. When George was entering high school, the Coca-Cola Bottling Company built a distribution plant just three blocks from our house. George, like many of the young men in the neighborhood, found summer employment at the plant loading trucks and later as helpers on the delivery trucks. George quickly established himself as a conscientious worker and one of the strongest of the young employees. The young summer employees used to stage contests to see who could carry the most cases of Coke; who was the fastest to load a truck and who could carry a skid (the platform used to store cases of Coke) the farthest. George always won these contests. The two helpers the drivers requested most were George and Jim Arneberg who became a Leo High School legend as a football player.

Working in the summer for Coca-Cola helped George to develop a very muscular body. In addition, the summer between George's junior and senior year at Notre Dame, he worked for a Notre Dame supporter building a damn on this man's property near Lake Delavan, Wisconsin. Watching the casual feats of strength George performed as he wheeled wet cement up a ramp to be dumped into the framed foundation was something to see. The year-round concrete men, who did this as a normal part of their work, would have their wheelbarrows loaded with cement, then try to get a head of steam before they began their upward push up the ramp. They would struggle to make it to the top of the ramp before gratefully tipping the wheelbarrow to allow the cement to flow into the frame. By contrast, George, stripped to waist in the hot sun, would run up the ramp. When he reached the top, he seemed to push the wheelbarrow into space before turning it, allowing the cement to flow into the frame. The year-round cement workers were regularly stunned at such strength.

Staying in shape was never a problem for George because, like most athletes of that time, he played sports the year round. In high school, at Holy Cross and up to his final year at Notre Dame, George was a varsity, two sport player - football and basketball. Even in his senior year at Notre Dame, after the football season he played basketball with amateur teams in Chicago.

Early in his career with the Bears, George had a conversation with Luke Appling, who for years, was the All-Star shortstop with the Chicago White Sox. George asked Appling how he stayed in such good shape year after year. Appling told George that the secret of his conditioning and longevity was to never get out of shape. He explained to George that most of the football and baseball players he knew took it easy in the off-season which resulted in their putting on excess weight. Then when they reported to camp they would have to torture their bodies to lose weight and get in shape for the season.

Appling went on to explain that as the player aged, this getting-back-in-shape routine became harder and harder, which eventually cut short a career by several years.

George took Appling's advice to heart and vowed to never get out of shape. He was aided by the discovery of handball as a sport he enjoyed. He played (singles and doubles) usually about four times a week. Oftentimes he would run the indoor track as a further way of staying in shape.

George Connor Day

In June, 1993, a group of George's friends decided to honor him with a special day. A committee was formed chaired by John Lattner, Notre Dame's fifth Heisman winner and a close friend of George's. After months of meetings, the committee selected September 15th as the day to honor George.

Three hundred plus people attended the reception held at Hawthorne Race Course's Gold Room to honor George for his outstanding football career, his exemplary life and his devotion to his family, friends and school. The spacious room allowed the crowd to mingle freely and allowed each person there to personally greet George and have a few minutes to chat.

George's life-long friend and a noted Chicago sportswriter, Bill Gleason, emceed the evening's program. Known for running a fast-moving program, Gleason did just that. He called on Sue, Jack Brickhouse, Brother Michael (President of De La Salle), Jim Gay (Principal) and George, Jr. as speakers before introducing George. In his brief remarks George Jr. said, "Unlike most of you in the audience, I didn't have the pleasure of seeing my father play in person. Growing up I tried to emulate, him but since I was given the true Connor body, I wasn't able to realize some aspirations. If you want to see a true Connor body look at myself, my uncle Jack and my cousin Kevin and you'll see what I mean – it's not made for the NFL. In looking at life and being with my father, I began to realize that I could emulate him on another playing field – that's the playing field of life. There are a couple of things I would like to share with you that I have shared with him, things that I admire about him. One is his sense of humor, two is his helping others whether it be his work with Maryville or other charities in Chicago, and finally is his devotion and faith in God. Those are the qualities I try to take with me in my life. Dad, I want to tell you I'm proud of you. I love you. It's a great night for you."

In introducing George, Gleason said, "Most of you know that George and I were children together at Meyering Park playground at 72nd and Calumet Avenue. We were at St. Columbanus school together. I have written much about him. He and I have written a lot of things together and I'm not going into that. All I want to say is what so many people here feel. George has never forgotten his friends from the old neighborhood. He's never forgotten the guys he played softball and basketball with. He's never forgotten the people who cared for him. He's always there for us. And George, I'll make this very brief. I just want to say, I love you."

In his response, George was never better. In speaking before an audience George always had the ability of sensing the "feel" of the crowd and the purpose of the gathering. He did that evening. He spoke of his youth and what our parents meant to him. He briefly traced his career, acknowledging certain people that were important to him, while blending in his remarks with humor.

George concluded by saying, "I've had a great life and have had a lot of great things happen to me. God blessed me along the way with a lot of talent. A lot of it was hard work and I had some great coaches. I had a great career at Holy Cross College, Notre Dame and the Chicago Bears. I have a lot of friends in my life. I'm blessed with a great wife and family. I'm greatly blessed with the greatest friends in the world. I want to thank each and every one of you and in particular the committee. I don't know why you're having this party – I guess I know why. I'm a sincere guy, I have a lot of friends – I've been giving all my life and am thankful for all that God has given me and I hope this is not the last hurrah."

Reunion in Canton

It is customary for the Pro Hall of Fame to invite the 10th, 20th, and 30th year anniversary classes back to the Hall in Canton, Ohio as guests. In 2000, NFL Commissioner Paul Tagliabue conceived the idea of Pro Football's Greatest Reunion as the kickoff of the 2000 season, the first of the new millennium.

The reunion, held in late July, turned out to be the largest gathering of Hall of Fame members from any one sport ever assembled for a single event. Of the then 135 living Hall of Famers, a total of 106 attended the multi-day celebration.

There was some doubt whether George would be able to make the trip because of recent, major back surgery. His post-surgical therapy was long and difficult and George was still using a walker. But the reunion coincided with the 25th anniversary of George's induction and as his boys say, "There was no way he was going to miss being in Canton." One piece of good fortune played a part in George's being able to make the trip. His good friend, Richie Perillo, loaned a John Madden-type bus to George, along with his driver for the trip. The size and layout of the bus allowed George to have plenty of room to maneuver and stretch out if needed. George, Sue and the two boys, George and Al, invited some good friends to accompany them on the trip. They were particularly thrilled when Carol O'Brien and her daughter Kelly accepted the invitation to share the trip with them. The reason they were so happy was that Carol and her husband Buddy were George and Sue's closest friends. Buddy had died a short time earlier. As young George and Al say, "It was very meaningful to have Aunt Carol and Kelly along for the trip, especially in light of Uncle Buddy's recent death. Having them with us helped make the trip one of those once in a lifetime experiences."

The contingent of 15 or so met outside Butch McGuire's to board the bus. Among the group were close family friends Chuck Carey, John Kinsella, Pat Shea, Dr. Mark Morasch and George's niece, Mary Mints. George's good friend, Tony Golden, had a banner made with the Hall of Fame logo on it and the words, "Friends of George 'Moose' Connor . . . Canton Here We Come!!" that was placed in the front of the bus. The sign proved to be invaluable when the bus arrived in Canton. The town was jammed with people. There was a parade, fireworks and traffic was at a standstill. When the nearest policeman spotted the sign and the official Hall of Fame logo, he stopped traffic and waved the bus on its way. George was convinced on recall that "the banner on the bus was a Godsend, as our bus was given priority wherever we went. I guess the police thought our bus was the official one of the Hall of Fame."

"When we arrived at our hotel," continued George Jr., and Al, "Dad was pooped from the trip and said he had to get some rest. He was gone less than an hour and then he was back with the group raring to go. He had that determined 'look.' Nothing, no pain or aches, were going to stop him from being a part of the celebration. He was determined to play the entire game."

With 106 Hall of Famers in attendance plus the new induction class including such stars as Joe Montana and Howie Long, there were sports celebrities everywhere. For an avid sports fan, it was paradise. Young George and a pal decided to take advantage of the celebrity-laden area and seek some autographs. They spotted Dick Vermeil (the coach of the St. Louis Rams) and Bill Walsh (the retired coach of the San Francisco Forty-Niners) and approached them for their autographs. When George identified himself as George Connor's son, the coaches immediately wanted to know where they could find his dad. When George told them, they forgot all about the autographs in their haste to pay their respects to big George.

In the country club where George's family was housed, there were separate parties being held throughout the place. Montana, Long and the other new inductees each had their own party. George and his contingent had their own party. When some of the other Hall of Famers heard where George was, they stopped to say hello. There were visits from Montana, Joe Namath, Mike Ditka and many others. As Al Connor says, "It was a unique blending of generations." George himself said, "My time in Canton was one of the greatest experiences of my life. I love all those guys. It was a thrill to be with some of my old pals and getting to know some of the younger ones whom I had not met before. I wouldn't have missed that trip for the world."

These reunions have been so enjoyable for so many people that the Hall of Fame will hold another reunion in late July of 2003 as part of its 40th anniversary celebration. "Ever since the first reunion, it seems that whenever I run into a Hall of Famer he asks, 'When will we do that again?'" Commissioner Paul Tagliabue recently said.

CHAPTER FIFTEEN

Summing Up

George played four years of college football, two at Holy Cross and two at Notre Dame. His pro career spanned eight years, all with the Chicago Bears. During those years, he accomplished much and was the worthy recipient of many awards:

1942   National acclaim in the famous Holy Cross upset of Boston College as a 17-year-old freshman. The youngest player (17 years old) ever selected to the All-Eastern team.

1943   All-American at Holy Cross and recipient of the George Bolger Lowe Award as the outstanding football player in New England.

Captain and leading scorer of the Holy Cross basketball team.

1946   Consensus All-American for the 1946 Notre Dame National Championship football team.

The first recipient of the Outland Trophy as the best interior lineman in the country.

The first recipient of the Lineman of the Year Award.

First-round draft choice of the New York Giants.

1947   Captain of the Notre Dame National Championship football team and consensus All-American.

1948   A starter for the East squad in the East-West Shrine game.

A starter on the 1948 College All-Stars.

Signed to play pro ball with the Chicago Bears; became the highest paid lineman in pro ball.

1949   First of the big, mobile linemen to play linebacker.

1950   Named to the All-Pro team.

1951   Named to All-Pro team on both offense and defense.

Selected for the first Pro-Bowl game.

1952   Selected as Captain of the Chicago Bears.

Named to All-Pro Team on both offensive and defensive team.

Selected to play in Pro-Bowl.

1953   Named to All-Pro team on both offense and defense.

Selected to play in Pro-Bowl.

1954   Selected to play in Pro-Bowl.

1955   Named to defensive All-Pro team.

1963   Inducted into the College Football Hall of Fame.

1974   Inducted into the De La Salle Sports Hall of Fame.

1974   Inducted into the Holy Cross Football Hall of Fame.

Inducted into the Chicagoland Sports Hall of Fame.

1975   Inducted into the Pro Football Hall of Fame.

1995   Named to the Pro Football All-Time Two-Way team.

2000   Named by a national board of sportswriters on the All-Century team.

2000   First lineman honored as a Football Legend by the Heisman Foundation.

The hard facts listed above, much like a balance sheet, do not capture what is behind the official record. The facts alone cannot measure the elements that make such records possible, elements such as George's heart, his effort, determination and leadership. In George's case, there were many characteristics about him which made him the outstanding football player he was.

There is no question that George was a big man for his day. There is also no disputing the fact that he was one of the fastest and most mobile, big men of his time. However, there are many players who are big and agile who never make it big in pro ball, let alone become one of the best not only of his time, but of all-time.

First among the traits that made him what he was as a player was his fierce determination to do the job at hand. Throughout his life George exhibited an incalculable resolve to attain a goal he set his mind to. One only has to look back on his life to see that George showed this trait throughout. Perhaps in some unknown way, this capacity to strive beyond the ordinary was ingrained from birth. Whatever the cause, George's dogged determination is a quality which defined him.

A second characteristic that made him a great player is the intensity level with which he played. He knew only one way to play football – to give his very best on every play. The idea of cruising or taking it easy for a few plays was foreign to him. Playing at a consistently intense level resulted in a reputation for being tough. There was no doubt that George was tough. When he hit an opponent, it was meant to be a hard hit and to be felt. As his college coach, Frank Leahy, used to say, "I want you to thump your opponent so hard that he will wish he was in the stands watching the game." George definitely believed in this adage but he played within the rules.

Third, George loved to compete. From the time he was a young lad and all through his career, he loved to compete no matter what the game was. According to son Al, his dad's competitive nature even extended to ping pong. "We went to Aunt Marilyn's (Sue's sister) house for some holiday. Our cousin Mary, who was in her twenties at the time, challenged Dad to a ping pong game. Dad accepted the challenge. He was probably in his late fifties at the time but it didn't stop him from diving for shots and playing like it was the Super Bowl – he just didn't want to lose. Dad won 23-21. I think he had to get a cortisone shot the next day for his aches and pains."

In addition to the physical attributes George brought to bear as a player – his speed, agility and strength, he possessed a keen mind for analyzing the strategy of the opponent. Further, he seemed to have an uncanny instinct as to where the play was going.

George was not only one of the best players at every level, he also was a leader. He was elected captain of his football teams at De La Salle, Holy Cross, Notre Dame and the Bears. George took this leadership role seriously as he demonstrated on many occasions. His leadership style was not the vocal type. Rather he led by example on the field and off the field. He was never afraid to talk directly to the coach if he thought there was a good reason. As George Dickson, his Notre Dame teammate put it,

> George was a great team captain; he unified and he encouraged, he represented the team to the coaches and the coaches to the team equally with a balanced and forceful approach. He was a superior leader because he was a superior player and a superior man. George was as friendly and as concerned with the fifth or sixth-team members as he was about the starting eleven. He was a friend to all and an inspiration to all.

In any analysis of George, the term loyalty must be high on the list. In my conversations with his friends from various walks of life, the one word used by everyone is "loyalty." First and foremost, he was loyal to his family. He was a faithful husband, father, brother, uncle, nephew and cousin. George never forgot his roots. His grammar school pals remained his close friends. He stayed in touch with them all his life.

In 2002, the second Gene Sullivan Awards Night banquet at Hawthorne Race Course featured a "George Connor" award. When asked which one trait he would like the award to represent, George thought a minute and replied, "loyalty." It meant that much to him.

A good example of George's loyalty and appreciation of old friends was evident recently. It has become a custom for long-time friends who grew up in St. Columbanus parish to meet three or four times a year for lunch. At a recent luncheon, George made a presentation to one of his heroes from our old neighborhood. George told the 40 or so men who had gathered that day that growing up he had several role models. He said the best was Walter "Pug" Boyle. He then presented Walter with a Pro Hall of Fame cap and said, "Walter, you are in my Hall of Fame."

Was He Tough?

At a sports function, I introduced my son Kevin to Don Kindt, George's great friend and teammate from the Chicago Bears. Kevin always likes to hear stories about his Uncle George so I said to Kindt, "Don, Kevin would like to know if his Uncle George was tough."

"Was he tough?" Kindt repeated in a tone that implied it was an absurd question. "Was he tough?" Kindt repeated. "Kevin, let me tell you how tough your uncle was." Kindt told of playing defensive back with George playing linebacker and how the one thing he feared in a game wasn't being hit by an opponent. "That was nothing," explained Kindt, "it was being hit by George that scared me. He came to the point of attack with such fury that anyone who got in his way, he annihilated, me included." I could see Kindt was just warming to the subject so I slipped away to watch Kevin and Kindt in a very animated discussion. I knew Kevin would be in for at least a fifteen-minute recital of how tough George was.

I began to think of what it means to be tough and particularly, George's toughness. When one thinks of a person being tough, it can mean many things. If a person plays major college or pro football and survives, that person can correctly be called tough. Let's call it survival toughness. Another level of toughness in terms of football would be a player who starred at whatever level of competition he was in. Such a person would have to be tough to reach stardom. However, there is, in my opinion, a higher level of toughness that few attain. At this level a player is a dominating and intimidating physical force who blocks and tackles so hard that opposing players hate to come into contact with him. That was George's level of toughness.

But George's toughness was much more than physical. He had a mental toughness that refused to let any obstacle, be it an opponent on the football field, some physical setback or one of the many surgeries he endured, get the best of him. He simply refused to quit – he didn't know the meaning of the word because he never quit on anything in his entire life. Was he tough? He was the toughest man I have ever known.

Gunslingers

As tough as George was on the field of battle, he was equally as amicable off the field. Once he took off his helmet, shed his warrior pads and his competitive juices no longer flowed, he became the easy-going, fun-loving person that his family and friends were used to seeing. It was good that he was that way because George, like so many big men and particularly pro athletes, was harassed from time to time by some obnoxious guy who tried to goad him into a fight. Like in the old western movies, where the man known to have the fastest gun was

236

baited by some young gunslinger who wanted to make a name for himself, so too, George had to face his challenges. Had George not been so easy going, he might have seriously hurt someone.

The attempted confrontations usually occurred when there was drinking. George says he could sense it when someone near him was about to challenge him. The opening line of the intruder was predictable – something like, "You're not so tough," or "I'd like a shot at you." Fortunately, George showed infinite patience at such times. He usually told the guy he was with friends that didn't want any trouble and urged the guy to forget it and go back where he came from. Sometimes that worked and other times his friends would intercede and talk the intruder out of his attempted confrontation. There was one time when he used his ingenuity to thwart a would-be fighter. As George told it:

> I was sitting with my wife at the bar in a very nice restaurant when I spotted this guy coming towards me. He was about 6´ 2˝ and well built – he looked like an ex-Marine Drill Sergeant and I knew instinctively what was coming. Sure enough, he tapped me on the shoulder and when I turned to face him without any preliminaries he said, "George Connor, I want a piece of you, why don't we go outside and fight." Without giving him my usual comeback, I replied, "As you may know, I'm a professional and I get paid good money to handle guys like you but I'm busy right now so I'll tell you what we'll do." I asked the bartender for a deck of cards and then said, "We'll cut the cards and the high man wins. If you get the high card you can always say you beat George Connor." The people around us who heard my proposal all laughed. The guy's face turned red. He turned and walked out.

Today's Game

George remained an avid football fan all his life and watched most Bear and Notre Dame games on television. He was happy with what the Bears have accomplished over the past few years, particularly the way the defense has played. Being an old linebacker, he watched how the Bear linebackers play and was impressed with their trio of linebackers particularly Brian Urlacher. He was also impressed with Dick Jauron, the head coach and the way he handles the team.

The Notre Dame games are a different story. George didn't think much of Bob Davie as a coach and got frustrated the last few years watching the Irish play. Oftentimes he turned off the games in disgust. George liked what he saw in the new Notre Dame coach Tyrone Willingham. George said, "For the first time in years the team is playing Notre Dame type football. They are disciplined, hit hard and never give up. When things go wrong, there are no excuses."

Like most former players he detests showboating of any kind. When discussing this subject he likes to tell the story of the time he and his pal Ziggie talked about Notre Dame players hot-dogging it. According to George:

> Ziggie told me he was so mad at Notre Dame players acting like cheerleaders that he wrote a letter to one of the tackles on the team and told him that he too played tackle at Notre Dame. Ziggie wrote, "If you look on the sidelines you'll see cute little boys and cute little girls dressed in cute little outfits – they're called cheerleaders. There job is to lead the cheers. Why don't you let them do their job and you stick to playing football which is your job." Ziggie concluded by saying, "You know, I never heard back from the guy."

Public Speaking

When George completed his first year of football at Notre Dame in 1946 as an All-American on a National Championship team and first winner of the Outland Trophy, he was in demand as a speaker at various functions in the area. The fact that he was still in school limited the number of times he could accept offers to speak but nonetheless, he gained valuable experience in public speaking. After his final season at Notre Dame when he was again named All-American and the team won their second National Championship in a row, George was again in demand as a speaker. And graduating that January, he was able to appear at more functions.

After George joined the Chicago Bears in 1948 he continued to speak at and attend as many functions as his schedule would permit. With the experience he gained at speaking before an audience and as time went on, George became an accomplished after-dinner speaker. He became known for his ability to think on his feet and give an outstanding talk without much preparation. His facility to adapt to a particular audience was uncanny. One year at a Notre Dame Rockne dinner he was seated next to Father Ray Klees, the chaplain of the Chicago Club of Notre Dame who was also to be one of the speakers that evening. The two were chatting as Father Klees observed that George would periodically jot something down on his program. Curious, Father Klees asked George if he had his talk prepared. "I'm doing that now," replied George. "I have to write my talk down and then review it several times before I speak. You're just thinking of your talk now?" Father Klees asked. George told him that he liked to be at the place where he was going to speak, meet some of the people and get a feel for the atmosphere, and then think of what he wanted to say. "My notes are a few reminders," explained George.

I have been with him a sufficient numbers of times at various functions to verify that's exactly what he did when he was a speaker. Many times beforehand I would ask him what he planned to say. His stock answer was, "I don't know, I'll think of something after I'm there." More times than I can remember I sat in the audience and wondered what he would say. Without fail, George would deliver a marvelous talk, usually the best of the evening.

In his talks, his sense of humor and candor were always evident. For years at the Notre Dame of Chicago Rockne dinner, there was a George Connor award. The audience looked forward to George's remarks because they knew that George would direct some blunt remarks to the then coach. One year Chris Zorich, who had played nose guard on the Irish team, was to receive the award. Oftentimes during the season, Lou Holtz, the Notre Dame coach, would have Zorich play a hit and hold game instead of charging straight ahead. After praising Zorich's play during the year, George said, "Chris, you're going to love playing with the Chicago Bears because they will allow you play north-south (straight ahead) rather than east- west (sideways)." The audience howled as Zorich's style of play had been a bone of contention with the Irish fans for most of the season.

Lou Holtz might have been the only one in attendance who did not enjoy the comment. A few days later Moose Krause called George to tell him that Holtz was not happy with the remarks and suggested he write Holtz a letter. George immediately wrote a conciliatory letter to Holtz explaining that his remarks were in fun and not meant to be a slam at Holtz's coaching. Much to Holtz's credit, he sent back a friendly letter and ended his letter, "Who am I to say what a Notre Dame legend can or cannot say?"

CHAPTER SIXTEEN

Coaches, Teammates and Friends

From the time George first began to play competitive athletics in grammar school and at De La Salle high school, he developed a close and lasting relationship with his coaches and teammates and continued to do so at Holy Cross, Notre Dame and the Chicago Bears. He never forgot a teammate and stayed close to them through the years. For example, when his grammar school teammate, Jerry Richards needed help to land a particular job, George used his contacts to secure the position for him. When the wife of his Notre Dame basketball teammate, Jimmy O'Halloran was looking for a position in the Chicago Public schools, George again came through by securing a position for her. Twenty-five years after he did so, George received a card from Jimmy and Eleanor O'Halloran who were in Hawaii on a second honeymoon, thanking George for getting the job for Eleanor. There are many such stories of George helping a teammate.

As Chairman of the Chicagoland Sports Hall of Fame he made sure his high school coaches, Sparky Adams (basketball) and Joe Gleason (football) were inducted. George's two primary line coaches during his career, Moose Krause at Notre Dame and Hunk Anderson of the Bears, were intimate friends of his as long as they lived. George stayed close to Frank Leahy too. For all three coaches, he served as a pallbearer at their funerals.

Like all of us, George has lost some dear friends along the way. None played a bigger part in his life than our brother Chuck, Moose Krause, Ziggie Czarobski, Elmer Angsman and Creighton Miller.

Chuck

In mid-February, 1975 tragedy struck the Connor family. Our beloved brother Chuck passed away. He had been ailing for some time but when his death came, it hit everyone in the family very hard. His wife, June, and the four children, Colleen (Mann), Cathy (Zuro), young Chuck, and Maureen (Kelly) all adored him as did we all. Chuck was such a good person that he is hard to describe. I recall an author saying about Hobie Baker, "He was an improbable combination of virtues made palatable only by his charm and self-effacing manner." The same could be written about Chuck.

Perhaps the highest praise of Chuck was given by his long-time friend and Notre Dame classmate, Michael Romano. At the Leahy Lads' yearly reunion held in 1994, almost twenty years after Chuck had died, Romano said to me, "I still miss Chuck. You know I love you and George as brothers but Chuck was the best. I don't mean just the best of the Connor boys, I mean the best there was." Michael's sentiment pretty much says it all.

Several times a year George and I had the same brief conversation about Chuck. The words spoken vary a little each time but in essence they are the same. George initiates the dialogue by asking, "Do you ever think of Chuck?" My response is, "All the time." To which George replies in almost a whisper, "Yeah, me too." We leave it at that as no others words are necessary. We both know the deep feelings about Chuck that the other carries in his heart.

Moose Krause

George had many great coaches and was close to most of them but without a doubt the one he was closest to was Moose Krause. It's almost eerie to compare the two. Both grew up on the south side of Chicago; both attended De La Salle Institute; both were called Moose; both wore the same suit size; both had an older brother play alongside him in high school; both starred in football and basketball; both had a Holy Cross connection (Moose as a coach – George as a player); both were All-American tackles at Notre Dame; both had a delightful sense of humor; both were intensely loyal to their friends and schools and both had a special love for the University of Notre Dame. With those similarities, it would seem inevitable that they would either dislike each other because they were too alike, or they would form a special bond like father and son or brothers. It was the latter.

They first met when George was still at De La Salle and Moose, a coach at Holy Cross, came to our house to recruit George. As George tells it, "Moose said, 'Son, I'll be with you night and day for four years while you're at Holy Cross.' Then when I'm on a train going east to attend Holy Cross, Moose was headed west to come back to Notre Dame." George always took great delight in kidding Moose with that story.

Moose was George's tackle coach the two years George was at Notre Dame. He coached George for one year in basketball. Through the years that followed his graduation, George stayed in close contact with Moose and their friendship flourished. Shortly after Moose retired as athletic director at Notre Dame, George was with Moose at a function at Notre Dame. He noticed Moose's car parked in front of the entrance and when he saw Moose, he said, "Moose, give me the keys to your car." "Why do you want my keys? inquired Moose. "Just give me the keys," answered George.

With Moose's car keys in hand, George went to the car, checked the mileage and gave the car a quick inspection. When George returned he said to Moose, "Your car has over 100,000 miles on it. It has some dents and is not a car my coach should be driving. You're getting a new Cadillac." "I'm getting a new Cadillac?" asked Moose incredulously. "That's right," George responded.

George and his fun-loving sidekick Ziggie, the other tackle under Moose, formed a small committee, wrote some letters soliciting funds to a select group of Moose's friends and arranged a party. They charged admission to the Chicago party with all proceeds going to the fund to purchase a new Cadillac for their coach. Soon after the party, George and Ziggie presented Moose with his new car, the first of two cars George was responsible for as gifts to Moose.

When Moose retired as athletic director at Notre Dame, he was assigned one of the wooden booths atop the old stadium in recognition of his emeritus role as athletic director and for his long and faithful service to Notre Dame. George, Creighton Miller and Bishop William Crowley of South Bend became permanent guests invited to all the home Notre Dame games. From time to time Moose would have family members, former teammates and other friends as guests in his booth. It was considered a great honor to receive an invitation from Moose to spend time in his booth watching one of the games. When Moose heard I was writing a book, *Leahy's Lads*, I too became a permanent guest in the booth. George and I often looked back on the times we spent with Moose in his booth as some of the happiest of our lives.

Moose ran the place like a drill sergeant. There were orders covering when to arrive, where to sit and God help you if you weren't paying attention during a crucial part of the game. The fun part began as soon as we were in our seats, usually an hour or so before the game started. Moose would ask me if I had my tape recorder ready so as to record his favorite stories. Then he would start the same way each time; "George, tell them about the time I recruited you," or some other story he wanted George to tell. The stories flowed until game time and, if the game got dull, there were more stories. It seemed that George told the one story about Moose and Rockne at almost every game and Moose would laugh just as much with each telling. As George told the story – Rockne asked Moose when he first reported to Notre Dame what number he wanted to wear. Moose told him number 69. When Rockne asked him why 69, according to George, Moose said, "So I'll have the same number if I'm right side up or upside down."

Creighton Miller also had a favorite Moose story which he told many times. According to Miller, a sportswriter asked Moose before a game, "How many men are you going to dress today?" Moose was said

244

to reply, "I'm going to dress 22, the rest are going to have to dress themselves." Moose loved the stories where he was the butt of the joke.

George had notified Moose early in one of the seasons that he would not be able to attend a particular game because he was the speaker at some function at the Pro Hall of Fame in Canton, Ohio. When the usual group assembled in the booth at the game, Moose asked me where George was. I knew Moose was aware of the reason for George missing the game but I explained that George was in Canton and why. Moose said, "There can't be anything in Canton more important than being here in the booth so you tell George, he's out – no more booth for him." The others in the booth, going along with the spirit of Moose's fake tirade, started to plead George's case. They told Moose that George had been a faithful guest and that this was his first offense and asked if he could be forgiven. Going along with the mock trial of George, Moose finally relented and said, "If he apologizes and sends some gift, like a box of cigars, I'll consider letting him back in." I reported this to George who sent Moose a note of apology along with a box of Moose's favorite cigars. George was back in the booth for the next game and never missed another booth appearance.

Moose's birthday is February 2, "Groundhog Day." One year, George called me and said, "I'm really in trouble. I missed Moose's birthday." A few weeks later I saw Moose at some function and mentioned to him that I had heard from George that he was in trouble because he missed the birthday. Moose said, "He is in deep trouble. Here it is my birthday and no call, no card, no cigars, nothing." I reported this to George who said he would come up with a plan to get back in Moose's good graces.

In early June, around the time of the yearly Notre Dame Monogram Club dinner, George was ready to put his plan into action. He lined up "Big Mike" Smith, one of Moose's former basketball players along with about 15 others who George knew would be in South Bend for the Monogram dinner. The group was to assemble at a restaurant to have a surprise lunch with Moose. George had a double extra large white jacket made for Moose with a logo of "Moose Krause

Day" with a drawing of a ground hog stitched on the front of the jacket. Along with the jacket, George had white T-shirts with the same logo on the shirts for the participants to wear.

At the appointed time, Moose entered the restaurant thinking he was having lunch with just George and Mike Smith when he was greeted by the gathering of former players, all wearing the "Moose Krause" T-shirts. George, acting as sort of emcee, told Moose this was a delayed birthday party and presented Moose with his jacket and a box of cigars. No one loved a party and an audience more than Moose. He addressed the group telling them what great players they were and how much he enjoyed their company. As he was thanking George for arranging the party, I leaned over to George and whispered, "If he goes on the attack, you'll know you're in his good graces again." When Moose sat down, he turned to George and said, "That was great but don't be late next time." George whispered to me, "You're right, he's on the attack. I'm in."

Moose had been driving his Cadillac for several years and it started to show signs of wear. George didn't have his pal Ziggie to work with (Ziggie died in 1984), so he formed a small committee with the purpose of raising some money to buy Moose another new car. George had me write a letter to a select group of Moose's friends explaining that we were requesting funds to buy Moose a new car and that it was to be a surprise. The response was overwhelming. In no time at all we had enough money to purchase the car with enough left over for Moose to take a vacation or have several years of gas money. At our annual Leahy Lads' reunion, George and I, along with John Lujack representing the group, presented Moose with his new car which he proudly drove for several years.

When Moose died it was a blow to all of us who knew him. George was particularly devastated. As he said, "Losing Moose was like losing a brother, a father, a confidant and close friend all rolled into one." At Moose's wake, held at the Sacred Heart Basilica at Notre Dame, George and I paid our respects to the family along with a Who's Who of Notre Dame sports. After we viewed Moose in the casket and returned to our seats, George said, "Did you see the cigar Moose had in his hand? That's not Moose's kind of cigar, it's too small." With that he pulled a huge cigar out of his pocket, the kind Moose was known to smoke, and asked me to see to it that Moose had the right kind of cigar to hold. I went to Phil Krause, Moose's youngest son, and he replaced the small cigar in Moose's hand with the large one. George was content knowing Moose had his favorite cigar.

George talked about Moose often, particularly of the fun days in the booth with him. It became a tradition with George and me that on Moose's birthday one of us would place a call to the other to say, "Happy Moose's Birthday." A few years ago, after we had exchanged our usual call, George said he was going to call Moose's daughter Mary (Carrigan) who is a favorite of ours. George gave Mary our usual Moose's birthday greeting and told her he was sorry he had to miss the dedication of Moose's sculpture (Moose on a bench outside the Notre Dame Joyce Center). He told her he intended to drive to Notre Dame so he could sit on the bench with Moose and have a cigar. Mary, in that friendly way she has, replied, "Give me a call, I'll go with you and we'll both smoke a cigar."

George and Ziggie

George and Ziggie's close friendship didn't end when their playing days at Notre Dame were over. On the contrary, that was just the beginning of a life-long friendship. George loved being with Ziggie and who wouldn't? Ziggie was so entertaining that you knew when you were with him, laughter would be there too. When Ziggie's playing days were over, he put on a considerable amount of weight which somehow seemed to fit his whimsical nature. George has been asked innumerable times if Ziggie was as funny as the stories about him seem to indicate. As George puts it, "All I can say is he was funnier than anyone could describe. You had to be around him to know."

Make no mistake, Ziggie was very bright. He was unbelievably quick-witted and added to that, he thought funny. He could come out with an original quip so fast that you would swear the conversation was rehearsed. A perfect example of this was the time Ziggie encountered General Omar Bradley, the famous five-star general of WW II fame. George and I had Ziggie as our guest for the College Hall of Fame induction ceremonies at the Waldorf Astoria Hotel in New York. We were in our tuxes riding the elevator to the lobby when the door opened and a very distinguished looking man and his lady stepped into the elevator. Ziggie immediately put out his hand and said, "General Omar Bradley, I'm Ziggie Czarobski and these are my two Notre Dame teammates, George and Jack Connor." The General shook hands with us, introduced us to his wife and asked where we were going. Ziggie filled him in. When the elevator door opened at the lobby, the General said, "Men, I enjoyed meeting you," and turning to Ziggie he added, "Ziggie, I enjoyed all your games." In an instant, Ziggie answered, "General, we enjoyed all your wars." Last seen, the General was walking through the lobby doubled over in laughter.

Ziggie was so loveable that he could do and say things that were at times outrageous, yet because it came from Ziggie, he would not only get away with it but somehow it became part of his charm. One year when he was the main speaker at a large food company's yearly dinner for all its employees, his first words were, "I have to tell you, that was the lousiest meal I ever had." The audience couldn't stop laughing.

The Leahy Lads who lived in the Chicago area saw him often. He would frequently call each of the teammates, as he nicknamed us. When he called you heard an unmistakable voice say, "This is 76." He would tell us about a gathering he was having and give the date, time and place to meet. All of us were working, so to a man, we would scramble to re-arrange our schedules to make sure we could attend because as his Notre Dame teammate John Lujack used to say, "Ziggie was so entertaining, you never wanted to miss an opportunity to be with him." And he never disappointed us.

At George's suggestion, Ziggie was selected by the National

Coaches, Teammates and Friends

Football and Hall of Fame Foundation one year to give the "comic relief" talk at the induction dinner in New York. The proceedings at the dinner were so emotion-filled that the administrators of the Hall of Fame found it helped ease the tension by having a celebrity known for his wit give a short talk. At the black-tie dinner with about 1,000 people in attendance, including Terence Cardinal Cooke, the Archbishop of New York, Ziggie began by saying:

> Your Eminence, seeing you here tonight reminds me of my good friend, Father Paul. Father was having some problems with his vocation so he asked his bishop if he could have a leave of absence from his duties in order to sort out his life. He explained to the bishop that his sister had a cabin in the mountains outside of Denver where he could go and meditate. The bishop granted his request.
>
> Several months later the bishop was in Denver on some church business when he recalled that Father Paul was in the area. He found the phone number of the cabin and called. Father Paul was delighted to hear from the bishop and invited him to make the drive up the side of the mountain to the cabin. When the bishop arrived at the cabin, he was greeted by Father Paul, who now had a beard, was dressed in a toga with a string of beads around his neck, and wearing sandals. When Father Paul and the bishop settled into the two chairs on the porch of the cabin with a great view of the mountains, the bishop asked, "Father Paul, how is your time of meditation coming along?" Father Paul replied, "It's wonderful, Bishop. I have this beautiful view, my rosary and my wine. Speaking of wine, would you like some?"
>
> "Yes, I would," said the bishop.
>
> Father Paul called out, "Rosary, would you bring us two glasses of wine?"

There was a moment of silence as all eyes went to the Cardinal. Cardinal Cooke started to smile and then erupted in laughter that spread throughout the audience. Ziggie owned the room for the rest of his talk.

George and Ziggie were together often. They were on the program as speakers at hundreds of banquets all over the city and nearby suburbs. Most of the time Ziggie played the role of the "court jester" but underneath the comic exterior was a heart as big as his body. He was known to stop and watch kids play some sport without any equipment, would talk with the boys and tell them he would be back. He would then arrange one of his famous Ziggie luncheons, raise funds from the lads at the luncheon, return to the area of a few days previous and unload a car full of sports equipment for his newly adopted team.

It was difficult to see Ziggie during his last days. That once robust body showed the signs of the cancer that raged within him. When Ziggie died, as per his request, he was waked at his beloved Maryville Academy. Father John Smyth said it was the biggest wake he had ever seen. "Helicopters were landing on the grounds and the people kept coming and coming." Ziggie always attracted a crowd when he was alive and he continued to do so even in death. The funeral Mass was officiated by Father John with Ziggie's nephews as pallbearers at nearby St. Cecilia's Church in the Round. The first six rows of the church were filled by his Notre Dame teammates.

At the conclusion of the Mass, it was a touching sight to see his Notre Dame teammates march out of the church with tears in their eyes as they sang the Notre Dame Victory March. Outside the church, George started to laugh which prompted Doris, Ziggie's wife, to ask, "George, why are you laughing?" George replied, "Ziggie did it again, he got the last laugh. The pallbearers left the casket in the church – Ziggie is still there."

When Ziggie was buried on the hill overlooking his beloved Maryville Academy, it was on the 6th day of the 7th month. Very fitting for George's great friend, number "76."

George and Elmer

The friendship of George and Elmer Angsman dates back to when they were in high school, George at De La Salle and Elmer at Mt. Carmel, both high schools on Chicago's south side. George was a year ahead of Angsman in school. When George left the area to attend Holy Cross in Worcester, Massachusetts, followed by his naval service and two years at Notre Dame, they didn't see much of each other. When George signed with the Bears, Elmer was already a Chicago Cardinal fixture as part of that team's famous "Dream Backfield" of Christman, Harder, Trippi and Angsman.

With both Elmer and George now in Chicago, they quickly resumed their friendship. They saw each other often around town and at the Lake Shore Club and Bob O'Link Country Club. Since the Bears and Cardinals played each other every year and sometimes twice a year, George and Elmer saw a lot of each other on the field of battle. They each liked to upstage the other when they played. For example in one game, with the Cardinals close to the Bear goal and George backing up the line, it was the perfect time for the Cardinals to run a quick trap up the middle to take advantage of Elmer's well-known quick start. Just before the snap, George edged over to the suspected area and when Elmer did get the ball on a quick trap, George was in the hole to meet him. As they were on the ground after George's hard hit, Elmer said, "George, what the hell are you doing in this spot? You're not supposed to be here." Sometimes it was Elmer who got George with an unsuspected block but whatever the case, the two played like mortal enemies on the field. Off the field, they were the best of friends.

Elmer was always very attentive to George in the course of his many surgeries. Several years ago when George had had a serious surgery to remove a growth in his hip muscle and was heavily sedated, Elmer called him to inquire how he was doing. "They found a mass of debris in my hip, but the biopsy shows it was benign," responded George.

251

Not sure what George meant, Elmer inquired, "A mass of debris, what the hell is that?"

George replied, "I don't know. All they said was there was part of a red jersey with the number 7 on it and something about cleats or teeth." (Elmer wore the number 7 on his red, Cardinal jersey and he had lost eight teeth in his college days at Notre Dame). Several days later when George was coherent and asked about his comments to Elmer, he remembered nothing of the conversation.

The relationship between the two can best be described by relating what happened after another of George's surgeries. The morning after the surgery, I went to the hospital to see him only to find Elmer already there caring for George, wiping his brow, helping him to the bathroom and other chores a nurse or aide would usually perform. Elmer did this for two straight days. I could tell from being with George so often after surgeries that he was so heavily sedated that he was out of it. On the third day, I visited George and he was obviously feeling much better. He said, "I'm disappointed. Here it is the third day after surgery and I haven't heard a word from Elmer." I told George how Elmer had cared for him the previous two days. George let out a soft groan and said, "I should have known better than to doubt Elmer," and added, "What a great friend." As George has said on many occasions, "If you have Elmer Angsman as a friend, you have the best."

On April 11, 2002, I was on my way home from visiting George at the facility where he was at the time and checked my cell phone for messages. There was a message from Elmer inquiring how George was feeling. I immediately placed a call to Elmer knowing he was still in Florida. He answered on the second ring. I gave him a good report on George and then we talked briefly about when he was coming back to Chicago. Later in the day, I received word that Elmer had died while playing golf at Iron Horse Golf Course near West Palm Beach. I learned from Ralph Steinbarth, Elmer's good friend and playing partner that day, that Elmer had received my call when he was at the 14th hole. He hit his second shot at the 16th hole and dropped dead.

Elmer's death, as with the deaths of Chuck, Moose and Ziggie, hit George hard. In an effort to ease his pain, I said, "George, you can take consolation in knowing that you were one of the last persons Elmer thought about before he died." George nodded and said, "I loved Elmer and I know he loved me," which was a perfect description of their life-long relationship.

George and Creighton

Creighton Miller had established himself as one of Notre Dame's greatest backs as the nation's leading rusher on the 1943 Notre Dame national championship team. George, at this time, had just returned from the South Pacific where he served as a Navy ensign.

When George was playing at Notre Dame, Miller attended most of the games and more likely than not, was with George after the games. When their teammate John Lujack was married in Davenport, Iowa, both George and Miller were in the wedding party. At the church the morning of the wedding, Miller encountered Frank Leahy and his wife Floss as they hurried up the steps of the church. With his ever-present sense of humor, Miller said, "Coach, you're late, take ten laps around the church."

Through the years George and Creighton were together often in various cities around the country – Chicago, Cleveland, San Francisco and Fort Lauderdale. They shared much in common: both had a good sense of humor, a love of football and their Notre Dame teammates, and a care and concern for their friends. When George learned of Creighton's unexpected death in May, 2002, he kept repeating, "Oh, Fluffy," as if to say, "Why have you left me." Another dear friend gone.

CHAPTER SEVENTEEN

What His Friends Say

George's friends are legion. He had that wonderful trait of treating all people the same from the barber, tradesman, doorman, to the mayor, the bishop and the leaders of industry. George, as with all of us Connor kids, was brought up to respect people from all walks of life regardless of color or ethnicity. We were trained to respect those in authority but not be in awe of them. George learned his lessons well as those who know him will attest.

So many of George's friends played such a big part in his life, that it seems appropriate to include their comments in his story. (It should be noted that these interviews took place over the course of several years, all prior to George's death.)

Bud O'Brien, friend (deceased)

I met George in 1947 when he spent the summer at Lake Delavan (Wisconsin). Through the years we became very close friends. Our families became close as George and Sue, along with their boys, George and Al, spent a lot of time with Carol and me and our family at our place in Lake Delavan. George is one of the finest men I have ever known. He has a great sense of humor and a great feel for people. I admire his loyalty to his family, his friends and to the many causes he has supported. I can't think of a better person to have as a friend than George.

Jerry Richards, friend

George is the best athlete I ever saw. But more than that he is a great friend – he never forgets. He went way out of his way to use his influence to get me my job when I needed it most. He is the most loyal person I know. His football stardom and fame never affected the way he treated people.

George Dickson, Notre Dame teammate and NFL coach

George to me epitomizes what a true Notre Dame man should be. He is manly, intelligent and devoted to the church. He embodies everything I admire in a man. As a football player he was the best. As a long-time NFL coach I have watched most of the great ones play. If there was a group of 40 linemen/inside linebackers – players such as Chuck Bednarik, Ray Nitschke, Ernie Stautner, Joe Greene, Jim Parker, Merlin Olsen, Dick Butkus, Jack Lambert, Willie Lanier and all the best lined up and I could select only one player, I wouldn't hesitate. I'd select George. As an all-around player, he was the best. Like all great players he raised the level of play of his team-mates and he never cheated the paying public as he gave his best at all times. When he played, he imposed his will upon the game and clearly established himself as the class of the field. He is one of a kind – a player for the ages.

Fred "Curly" Morrison, Chicago Bear teammate

George Connor is without reservation one of my absolute all-time heroes. It was a great pleasure to play and be on the same team with George. He was a terrific guy and a lot of fun to be with. But more important, he was a leader who led in so many ways – mainly his competitive spirit. He didn't talk a lot but when he did, everyone listened. In tense moments, like before a game and George got up to speak, it really meant something to everyone on the team. Of all the players I played with and against in my seven years in the NFL, I don't know anyone who had less regard for his own physical well-being and who played more recklessly in a dedicated fashion than George. If I had to pick a linebacker today who was the best of them all, it would be George. He was a sensational player, a great guy and a great leader.

Andy Natowich, Holy Cross teammate

When we first saw him play at Holy Cross, he was the best player we had ever seen. I told him he should be playing for Notre Dame. I later played with the Washington Redskins and with the possible exception of Sammy Baugh, George was the greatest player I ever played with or against, and the best person.

Ed McCaskey, Chairman Emeritus of the Chicago Bears (deceased)

I have known George since he was a player with the Bears. He was a great one. I won't say George is one of my all-time heroes because that is reserved for the men I fought with in France during the war. But I will say that George is one of the finest men I have ever known – perhaps the finest. We have a great friendship which I treasure.

Dr. Edmund Rooney, grammar school classmate

The George Connor I know is a very humble man. He has stayed close to his family and friends which is the mark of a true champion. His personal life is unblemished. George's story is an inspiring one – he has already been an inspiration to many of us.

Alex Agase, Hall of Famer and honorary teammate

George and I roomed together in New York when we were inducted into the College Hall of Fame. I was like a country boy in the big city and George took me to many places in New York including the famous Toots Shor's. Everywhere we went, George was well known and was greeted with great enthusiasm. I was impressed – to this day I call him, Mr. New York.

Also, that weekend Ara Parseghian was conversing with Notre Dame people and he had the job as the next head football coach which I knew. When George found out I knew about it and didn't tell him,

I took a lot of kidding from him. George was one of the best football players of his time or any time – and is a great guy.

D.J. (Buddy) Romano, Chairman Emeritus of Romano Bros. Beverages and teammate

I've known George Connor as a football player and as a friend. As a football player he is by far the best I ever played with (I'm still seeing stars from when I tried to block him over 50 years ago) and the best and smartest player I've ever known or seen. But as a friend, he is even better. Anytime I was sick or needed help George was always there, and he was always there for his family and for anyone else who was lucky enough to be his friend. I truly love George Connor.

Creighton Miller, Notre Dame, Hall of Famer (deceased)

I've known George since 1945 when we met while he was home on leave from the Navy. George and I hit if off immediately and a friendship was formed then that has lasted a lifetime. I had heard George was a great player from his days at Holy Cross and when I saw him play at Notre Dame, I knew I was watching one of the best linemen I had ever seen.

George always called me 'Fluffy,' a name given to me by Frank Leahy. George was the only one who called me that and I liked it as it signified to me a special relationship between us. I saw George often through the years. I watched him play with the Bears and can say without hesitation that he was the best linebacker I ever saw and that covers all the great ones. But more than a great player, George is an exceptional person. He seems to be always doing something to help a teammate or friend. He has a good sense of humor and is a delight to be with. I consider him a dear friend.

John Lujack, Notre Dame and Chicago Bear teammate, Heisman Winner and Hall of Famer

George Connor was the best tackle college football has ever produced. He was equally good on offense and defense. George went on to become the best in pro ball and added a new position, linebacker, where again he was the best. We both started with the Bears at the same time and were roommates on the trips. Together with our mutual friend and teammate, Don Kindt, the three of us were inseparable. George and I had the Notre Dame experience in common, our birthdays are only three weeks apart and we shared common values. During the trips when we were together so much we talked endlessly about everything under the sun. We developed a closeness that is like that of brothers – it's hard to describe. George was not only the best I have ever seen but is also one of the finest men I know. It's always such a pleasure to see him at our reunions. He was a great teammate and is a great friend.

Monsignor Ignatius McDermott (Fr. Mac), President of McDermott Foundation

George Connor, not only tackled the legendary running backs of the 'Golden Dome Days' – George also buried those professional pyramids in the dust of Wrigley Field. It was like breathing for George to tackle the people problems of the youthful residents of Maryville Academy in Des Plaines (Illinois) with his All-American dedication.

Jerry Groom, Notre Dame teammate, Hall of Famer

George Connor was one of the greatest players ever to play football. The first Outland Trophy winner and All-Pro on both offense and defense. How many players have done that? George is the only one. That says it all. As a person, he is the best. He has been loyal to his family, his teammates, to Notre Dame and to all who know him. He is a dear friend and I cherish our friendship.

Harry Kalas, veteran television announcer

George and I did televison broadcasts of Notre Dame football games for five or six years. There are few Hall of Famers who are as down to earth as George. We had a lot of fun doing the broadcasts – he was great to work with – and even more fun being together before and after the broadcasts. He was a joy to be around and is a wonderful friend.

John J. Kinsella, friend

Sure, George was a great athlete. But his biggest victories weren't on any playing field or in a TV booth. His biggest victories are when he says hello to you – whether it's a first time or the 500th time. If you're a pal of George's, you've got a pal – an unselfish 'what can I do for you' pal. It's the thing that makes each meeting fun – a feeling not shared, I'm sure, by guys who played across the line from him. But for his pals, well, each meeting is fun because he just makes you feel so good.

Charles P. (Charlie) Carey, President, Chicago Sports Hall of Fame

I always knew that George Connor was a football legend because of his play at Holy Cross, Notre Dame and the Chicago Bears. But it wasn't until I witnessed a meeting between George and John Hannah, one of the best offensive linemen ever to come out of the University of Alabama and himself an NFL Hall of Famer, that I began to understand the impact George had on the game. Hannah told George that his Dad had played in the NFL against George and his father told him that George Connor was one of the best ever to play the game. The respect and admiration John Hannah had for George was something to see.

As I grew up, the name George Connor was a revered one in our house. My dad was a teammate of his at De La Salle High School, his roommate at Holy Cross College and they were the best of friends. After I was out of college and in the business world, I

262

began to see George often and we developed a wonderful relationship. George got me interested in the Chicagoland Sports Hall of Fame and became my mentor. I learned of his dedication, his feel for people and his caring nature. I am very proud to be his friend and can say without hesitation that George Connor is one of the finest men I know.

Rev. John P. Smyth, Executive Director, Maryville City of Youth

George Connor has dedicated his life to sports. He had a strong desire to see that sports winners were not forgotten. He was directly involved in the original Chicago Sports Hall of Fame. When that fell on hard times, he came to me and asked if there was any room at Maryville to house the memorabilia – a place where fans could come and reminisce as well as get a feel for the role of sports in the Chicagoland area. Together we found a way and the Chicagoland Sports Hall of Fame at Maryville opened in 1996.

Each year we induct new members into the Hall. George served as president of the board for several years and now serves as president emeritus. He has always been active with the nominating committee. I can honestly say that if it were not for George's drive, there would be no Chicagoland Sports Hall of Fame. The Hall has been an asset to Maryville. The annual induction ceremonies benefit the youth in our care.

George was a dedicated athlete, a devoted family man and always a supporter of our alma mater, Notre Dame. He has been close to Maryville for years and was present at almost all of our fundraising events.

What else can I say? George is a friend and true believer in Maryville's mission to keep youth from harm's way.

Richard M. Daley, Mayor, City of Chicago

My father (Richard J. Daley, Mayor, City of Chicago) and George Connor were great friends and had a deep respect for each other. In addition to their south side roots, their Irish heritage and their De La Salle education, they shared an interest in sports and a great love for the city of Chicago and its people.

George's Sons: George and Al Connor

There are a couple of themes that run through his life – how humble he was and what a down-to-earth person he was. He never talked about his football career and never pushed us into playing sports. Whether we wanted to play football or any sport was our decision. When we did play he never tried to coach us or interfere with our coaches but would answer our questions like the time I (George, Jr.) said, "Dad, I can get near the ball carrier but can't seem to get to him. What should I do?" He said, "Pretend the ball carrier is your brother Al and get him the way you always do." Particularly at basketball games you could hear the other fathers screaming and yelling but Dad remained silent. Maybe those fathers were trying to push their unfulfilled dreams on their kids. Dad had already made his mark in sports, and he was very conscious not to push us. He let us make the decision to play sports, and then he was our best fan.

He gave us a great lesson in the way he treated people – the doorman, the busboy and everyone he met. We ate out a lot and in addition to the waiters and waitresses, he always tipped the busboy. We asked him why he did this. Dad said, "They have a job to do and do it well – besides he might become the maitre'd some day."

While we know Dad was a great football player, it is the man we know after football who we love and admire most. We know him as a great father, a loving husband, a loyal friend and the finest man we know. He would do anything for a friend and expect nothing in return. His dry wit and great sense of humor has filled his family's life with tremendous joy and helps us get through more difficult times. Dad has had a Hall of Fame life.

Brothers

I have had numerous people tell me that they thought the relationship between George and me was as close as any brothers they know. It's difficult for me to judge this. But I do know that it's hard to conceive of my relationship with George being any closer than it was.

This sibling closeness was not confined in the Connor family to just George and me. Our sister Mary Ellen was very close to Chuck and George and I still continue to have a very close relationship with her. There is no question in my mind that our parents, in providing a loving home where respect and love for each other was the order of the day, were responsible for setting the stage.

For three years at Notre Dame, George and I were roommates

and then again when we both moved home after our college days. We were not only brothers but the best of friends. We shared confidences and were in tune with the needs, moods and wishes of the other without infringing on the other's space. We seemed to be able to "read" each other like an open book.

As the years passed, I could always tell George's mood by the way he addressed me. If he called me "the Agent" (from my FBI days), I knew he was in a kidding and playful mood. If I was "John F," I was probably in for some mild rebuke about some matter. If I was "Jack," things were normal. When I was "brother," I knew George was in one of his sentimental moods which happened with increased frequency in his later years.

George loved to tell people we were "The Corsican Brothers," from an old movie starring Douglas Fairbanks, Jr. In the movie, twins were separated at birth, with one raised in the country and the other in a city miles apart. When one brother was injured, the other brother felt his pain. When George would have one of his many surgeries, I would have post-operative aches and gas pains. After one of his surgeries he said to me, "You must be feeling good, I have no gas pains." "Yes, I know," I replied, "this is one of the best surgeries we've ever had."

George loved to tell the story of the two of us having lunch when we both worked a block apart on LaSalle Street. We always sat in the same booth and had the same waitress. The routine was the same. After scanning the menu, she would ask George what he wanted. George would select an item and then she would ask me what I was going to have. Five or six consecutive lunches I answered, "I'll have the same."

The next week for lunch as we sat in our usual booth, I noticed George had an odd look on his face. When the waitress asked George what he wanted, he said to me in sort of a challenging way, "You order first." I looked at the menu and gave my order. He studied the menu for an unusually long time before saying, "That sounds good. I'll have the same." Then we both burst out laughing.

Through the years it seemed no matter who ordered first or what the order was, the other invariably answered, "I'll have the same." In later years when he came out to Ridge Country Club for lunch and our waitress, either Josephine or Maureen, would take our order, he would usually say, "What do we feel like for lunch today?" If there were others at the table, he would tell the story of how it all started – "I'll have the same."

Epilogue

Esther Connor's loving care of her son George over 75 years ago saved his life. Together as parents, Mother and Dad gave George the foundation for his faith and values that would carry him through a lifetime.

Perhaps surprisingly to some, George maintained that it is the mother who gives a child the drive to excel in sports. It is George's belief that the mother is the one who, through her encouragement exhibited in so many ways, is the spark a child needs to do well in athletics. Given his personal history, it is understandable that George would think this way.

Whatever the incentive, George did indeed excel in sports. But more importantly he excelled in living his life as a Christian gentleman. I am sure Mother and Dad, if given a choice, would prefer the latter over the former.

It would seem that the best way to describe George's attitude as he journeyed through life is to recall his own words when a priest asked George before one of his many surgeries if he wanted to say anything or go to confession. George replied, "Father, I am on good terms with God. I know something can go wrong but whatever He has in store for me, I accept. I am in His hands."

George's strong Catholic faith and his love of family and friends have been the centerpiece of his life. His family and legion of friends would, I'm sure, totally agree and realize the vastness of his influence on us all. But even I was surprised by the writings of our 11-year-old granddaughter, Rachel. When given a school assignment to write about a hero, she selected "Uncle George." She wrote about the nice things he did for people and how he always made his family his first priority. In her eyes, this made George Connor a hero. Rachel ended her paper by saying, "He also played football."

Acknowledgements

As with the writing of *Leahy's Lads*, my family was immensely helpful in putting this book together. My thanks always to my children Kevin, Terri, Kacky, and Pattie, and to my sister Mary Ellen. Each in their own way contributed to the writing of this book. A special thanks to Kevin and Mary Ellen who painstakingly reviewed the manuscript and added some essential information.

When I decided to investigate self-publishing, Terri took on the roles of publisher and then later editor, putting that St. Mary's English degree to good use. She has worked tirelessly in seeing the book to completion and has my profound thanks. I can't imagine anyone doing a better job.

As the subject of the book, George was a joy to work with, as was his wife, Sue and their sons, George Jr. and Al.

My thanks to my cousin, Rita Ward, for loaning me her scrapbooks about George. Our mother and father, Dr. Charles and Esther maintained numerous scrapbooks while George was playing athletics. George's wife, Sue, carefully stored these, so my thanks to her for loaning them to me.

A special thanks to Mary Stimming for her editing advice. For someone who is not a football fan she brought to the enterprise a fresh approach, and was a joy to work with.

My dear friends Tom Gallagher, Joe Frechette, Buddy Romano and others were generous with their time in reading the manuscript and giving me their advice and support. They have my deep gratitude. My dear friend Bud Maloney, a retired sportswriter and a contributing writer for the *Blue-Gold* paper, was essential to the writing of this book. Bud, who has a special love of Notre Dame football, is a gifted writer, a World War II and sports historian and a researcher of facts without peer. He graciously shared his many insights about the book with me and has my deepest gratitude.

George's teammates at Holy Cross, Notre Dame and the Chicago Bears and his many close friends freely shared their thoughts and memories with me. They, too, have my profound thanks.

Marilyn Harrington of Visions Graphics was of enormous assistance to Terri and me throughout the entire editing and publishing process. Her suggestions were first rate, as are her skills. Thank you, Marilyn.

My thanks to Marty Joyce for all his computer advice and troubleshooting.

Saving the best for last, the love of my life, Alice, was always there with her encouragement, her love and her very helpful suggestions for the manuscript. Without her patience in putting up with my odd hours and moods and mainly her loving support, this book would never have been written.

Publisher's Note

After the publication and success of Jack Connor's first book *Leahy's Lads*, big brother George had a new schtick. Each time they attended a Leahy's Lads scholarship fundraiser together George was of course asked to say a few words.

He would begin, uncharacteristically, a little downcast. "I used to be somebody," he would say. The audience usually exchanged concerned and slightly panicky looks, as if to say "What's wrong with George?!"

"Yeah," he would continue, "I've played professional football. I've won some awards. I'm even in the Hall of Fame, you know." Long pause...

"Now I'm just the author's brother. But sometimes he lets me drive him."

No one was prouder of his brother's accomplishments than George Connor.

Terri Connor Brankin